THE LAST OF THE BLACK EMPERORS

THE HOLLOW COMEBACK OF MARION BARRY IN THE NEW AGE OF BLACK LEADERS

THE LAST OF THE BLACK EMPERORS

THE HOLLOW COMEBACK OF MARION BARRY IN THE NEW AGE OF BLACK LEADERS

JONETTA ROSE BARRAS

Photos by Darrow Montgomery
(unless otherwise noted)

bancroft
press

BALTIMORE, MARYLAND

Published by Bancroft Press
P.O. Box 65360, Baltimore, MD 21209
(800) 637-7377 (for general inquiries) and
(888) 40-READS (for book orders)
www.bancroftpress.com

Library of Congress Catalog Card Number 98-071561
ISBN 0-9631246-6-8
Printed in the United States of America

First Edition

1 3 5 7 9 10 8 6 4 2

Distributed to the trade by National Book Network, Lanham, MD

For Umoja Shanu, Afrika Midnight, and District residents

who took a wayward radical into their home

and helped her touch the real world

✦ CONTENTS ✦

Chronology

◆ THE CHRONOLOGY ◆

1936 ◆ Born in Mississippi

1958 ◆ Graduated from LeMoyne College

1962 ◆ Married first wife, Blantie Evans

1965 ◆ Came to Washington, D.C. for SNCC

1971 ◆ Elected to D.C. school board

1973 ◆ Married second wife, Mary Treadwell

1975 ◆ Elected to D.C. City Council

1977 ◆ Married third wife, Effi Cowell

1978 ◆ First elected mayor

1982 ◆ Re-elected mayor

1986	◆	Elected to third mayoral term
1990	◆	Arrested on drug charges, January
	◆	Defeated in bid for at-large Council seat
	◆	Convicted on one count of drug possession
1991-92	◆	Served six-month federal jail term
1992	◆	Elected to Ward 8 Council seat
1993	◆	Married fourth wife, Cora Masters
1994	◆	Elected mayor for fourth (albeit, non-consecutive) term
1995	◆	Congress created control board, March
1997	◆	Congress stripped mayor of power

The Sinner Becomes the Savior

· PART ONE ·

ON A BRIGHT SPRING DAY IN 1994, a confident Marion Barry strolled into Coolidge High School in upper Northwest Washington, D.C. Barry's walk, once described as a modified pimp roll, and frequently seen in African-American communities of the 1940s and 1950s, was more like a strut. The ease he exhibited entering the cavernous building telegraphed arrogance matured from years of confronting enemies. Never knocked out, and only occasionally knocked down, he anticipated yet another victory this day.

Dressed in an African-inspired suit, accented by the Kente cloth and matching kufi that had become his standard uniform for the previous two years, Barry exuded the pomposity of a Third World dictator—sans military entourage. He had traveled to this middle and working class neighborhood of Ward 4 to formally declare himself a candidate for mayor of the District of Columbia. The venue transmitted Barry's audacious intentions to campaign citywide, rather than confine himself to the low-income communities he had repeatedly mined throughout his career.

Ward 4 was home turf for mayoral incumbent Sharon Pratt Kelly, and with his appearance, Barry symbolically struck the first campaign blow. Hours earlier, a beehive of workers swarmed the streets surrounding the school, hanging posters with Barry's name printed in large white letters against a kelly green background. They passed out matching brochures on which appeared a miniature map of the city, framing the Star of David, a Christian Cross, the Islamic half-moon and star, and kids jumping rope.

Just below were hands—black and white hands clasped together—then the slogan "A City Healed and On the Move." The brochure properly, although some might say whorishly, touched all segments of Washington's diverse multi-racial and multi-ethnic community, attributing to Barry's campaign an inclusiveness that clashed with his reputation as a race-based politician. Like redeemable coupons sought for their timeless value, the word was passed around by campaign volunteers: Marion Barry was coming to the neighborhood. That announcement alone garnered at least fifty gawkers, who ordinarily would not have made their way to the auditorium.

A magnetic Barry easily attracted the curious, and most African-Americans liked seeing him up close and personal. Many simply wanted to touch him, say a few words to him, and run home to tell friends and family members. A middle-aged African-American man from Detroit, in town for the National Teacher of the Year Program, once waited hours during a prayer breakfast just to shake Barry's hand as he circulated through a crowd of government workers and civic activists. The man left smiling and satisfied—as if he had kissed the papal ring.

◆ ◆ ◆ ◆ ◆ ◆ ◆ ◆ ◆ ◆ ◆ ◆ ◆ ◆ ◆ ◆ ◆

A blend of race, cultural pride, and history underlie the admiration and respect most hold for Barry. A wily, controversial personality, with indisputable civil rights credentials, he is lauded for his skill at out-maneuvering the "white establishment."

Barry *is* Anansi the Spider, a mythic figure found in African and diasporic folklore. Stories abound of Anansi—including one where he steals the sun and dupes the Tiger into letting him ride his back. Whatever role he plays, Anansi is always crafty and cunning, surviving by his wits, indeed bamboozling other animals for his own profit. Occasionally, because of over-confidence, he falls into his own traps. In numerous stories, Anansi turns into a spider just as he faces great danger. His name conjures up two West African proverbs: "Woe to him who would put his trust in Anansi—a sly, selfish, and greedy fellow"; and "The wisdom of the spider is greater than that of all the world put together."

◆ ◆ ◆ ◆ ◆ ◆ ◆ ◆ ◆ ◆ ◆ ◆ ◆ ◆ ◆ ◆ ◆

Cathy Hughes, a short, assertive, light-skinned black woman, once counted herself among Barry's supporters. Hughes, the owner of eight radio stations in the Washington region, has a keen interest in promoting the cause of African-Americans. But she locked the door on Barry's return, dismissing him merely as a "master pol."

"Even if he can't help," she said, "he'll create the smoke and mirrors to make it seem like he is…There's something about him that people connect to. He's a [Louis] Farrakhan-type figure," she continued, referring to the Nation of Islam leader. "It's not what they've done for the people, it's their ability to channel the people's frustration." Or at least create the illusion they have diverted the public's attention.

The cultural narrative Barry tells is bifurcated: a parallel plot of African-Americans as both victims and victors. "The narrative is one of the primary ways in which a culture patterns our lives," says Roger Betsworth, professor of religion at Simpson College. "Through narrative, cultural communities communicate, perpetuate, and develop knowledge about and attitudes toward life. The cultural narrative establishes the world in which an ordinary story makes sense. The history, scriptures, and literary narratives of culture, the stories told of and in a family and clan, and the stories of popular cultures—all articulate and clarify the world of the cultural narrative in which they are set. Thus a cultural narrative is not directly told. The culture itself seems to be telling the cultural narrative."

The African-American cultural narrative as told through Marion Barry depicts blacks bending to the white whip across their backs, suffering, pushing the proverbial rock up the hill like Sisyphus, only to have it slide over them just as they near the summit. This narrative laments the African-American's ostensibly insurmountable obstacles to achieving a starring role in the master American narrative—the journey to wealth and influence. Simultaneously, through rhetoric and behavior, it advocates an undying belief in African-Americans' ability to overcome, master, and control their destinies—to win, or at the very least, snatch a piece of the American dream. It is the old slave narrative writ large, the one of Frederick Douglass, of the abolitionist David Walker, and of Sojourner Truth.

The scene and script of this narrative are as confusing as that in the movie *Chinatown*, where Faye Dunaway tries to explain to Jack Nicholson that the young blonde with her is both her sister and her daughter—the product of an incestuous relationship with her father.

Blacks, for their part, do not see the narrative's contradictions. They simply accept their schizophrenia as normal. They are outsiders playing the part of consummate insiders, constantly negotiating deliberately constructed hurdles, camouflaging their true nature and feelings, and outsmarting mainstream white America.

Barry personifies this Anansi duality, and for this he is exalted. "Marion has tricked the system in many ways, and black people in cultural terms have a proclivity to have glee about people who do that," explains University of Maryland political scientist Ronald Walters. "Because of our situation, we've always elevated black people who could do that, whether he was the hustler, the preacher, or whoever. We also elevate people who were defiant of the system...We've respected those people who can stand up to the system, and Marion has told almost everybody in this town where to get off."

But all laurels are not woven into his wreath. Some blacks are leery of Barry. Having found their way inside corporate boardrooms and suburban neighborhoods, they temper their praise of him, labeling his race-based politics divisive, his governance style and political instincts narcissistic. Still, their cultural connections demand that they respect and marvel at Barry as Anansi.

He is both icon and iconoclast—a man of two minds and many faces who, in astrological terms, epitomizes his sun sign of Pisces. Depicted as the two-headed fish, with each head destined for an opposite direction, Pisceans are said to suffer a sort of multiple personality disorder. They are both secular and sacred, magnanimous and selfish, intelligent and downright dumb, appealing and repulsive. Barry once described himself as sensitive and compassionate. He even added that some people label Pisceans as "wishy-washy".

"People say they equivocate—one fish going one way, one the other way. I describe it differently—top fish and bottom fish. I'm the top fish," he told *Washingtonian Magazine*. "Some people say that I'm too arrogant. I don't think so. That I'm too self-assured. I don't think so. I think you've got to be that way in order to survive in this society. If a person isn't that way, the people around them won't be self-assured and confident, either. If you act weak, they'll act weak." The one Barry trait that people seem awed by, and is disputed by no one, is his charisma.

◆ ◆ ◆ ◆ ◆ ◆ ◆ ◆ ◆ ◆ ◆ ◆ ◆ ◆ ◆ ◆ ◆

The large Coolidge High School auditorium swallowed the coterie of supporters, media representatives, and the curious who came to watch Barry throw his name into the puddle of mayoral wannabes. Except for Rev. Willie Wilson, District leaders treated the high school site as if it were under quarantine. Barry campaign workers worried what message might be sent to the larger voting public by Barry's inability to attract credible and recognizable leaders to his "big announcement." Once upon a time, Marion Barry was to the District what Melaquiades was to Gabriel Garcia Marquez's Macondo, bringing new ideas and resources to the city. Barry was the city's most potent magician. He awakened its soul and taught it how to fight. When he raised his hand, people converged, filling once-empty streets and sparsely attended meeting rooms. He whispered his desire to speak with someone, and the person raced to the scene, appropriately genuflecting.

Such deference may have been justified. In his life, Barry had met monstrous challenges and demolished each one. He rose above the abject poverty and suffocating discrimination of his Southern beginnings. He led protest rallies against members of black-hating white citizens councils. He corralled governance of the nation's capital city. He was the benevolent chief before whom people lay their burdens.

And while Barry didn't resolve every difficulty, his petitioners left buoyed, believing their hardships short-lived and good times just around the corner. Sam Smith, author of "The Great American Political Repair Manual" and "Captive Capital: Colonial Life in Modern Washington," once said that "Marion Barry could speak to, and would listen to, more people in D.C. than most...You had to include Barry, because Barry could make things happen or help keep them from happening. So it was Marion Barry to the Urban Coalition, Marion Barry to help the Commissioner cool a disturbance, Marion Barry to help press the latest protest on freeways." Barry, unlike most chiefs, did not demand payment in cowrie shells or other valuables for his service. His only requirement was to follow him—and follow him they did.

◆ ◆ ◆ ◆ ◆ ◆ ◆ ◆ ◆ ◆ ◆ ◆ ◆ ◆ ◆ ◆

If the African-American cultural narrative is being told through Barry, then his life is the District's subplot. He is the protagonist that symbolizes its hopes, dreams, and human frailties. Like Barry, the real Washington, D.C.— not the federal enclave viewed by tourists from trolley cars and through camera lenses—showcases a deceptive duality. It possesses a cosmopolitan patina, but beneath the surface it has a Southern heart, still aching over the destructive impact of the slavery era, the slights of Jim Crow, and the meager offerings of post-civil rights integration.

Like African-Americans who want to be separate from the mainstream culture yet part of it, the District does battle with its unpolished rural shadow, pushing to join the 21st century, to trust its white counterparts. But always, just as it is becoming comfortable with its northern personality, its life beyond the fields—just when the smell of cotton seems to be leaving its nostrils—something happens to remind it of its Southern core. There is no escaping history. Marion Barry is both history and history teacher.

◆ ◆ ◆ ◆ ◆ ◆ ◆ ◆ ◆ ◆ ◆ ◆ ◆ ◆ ◆ ◆

Someone in the crowd at Coolidge High School hoisted a poster that read "Mandela in April; Marion in September." To the uninformed, the comparison to South African President Nelson Mandela seemed an outlandish and inappropriate use of a sacred, untarnished icon. In propagandist terms, the poster was unadulterated band-wagoning, ascribing to Barry the same characteristics and motivations as Mandela, the father of a new nation. But the connection wasn't far-fetched, considering Barry's place in black political history. "D.C. is the bellwether for black politics," says the University of Maryland's Walters.

Marion Barry had been part of that first generation of civil rights activists thrust from picket lines either by their own ambitions or community approbation into the high-stakes game of traditional politics, which since Reconstruction had cast African-Americans as oppressed outsiders. Following passage of the 1964 Civil Rights Act and the 1965 Voting Rights Act, a surge of blacks moved into elected office, most in small towns like Pritchard, Alabama. Passage of the two landmark bills followed dramatic and unprecedented events, forcing the country to examine its moral conscience and its system of justice. With this as back-drop, liberals and moderates in the country pushed for changes. Civil rights activists and radical African-Americans together wrote a transracial narrative that would attempt to bury W.E.B DuBois's prediction—that *the* problem of the twentieth century would be that of race.

By 1966, Robert Weaver, a black man, sat in the cabinet of President Lyndon Johnson. Later, President Jimmy Carter appointed Andrew Young U.S. ambassador to the United Nations. Blacks also took control of major cities: Carl Stokes was elected mayor of Cleveland in 1967. In 1968, nine blacks were elected to Congress. The same year, 1,185 black candidates were elected to various offices around the country, compared with 280 just five years earlier. Mayors Kenneth Gibson (Newark), James McGee (Dayton), Ernest Morial (New Orleans), Coleman Young (Detroit), Maynard Jackson (Atlanta), and Tom Bradley (Los Angeles)—all took office between 1970 and 1975. By 1976, 3,979 blacks held elected office throughout the country. In 1979, when Barry, the radical with the lethal tongue and fiery brand of racial politics, won the mayorship of the nation's capital, the event's symbolism couldn't be ignored: Civil rights activists and black power advocates finally had arrived, and with them would come a shift in the way the country did business.

But while the population in the nation's largest cities was shifting from majority white to majority black and Hispanic, the conditions in which people of color lived had not improved dramatically.* Still, control of the capital of the free world offered many blacks the promise of better times. Washington, D.C. became a Mecca, the place where African-Americans were destined to showcase their ability to govern and become viable participants in America's free enterprise system.

In 1979, Washington, D.C.'s newly elected leaders represented a more radical wing of the movement than those blacks elected to leadership immediately after the signing of civil rights legislation in the mid-1960s. Many blacks elected to office boasted mainstream credentials such as law degrees from prestigious universities. But while Barry had a master's degree in chemistry, he and his minions were the field workers compared with other elected officials.

Yvonne Scruggs, head of the National Black Leadership Forum, attributes the paucity of mayors from the protest tradition to its "threatening" nature. Barry exemplified those radical leaders who demonstrated a "greater willingness to take risks, a greater degree of combativeness, a more heightened sense of urgency, a great deal more personal loyalty with people who supported them," says Scruggs.

"They got where they were by clawing and scratching," she continues. "Nobody gave them anything. They started out advocating and they were always advocating as the underdog. The style they developed was more confrontational, less ameliorative, more driven by quid pro quo than compromise...People like Marion Barry understood that the only way they got power was [being] in your face and making it clear that there would be consequences if you didn't help them. That's what Marion operates on."

When Barry first took office in 1979 as mayor of the District, he was exactly what most of black America needed. Consequently, he was catapulted to the historical stature comparable to New York representatives Adam Clayton Powell Jr. and Shirley Chisholm, California congressman Ronald Dellums, Georgia state legislator Julian Bond, and mayors Coleman Young in Detroit, and Richard Hatcher in Gary, Indiana.

◆ ◆ ◆ ◆ ◆ ◆ ◆ ◆ ◆ ◆ ◆ ◆ ◆ ◆ ◆ ◆ ◆

A photographic montage flashed on the screen at Coolidge High School. A premeditated attack on the audience's emotions, it covered Barry's dirt-poor origins, and moved ahead to his work in the civil rights movement and his service to the District of Columbia. It was produced by Jeanne Clarke, who gained notoriety in the 1980s when she first tried to employ Effi Barry, the mayor's third wife.*

In concert with Barry and his wife, Clarke selected pictures of Barry during his days at Youth Pride, Inc.—photographs of Barry encircled by youths and senior citizens. There he was at the Martin Luther King Jr. Birthday Parade and during a protest march, in the council and jumping over the broom with Cora Masters, his fourth wife.

◆ ◆ ◆ ◆ ◆ ◆ ◆ ◆ ◆ ◆ ◆ ◆ ◆ ◆ ◆ ◆ ◆

Politics at its finest is the art of packaging and spinning. A skillful politician repackages himself every two or four years, inducing selective amnesia in the electorate. The public is artfully manipulated into looking out the window while the politician quietly frames selected snapshots, blocking views of his career's entire landscape.

Barry practiced political packaging and repackaging all his life. In the South, this is called rebirth. At Coolidge, Barry and others called it redemption, resurrection. The sinner was recast as savior. The past disappeared and the present was all there was, shiny and brand new. No one in the District, maybe even in the country, had been better than Barry at making the old new, or even making pieces of the past disappear before attentive eyes.

The montage was just one tool in a massive arsenal Barry intended to employ, hoping, through revision and camouflage, to reduce the impact of history. He wanted District voters and the nation to forget that fateful day in January 1990, when his world collided with a steam-rolling investigation by the FBI and the U.S. Attorney. That was the day he ignored his instincts, listening instead to the voice just behind his pants zipper, when former model/paramour Hazel Diane "Rasheeda" Moore called and invited him to her room at the Vista Hotel in northwest Washington, D.C..

There, Barry permitted himself to be seduced by both her and the FBI-supplied crack pipe, thereby collapsing a drug-free facade he had taken half a decade to construct, and nearly demolishing a political career he had taken a lifetime to erect. He had struggled for years with a carnivorous addiction. His battle had become the talk of the town. The press, almost weekly, reported sightings of the drug-using mayor.

Back in the 1960s everyone did it—or so it seemed. Unlike President Bill Clinton, who said he never inhaled, Barry most certainly did. His friends say he was never a big drug user. Alcohol and women, they assert, were his thing. But sometime between an occasional joint in the sixties and 1987, Barry's nose was opened. That was the year the number of sightings of Barry buying drugs, doing drugs, and drugged out seemed to have outnumbered sightings of Marie Laveau after her death.

An exotic, New Orleans quadroon with undeniable beauty and power, Laveau used herbs and various potions, including ingredients like dead animals and blood, to aid the elite and wealthy of Louisiana and other parts of the South. Crescent city residents never admitted that Laveau died. For years, they swore they saw her at various voodoo ceremonies, walking the streets, sitting at sidewalk cafes.

In the District, residents saw Barry at strip clubs snorting powdered cocaine, on yachts in the Caribbean, high and singing sexual songs in women's ears, at the Ramada Inn Hotel on Rhode Island Avenue, with a man from the Virgin Islands. Later, traces of crack were found in the room. His cabinet members saw his stupor, using the then fashionable phrase "Beam Me Up, Scotty," to describe the mayor's drugged state. Despite all of this, however, there were residents who saw the old Barry—the dashiki-wearing activist who strolled into the District like Wyatt Earp ready to clean up the town, bringing order and independence. But in 1989, that Marion Barry was as mythical as Marie Laveau. For all practical purposes, he was dead, or at least comatose. The other Marion Barry was caught on tape January 18,

1990, sitting on the bed in a hotel room, handcuffed, repeating almost like a mantra, "The bitch set me up! The bitch set me up!"

Who could forget the trial that became a circus, replete with hordes of onlookers, international media, and a black woman lawyer playing ring master? Who could forget the federal judge who made no attempt to shield his disdain for the popular mayor and the people who supported him, meting out the most stringent sentence possible? Who could forget Barry's desperate, cliff-sliding grab to retain power—his unsuccessful efforts to persuade the Rev. Jesse Jackson to hold his place?

Barry met with Jackson at the Frank Reeves Municipal Center on 14th Street Northwest just weeks after the arrest. The two men tried to decide whether Barry should abandon his re-election bid for a fourth term. Their inner circle of advisers joined them, while the spokes in Barry's machinery, mostly workers in his Office of Constituent Services, waited several floors below to receive word about his political future—and their's.

There in the conference room was Anita Bond, head of Constituent Services and one of Barry's political strategists. In attendance, too, were Barry operatives who had been at his side since his school board days. Also present was Lawrence Guyot, a former Student Nonviolent Coordinating Committee activist who had worked with Barry in the South and helped found the Mississippi Freedom Democratic Party. The party gained national notoriety when it challenged the state's delegation during the 1964 Democratic Convention in Atlantic City.

"Marion agreed when he could not run for office for mayor that Jesse Jackson would be the next mayor of Washington," Guyot recalls. "I left and went to a speaking engagement in Hartford, Connecticut. I went before seven TV cameras and ten radio stations. I said, 'Jesse Jackson's gonna be the next mayor.' I got back five days later. Jesse had changed his mind."

It wasn't surprising that Jackson bowed out. For a man who one day was in California and the next day in the Middle East trying to free American marines held captive by terrorists, being mayor of a city would have been like being inside a prison cell. He had never managed anything in his life.

In 1990, desperate to retain some portion of his political empire, Barry decided to run as an at-large D.C. Council member against an old and nearly feeble ally, Hilda Mason. It was the only political race he'd ever entered in the District which he did not win. Finally, after exhausting his legal appeals, and bereft of a potential office to claim, Barry rode off to a Virginia prison, humiliated and humbled.

Who could forget such a dramatic and traumatic saga?

◆ ◆ ◆ ◆ ◆ ◆ ◆ ◆ ◆ ◆ ◆ ◆ ◆ ◆ ◆ ◆ ◆

Around the world, Barry's leap into the mayoral race in 1994 was seen as audacious and unfathomable. At home, in the District, the reaction wasn't all positive, either. "If he were truly rehabilitated, he would not run," said Jim Nathanson, Ward 3 Council member. A short Jewish man who once taught in D.C. public schools, Nathanson articulated his constituents' view of Marion Barry "as a guy who broke the law and devastated the city in some way. They feel that he has no business running for mayor…" Nathanson's Ward 3, which was predominantly white, included the city's wealthier residents. They often seemed out of step with the city's seven other wards, and most blacks ignored Nathanson's comment.

Joe Johnson, who was pulling together a mayoral campaign organization for D.C. Council at-large member John Ray, was flabbergasted at Barry's announcement. Johnson had apparently experienced the sting of Anansi. "We were courting Marion, trying to get him to get behind John [Ray, who had run and lost in three previous outings for mayor]. Meanwhile, he was putting together his machinery. Carl Rowan Jr. kept saying, 'Marion's going to run.' And I kept saying no, because we had been talking. Then I heard he was picking up petitions."

But what group of voters in their right minds would elect a man like Barry who admitted having been addicted to drugs, alcohol, and sex? How could anyone forget or forgive the disgrace Barry had brought on himself and the nation's capital? Everywhere, Barry's potential candidacy caused consternation. Many were worried about congressional reactions. Congress, by constitutional authority, maintains control of the District's finances and laws. All city budgets are passed by federal appropriation, although more than eighty percent of the revenue used to finance the local government's five-billion-dollar annual budget is raised from District taxes. Moreover, any law passed by the city council must be reviewed by Congress, which at any time can overturn local legislation. The relationship between the District of Columbia government and Congress, even under what's called "limited Home Rule," is reminiscent of that between slave and slave master. Many political observers still refer to the nation's capital, whose congressional representative cannot vote, "as the last plantation."

John Hechinger, former D.C. Democratic state committee man and one-time Barry supporter, recounted the Biblical story of the Garden of Eden to illustrate how many regarded the Barry mayoral bid: "The Lord gave Adam and Eve redemption, but he didn't let them back in the Garden," he said.

The day following Barry's launch, District resident Andrew Frazier offered what turned out to be an astute assessment of the situation: "I believe Marion Barry has redeemed himself. However, for the sake of the District and its relationship with Congress and the world, I think he should not run for mayor." D.C. council member Frank Smith, who had known Barry since their days together with the Student Nonviolent Coordinating Council (SNCC), told *The Washington Post*: "It's hard to ask a guy with an ego like his just to stay on the sidelines. He can't resist."

But Mary Cox, the black lawyer who had defended Marion Barry in 1990, and made him her cause, came closest to understanding how most African-Americans in the District and throughout the country viewed the 1990 Vista affair. Speaking to *The New Yorker*, Cox said that law enforcement officials had "treated Jeffrey Dahmer [an infamous mass murderer] better than they treated Marion Barry. The black male is depicted as an animal. Whether it's Michael Tyson or Michael Jackson…every year we see a black male sacrificed. Marion Barry represents the ordinary black man, not the black middle-class man—the way he walks, the way he talks, his skin color. There is a natural connection between Mr. Barry and men who have had troubles. He is not Andrew Young or Julian Bond. By birthright, he connects to the ordinary man. So when the system holds up his weaknesses, [people] react. It's a class thing."

Even so, most doubted Barry could make it back to the mayor's office. To pull off a comeback like that would be a remarkable political feat.

◆ ◆ ◆ ◆ ◆ ◆ ◆ ◆ ◆ ◆ ◆ ◆ ◆ ◆ ◆ ◆

A "Draft Barry" movement had begun months earlier. While Barry, in true Anansi fashion, promoted the public perception that the draft was *independent*, it actually had his imprimatur. A local Baptist minister, the Rev. Robert Hamilton, served as the group chairman. And Barry directly asked Eydie Whittington, a slender political novice whose mother had been active in District politics, to serve as its treasurer. "I don't think he trusted anyone else with the money," she said.

Many campaign decisions, even at the earliest stages, were made in concert with Barry, including a series of telephone polls and surveys that offered tangible evidence of support for the candidate. The draft movement permitted Barry to skirt laws and potential embarrassment if polls indicated he couldn't win. Technically, such a committee, under District campaign finance laws, can only study the feasibility of a candidacy.

When the candidate officially enters the race and starts collecting money, however, a formal campaign committee must be organized. Barry's draft effort flaunted the rules, raising money and telling donors that the funds would not be reported publicly. Consequently, those who were concerned about their image needn't worry, because no one would know if they contributed. If support proved to be thin, Barry, with the help of the draft committee, could ease out of the public limelight without ever declaring his desire to recapture his former office, without suffering yet another public humiliation.

However, even before he entered the race, the draft movement had the desired effect on his opponents. Democratic pollster Ron Lester, who had been hired by incumbent Sharon Pratt Kelly, said his candidate's numbers took a nose dive the moment Barry entered the race, and "she never recovered."

Kelly's popularity as mayor had begun to drop months earlier, which may have been the primary reason Barry seized the moment. While promising major reforms, Kelly had only delivered lip service, frustrating residents in Ward 3 where the largest pocket of white voters live—they had been Kelly's primary base of support. The black poor and working class never warmed to her, citing her elite background and light skin—intra-race prejudice among blacks in the District was as pervasive as that between blacks and whites.

Kelly, in sharp contrast with Barry, was in the good graces of Congress, which provided the District an unprecedented amount of additional federal aid (one hundred million dollars), as well as permission to sell more than three hundred million dollars in deficit reduction bonds. Still, at the start of fiscal 1994, financial experts were predicting that the District would face a cumulative deficit of nearly one billion dollars by 1999. Congress ordered the U.S. General Accounting Office to conduct its own audit of the city's finances. Just weeks after Barry launched his campaign for mayor, the GAO issued a stinging indictment of Kelly's administration, lambasting her handling of the city's fiscal affairs and management of various agencies. Auditors accused her of using gimmicks and violating the federal anti-deficiency act, which prohibits over-spending of a federally approved budget.

Notwithstanding Kelly's colossal failure, Dwight Cropp, the former secretary of the District, called Barry's mayoral launch predictable: "Marion, since about 1982, when he defeated Pat Harris—which he was not supposed to do—viewed the office of mayor of the District of Columbia as his God-given job. I knew that, even though he was forced to leave office, he was going to come back. In his mind, that job was his job, and he was coming back to claim his job."

A native Washingtonian, Cropp had joined the first Barry administration and stayed through part of the second when, disillusioned, he left to become an administrator at the University of the District of Columbia. But that was a skillet-to-fire move, and Cropp found himself working for Barry again. After ten years of an on-again, off-again professional relationship, Cropp made the final break in 1990.

"I've known Marion long enough to know that [getting back in the mayor's office] was in his mind and it never left his mind. That's how he survived prison…I don't know how people didn't understand he was going to run for mayor," Cropp said. "Everything was staged for that."

◆ CHAPTER TWO ◆

THE ROAD TO BARRY'S POLITICAL REDEMPTION and resurrection began on a postcard perfect spring day. The pink light of early morning clung to the sky as Anacostia yawned. A smattering of people scurried to bus stops and the neighborhood's sole subway station. The parking lot and sidewalks adjacent to Union Temple Baptist Church bustled with hundreds of African-Americans, mostly elderly women and men. An impressive, though unobtrusive, blue and white structure on W Street Southeast, the church stands in the middle of the historic neighborhood known as Union Town. Several locations in Anacostia, which lay on the eastern shore of the river, offer a panoramic view of downtown Washington.

In a previous life, Union Town sported a pastoral, predominantly white veneer. When famed abolitionist Frederick Douglass bought his house—which he called Cedar Hill—he was the neighborhood's first black and best-known resident. During Douglass' day, throngs of African-Americans could be seen walking past his home on their way to land originally owned by James Barry. Barry (no relation to Marion) sold the land to the Freedmen's Bureau,* which, in turn, resold plots, priced at two hundred to three hundred dollars per acre, to former slaves, who then built their own homes in the community that became Barry Farms. For these people, Anacostia represented a new frontier. It provided an opportunity to stake their claim to the American dream. Severed from monument-filled Washington, Anacostia exuded a certain independence that offered its black residents an illusion of greater freedom from white dominance and control.

Today's Anacostia, like most of Washington, D.C., is predominantly black, contemporary ills corrupt its elegance. Douglass' old neighborhood is a lethal concoction of the worst of urban America, and of the fading traditions that permitted blacks to maintain a certain degree of dignity, despite decades of degradation and discrimination. Howard Croft, a former civil rights activist and professor at the University of the District of Columbia, once lamented that more than four hundred black youths, mostly male, had been killed in his Anacostia neighborhood.

Union Temple bridges the seemingly disparate territories—Douglass' and Crofts' neighborhoods. It is the post-civil-rights version of "The Church of What's Happening Now," existing in a vortex of radical activism and spiritual revivalism. Union Temple's pastor, the Rev. Willie Wilson, nearly always dresses in African-inspired clothing and preaches a brand of conservative-style self-sufficiency and cultural nationalism.

The cultural national philosophy was anchored in the Black Power movement of the late 1960s and 1970s, and saw blacks clinging to African motifs, asserting the superiority of their race, and insisting on African-American political empowerment and economic development undergirded by a "buy-black" philosophy.

A rather unique rendition of the Last Supper hangs in Wilson's sanctuary. Six of Jesus' twelve disciples are depicted as: Pan-Africanist Marcus Garvey, Nation of Islam Founder Elijah Muhammad, National Council of Negro Women Founder Mary McLeod Bethune, South African President and former political prisoner Nelson Mandela, Harriet Tubman, and Malcolm X.

Union Temple also wears its blackness on its windows, in its halls, and even in the chairs where the ministers and church leadership sit every Sunday. The wall to the left of the Sanctuary's entry boasts a hand-carved map of Africa. Plaques feature the Adrinka symbols found in Ghanaian culture.

Despite accouterments often associated with the disaffected, Union Temple isn't a basin for social rejects or for the poor. Its membership derives largely from the city's and region's thriving black middle class—those who each day face white corporate America and remain angry about perceived racial slights borne of familiarity and proximity. In a 1992 study, the University of California at Los Angeles' Center for the Study of Urban Policy found that many blacks with incomes as high as fifty thousand dollars considered themselves repeated victims of racism. "These are the people of high accomplishment and who have worked hard for what they have achieved," Lawrence Bobo, the UCLA sociologist who led the study, told Ellis Cose, author of *The Rage of the Privileged Class*. These are the people who, like the black underclass, resort to nationalism to defend or insulate themselves against the white establishment and its perceived attacks.*

All things considered, even an ordinary political observer might have predicted Union Temple's performance as conductor of Barry's political resurrection in 1992 and 1994.

♦ ♦ ♦ ♦ ♦ ♦ ♦ ♦ ♦ ♦ ♦ ♦ ♦ ♦ ♦ ♦

Outside the church on the morning of April 23, 1992, yet another religious group appeared to be heading off for a day of gambling at the casinos in Atlantic City, New Jersey, or for a shopping spree at one of the many retail outlets in North Carolina or Pennsylvania. A festive mood circulated, inspiring smiles, laughter, and light-hearted chatter. But a trail of television cameras and reporters with notebooks quickly altered the perception that pleasure served as sole connector. Clearly, the excited bunch of black women and men weren't interested in buying discount shoes or robbing one-armed bandits of their nickels and quarters. The group, which included lawyer Mary Cox, who had attended every day of Barry's 1990 trial, and Betty Banks, a nurse at the Washington Hospital Center, and Delores Weems, a school cafeteria worker, were destined for Loretto, Pennsylvania to bring Marion Barry back from prison.

A small northern town with only three main streets, Loretto, like a retired, born-again prostitute, flaunts an intriguing mix of religion and crime. The Catholic Church and a federal prison are its two anchoring institutions. Christians first staked the mountainous terrain in 1788 when Michael McGuire moved his family from Maryland. Not much later, in 1799, a Russian Prince, Demetrius Augustine Gallitzin, arrived. The prince had come to the country in 1742 and became the first Catholic priest ordained in the United States, according to Frank Seymour, Loretto's official historian. Gallitzin dreamed of establishing a religious settlement high in the Alleghenies. Perhaps he imagined the mountains as figurative ladders to heaven. Upon his death, Prince Gallitzin donated all his land to the order of the Franciscan Friars.

The Third Order Regular of Saint Francis, the group's formal name, still owns much of the land in and around Loretto. Steel magnate Charles Schwab also owned a large amount of Loretto's property. Though deceased, he lives on in the minds of the town's nearly five hundred residents, because he donated his land to the Carmelite Sisters as a site for a new convent. Schwab's body is buried in St. Michael's Cemetery.

The actual integration of sacred and secular began back in the 1980s when the good Friars started aborting Gallitzin's mission—in exchange for money. A new federal prison would be built. Seymour says Loretto residents were none too happy, but became participants in the marriage after a prenuptial agreement promised interaction between prisoners and townsfolk—sort of a covert conversion program. The honeymoon was short-lived and a long estrangement began, leaving the residents and church outside the prison wall. Today, the prison and church lead separate lives.

◆ ◆ ◆ ◆ ◆ ◆ ◆ ◆ ◆ ◆ ◆ ◆ ◆ ◆ ◆ ◆

The five buses and gaggle of cars, carrying more than three hundred passengers and a group of ministers, roared west on Interstate 70, through rolling green hills in Maryland, past the "Welcome to Pennsylvania" sign, making their way up the rough side of the mountains, and catching the leftovers of crisp winter air which would soon surrender to spring. No one knew anything of the local history. But even if they had been privy to it, it's doubtful they would have cared.

The folks from the District of Columbia were writing their own religious story that day, re-enacting their version of the prodigal son. Marion Barry, and only Marion Barry, was the center of their universe. The man who had helped so many of them get jobs, who had helped their grandchildren secure summer employment, and who had stood up to whites in Congress when black people's rights were being denied, deserved their praise and embrace, they believed.

"I've been for Barry since he came to my sixth grade graduation," Aletha Williams would say years later.

"I felt Marion could have been my son," said Ward 8 resident and current city council member Sandra Allen. "When he got locked up and the way they treated him, I felt like he could have been one of my boys and they could have done the same thing to them. The last thing I would want is for everybody to turn their backs on my children because they had made a mistake. I'm a firm believer that you could make mistakes and change. All of us at some time in our lives have made some kind of mistake that we don't want to think about. Some of us went to jail; some of us didn't. I felt that a lot of people were calling Marion a dog."

◆ ◆ ◆ ◆ ◆ ◆ ◆ ◆ ◆ ◆ ◆ ◆ ◆ ◆ ◆ ◆

About midway through his six-month term for narcotics possession, Barry was moved to Loretto from the federal prison in Petersburg, Virginia. The transfer came after accusations surfaced that Barry had received a "blow job" from a female visitor. The episode reportedly occurred in a prison visiting room where about 20 inmates were meeting with family and friends. Floyd Robinson, a white prisoner serving time for selling drugs, was with his wife and children. Initially, he told officials he saw the act, but later, Robinson said the woman "leaned over [Barry's] lap, and then I saw her go up and down." In other words, Robinson never saw the woman's mouth on Barry's penis. He simply assumed that's what she was doing.

The shift in Robinson's tale didn't prevent the *New York Daily News* from running a story under the headline "Sex? How emBarrysing!" Prison officials subsequently concluded that Robinson told the truth. But long before they issued their report, nearly everyone who knew the former mayor's antics disbelieved his assertion that the entire incident was yet another white establishment effort to break his spirit.

For most of his career, Barry had always been a lady's man. Many African-Americans who were the product of the 1960s and 1970s—both men and women—developed a fusion of bravado, intelligence, sexual freedom and promiscuity. The country was caught in twin revolutions—

While in prison, Barry attempted to remain connected with parts of his political operation, making collect telephone calls to anyone who would accept them. Ivanhoe Donaldson often joked that his buddy "never passed a telephone he didn't pick up and use." Donaldson had been the tyrant in the Barry administration. Short, brilliant, and impatient, he didn't suffer fools or incompetents gladly. And, he knew Barry better than almost anyone.

The two had met in 1960 at North Carolina's Shaw University, where SNCC was founded. Three years later, they were sent down to Danville, Virginia. Donaldson recounts that they had just arrived there when a police officer pulled them over, accused Donaldson of driving with a faulty hand brake, and then arrested him. Barry went to a nearby pay phone and called a lawyer to say that one half of the team of big-time SNCC organizers had been busted. The next day, Donaldson was released from jail—Marion made sure his partner didn't languish—and the two implemented their planned voter registration campaign.

But their friendship didn't forge under the fire of racial discrimination. It was much later before Barry and Donaldson became joined at the hip. Donaldson subsequently went on to organize political campaigns for Richard Hatcher, Andrew Young and others. By 1974, he had developed quite a reputation as a political strategist. Barry called him to be the architect of his council race, and he served in that role for nearly every subsequent election in which Barry was a candidate. In 1987, when Donaldson found himself on the wrong side of the law for stealing $190,000 in government funds, it pushed him to the outer reaches of the political limelight. But he remained a critical player, albeit behind the scenes, in District politics.

At the prime of Barry's career, Donaldson says, "Marion didn't need a phone book. He carried 2,000 telephone numbers in his head." Barry seemed to have something in common with Chicago mayor Richard Daley, who according to Mike Royko, didn't like "putting things on paper, preferring the telephone. Historians will look in vain for a revealing memo or an angry note. He stores his information in his brain and has an amazing recall for detail." Certainly, when federal law enforcement officers came looking for records, they found nothing incriminating with Barry's name on it. And because he stored so much of his information in his head, there wasn't even a telephone book to reveal the names of his closest associates. Federal officials and much of the public were left to guess.

Barry, the convicted addict, was hard-pressed to find two thousand people to take his calls from prison. He was lucky for the handful of District residents who refused to abandon him—among them Sandra Allen. And there was no doubting her loyalty. Her loyalty to Barry extended far back in time, and was matched by few others. To assure a prime seat in what she knew would be a jam-packed federal courtroom, she camped out on a public bench the night before Barry was being sentenced.

The entire affair— from arrest to trial to sentencing—had been a spectacle. While it predated the O.J. Simpson circus, it was still media overkill, considering the nature of Barry's offense. Nevertheless, camera crews and reporters from around the country and the world assaulted the District for the duration of the trial, reporting everything from what the mayor wore, to who sat behind him. The appearance at the courthouse of Nation of Islam leader Louis Farrakhan fueled the fervor. U.S. Judge Thomas Penfield Jackson refused to permit the firebrand to enter the courtroom. Eventually, Farrakhan gained access, but the tussle cast an even larger racial shadow over the proceedings.

◆ ◆ ◆ ◆ ◆ ◆ ◆ ◆ ◆ ◆ ◆ ◆ ◆ ◆ ◆ ◆

The legacy of Jim Crow influences both blacks and whites in the District, and Washington remains a deeply divided city—more Southern in its demeanor and outlook than Northern. Many District residents play a wicked game of pretense, speaking as if there are no racial or class fault lines. Yet, still lingering is the psychological impact of laws that forced blacks to urinate in separate bathrooms, enter far too many back doors, and tolerate being followed around department stores as if they were common thieves. All the affirmative action and black office-holders in the country can't fig-leaf that truth. It is a truth that asserts itself clearly at election time in the District.

Race constantly sits in the front seat, resolute and virulent, demanding attention. It is the District's primary way of looking at things, the prism through which civic life is most accurately viewed. It screams through housing patterns that keep blacks and whites separated by a park, a river, and monuments. It announces itself in academic programs that pamper the children of Ward 3 while allowing the majority of kids elsewhere in the city to languish. And it plays out in municipal services that are pinched east of the Anacostia River while lavished on the neighborhoods west of Rock Creek Park. While many pretend otherwise, the plain fact is that blacks and whites in the District distrust each other, perhaps even more than they do in other parts of the country. They are generally cordial, working side-by-side, even occasionally lunching together. But rarely do they mix for evening social events. And, while there is a great deal of civility, blacks in Washington often secretly plot the overthrow of their white counterparts.

And where race is not the partition, class is. A strange brand of classism and intra-race prejudice haunts the District. African-Americans in middle-class Ward 4, for example, thumb their noses at blacks in low-income Ward 8. In 1978, Barry ran against Walter Washington, a former federal bureaucrat who had served on the District Commission prior to Home Rule and who, as a member of the old guard, symbolized black privilege and entitlement. Barry was the carpetbagger. An interloper with sharecropper roots, he was "much too common" to lead the nation's capital. But, during those times, there were more of Barry's kind than Washington's, and a lot of guilty-feeling whites as well. Four years later, in his re-election bid, Barry's rural beginnings played well against the elite persona of Patricia Harris, a federal official in the Carter Administration. Political strategist Donaldson says Harris once required a church to rope-off its restroom for her personal use, preventing her own supporters access to the facility.

And in 1986, in her longshot attempt to unseat Barry for a third consecutive term, white Republican Carol Schwartz was doomed from the beginning—even whites have been reluctant to elect other whites in the predominantly black city. Pollster Ron Lester recalls that, in conducting a survey for a large corporation, he slipped in a question about whether the respondents would ever elect a white for mayor. Lester says the overwhelming majority of white respondents said no. "They respect the black majority and think the mayor should come from that community," he said, explaining the reasoning.

Barry always operated as if this political reality didn't exist. Dwight Cropp, the former city secretary, recalls one discussion with him just after he was first elected to the mayor's office in 1978. "I said something about why some persons, who happened to be white, were so critical of him. And [Marion] said, 'You know white people always stick together, and don't you ever forget that. They are going to protect their own.' That just blew my mind," Cropp said.

Barry knew what author Henry Louis Gates learned early. In his memoir, *Colored People*, Gates writes about a time in his young life when his brother, in their West Virginia hometown, was cheated out of a spelling award: "No matter what you did or how you did it, it didn't matter because it was their world, their sea, their tide, and your little black ass was about as significant as a grain of yellow sand."

But while many blacks felt as Barry did, and there were private discussions along these lines, complaints about Washington's racial polarization were rarely aired publicly. Peter Williams, D.C.'s former Common Cause executive director, likens it to a "roach crawling into the middle of the room. The people who live there are going to be too embarrassed to go and step on the roach. The people who are visiting aren't going to say anything. So that roach is going to crawl up the legs of a chair onto a table and no one is going to say anything."

During Barry's trial, though, a great many blacks said a great deal on the subject. In beauty salons, on street corners, and in offices, they protested what they considered the lynching of Marion Barry. Investigations of other black elected officials made for a tense national climate. Both Reps. Harold Ford and Floyd Flake were brought up on charges of fraud and misappropriation of federal funds. James Ursy, mayor of Atlantic City, was indicted on charges of bribery and corruption, pleaded not guilty, ran for re-election, and later was found not guilty. Congressman Ford's case ended in a hung jury, and the charges against him eventually were dropped. Rep. John Conyers, a Michigan Democrat, charged that blacks were being investigated, indicted, and convicted far more often than their white counterparts.

During the same twelve-month period between Barry's arrest, trial, and sentencing, Medgar Evers' murder case was reopened; David Duke, a former Ku Klux Klan member, ran for the U.S. Senate in Louisiana; Rodney King was beaten by four Los Angeles police officers; and more than four hundred black agents in the FBI filed equal opportunity complaints, charging discrimination within the bureau.

Where overt signs of racism didn't exist, discrimination because of class and poverty did. The Population Reference Bureau, a nonprofit group based in Washington, D.C., issued a report declaring that two societies were emerging in black America, one affluent and middle class, and the other poor. Thirty-one percent of the country's thirty million blacks, it said, had incomes below the twelve-thousand-dollar poverty line.

The United States in 1990 and 1991—the time of the Barry trial—was proving to be a difficult place for most blacks, and whites received the primary blame. The country was hot with racial hostility and antipathy. In the District, Barry was the heroic target, the victim of white supremacy, the person the government wanted to take down, the man who helped the poor when whites and wealthy African-Americans had turned away. He was the poster boy for the ills perpetrated against the black man. Consequently, instead of being excoriated for the transgressions revealed during his trial, he was hoisted on the shoulders of the community, celebrated and supported as if he were Jesus entering Nazareth.

Blacks pushed their way into the courtroom, giving physical expression to their dissatisfaction. The lynching of a black man, they seemed to be saying, would no longer take place under the cloak of darkness and secrecy.

◆ ◆ ◆ ◆ ◆ ◆ ◆ ◆ ◆ ◆ ◆ ◆ ◆ ◆ ◆ ◆

Though there would be rigorous security searches, Sandra Allen was determined to get into the crowded courtroom the day of Barry's sentencing. She desperately wanted to signal to Barry that he would not be forgotten by those who loved him. "The day before he was to leave to go to prison, I was in the Bahamas," recalls Allen. "I called him. I was supposed to have seen him before I went to the Bahamas, but we just kept missing each other. I called him to tell him that I was his friend and that he could feel free to call."

Now, in December 1991, Allen once again wanted access. She didn't know where the District's former chief executive had been hustled off to, and she was fearful. For a black woman of her generation, her fears were natural. Many African-Americans, especially those with extensive Southern roots, can recite countless stories of relatives or friends being beaten unmercifully, dying, or simply disappearing while in police custody. Their stories echo those of blacks under the apartheid regime in South Africa. Barry, a former civil rights activist, knew the dangers firsthand. Blacks were taken away in the middle of the night, only to be found the next morning hanging from some tree, drowned in some river, or gunned down in some field.

Allen had last talked with her former boss—by phone—a week before his prison transfer, at a Christmas party she and Bob Bethea organized at Hadley Memorial Hospital. "The idea came to us, on one of our trips back from seeing him," she said. "We were thinking about how he could keep in touch with his people. We decided to have a party with all the seniors so he could say 'Merry Christmas,' and so they would not lose touch with him and know he still cared about them."

Barry had long shown concern for the elderly. In fact, during his tenure as mayor, he elevated courting the senior vote to a fine art. The old folks held memories of suffering at the hands of white elected officials. Having someone who looked and talked like them seemed a special gift. To reach his old friends at the Christmas party, Barry "called my house collect. Being in the penitentiary, you don't have money to make direct calls," recalled Allen. "My mom hooked him up to the hospital. We had a speaker phone so he could talk to the seniors. They were so excited to hear him "

Finally, after a frightful wait, Allen received a phone call from Barry telling her he had been moved to Loretto. "I wasn't home, but he left a message with my mom." The transfer left Barry as humiliated as the initial arrest. He couldn't escape scandal—even in prison. Perhaps it was his own determination or the attention of prison officials, but the last portion of the mayor's sentence was served without controversy.

In April 1992, Barry prepared to return to the town where he had established his political bona fides. It was the place where the civil rights activist had metamorphosed into a shrewd politician—the place where he had become both cultural icon and iconoclast in only two decades.

◆ ◆ ◆ ◆ ◆ ◆ ◆ ◆ ◆ ◆ ◆ ◆ ◆ ◆ ◆ ◆

The buses and cars at Washington's Union Temple Baptist Church were there to escort Barry from prison, as if he were a king instead of a disgraced politician. The idea for a caravan hatched with Reverend Wilson, who had pitched a tent outside the courthouse during the Barry trial, conducting a continuous prayer vigil. Cora Masters, Sandra Allen, and Bob Bethea joined with Rev. Wilson. "I was interested in making sure that when he came back to Washington, he came back in style," recalls Allen.

African-Americans since the Northern Migration have understood the need to present a good image when traveling back home. The issue of style and appearance preceded Allen's concerns for Barry, and tends to dominate the African-American modus operandi. This culture, like some cultures in Asia, requires people to "save face" even in the most dire of circumstances. Blacks in America have been taught to maintain the appearance of dignity and prosperity at all costs, to never appear bowed or bent for anyone. After the great migration, when Northern blacks went home to visit in the south, they took the utmost care to appear prosperous.

Countless writers have described the scene of the Southern black— usually male—driving up a dusty, unpaved road in a Cadillac or some other equally expensive automobile, stopping at the door of the old shack where his family still lives. His mother, along with a crowd of nieces, nephews, aunts, and uncles would surround the vehicle, smiling, because their boy was doing well. He had conquered the North and the white folks who claimed to own it. And, he's brought a piece of it as proof—a car, a few dollars which seem like millions depending on how poor his family is, and a couple of slightly expensive suits with which to impress the local women.

But it's all show. Up north he's hurting, working two or three jobs—if he's working at all. He's living in a rat-infested tenement, scraping, saving every dime just to make this trip, to come back home in style. His secret hides safely behind his smile.

Barry's return would also be show. Everyone knew he didn't have a job, and no one knew how he might be greeted. He had wreaked havoc on the city's image, but some hoped that the repair of his image might signal the repair of the District itself.

The initial meeting to plan the caravan was held in the conference room at Union Temple with a cross section of people from throughout the city, including those adept at organizing bus trips for social events. They intended to begin the group's journey at Union Temple, but to have another church host a ceremony for Barry on their return.

"We asked Rev. Beecher Hicks if we could have the return home celebration at his church. Rev. Hicks wouldn't buy it," recalls Allen. Rev. Wilson says he still doesn't know why Hicks refused. Hicks had been one of the many clergymen linked to Barry's political machinery. Barry had established a cabinet-level Office of Religious Affairs, sealing the relationship while providing booty to clergymen who lent him support on controversial issues, or simply called out the troops when he needed them.

Throughout the history of blacks in the United States, there has been a covenant between the religious community and secular leaders in advocating the advancement of African-Americans. In contemporary history, Martin Luther King Jr. and his Southern Christian Leadership Conference stand as testament to what Lawrence Guyot, activist and co-founder of the Mississippi Freedom Democratic Party, calls the "ecclesiastical connection. Politics is religion writ large," he says, adding that "SNCC was part of the messianic expectation of black people in the South."

"Never has there been a society where they didn't say someone is going to come and slay our enemies—even in unwritten society, they had that belief. It translates into the Southern Fundamentalist. It is no coincidence," continues Guyot, "that some of SNCC's field secretaries were ministers."

"Marion is tied to both the religious ethos of black America and...the street. That combination gives him the credibility to go into the streets and do things that other people couldn't get away with doing," adds Guyot.

Actually, the link predated Barry. According to James Borchet, many District blacks lived in shacks well-removed from the main streets of the nation's capital, and adopted a common outlook on life: "Alley dwellers drew no sharp lines between the sacred and the secular. Like everything else in alley life, religion and folk life were intertwined almost completely."

But the Rev. Beecher Hicks, like many ministers in the District of Columbia, wanted to unravel the connection. He blamed Barry for the city's decline and was offended that he had lied publicly for so long about the extent of his substance abuse. In his view, Barry had deliberately deceived everyone, especially the District's youth who admired him and considered him a modern-day hero.

The Rev. Willie Wilson decided to help the bring-Barry-back caravan, partly because Cora Masters, his long time friend, was a member of his Union Temple congregation. In Wilson's view, Barry's arrest and trial caused a volcanic eruption that had the potential of destroying, at least temporarily, the morale of black communities throughout the world, where Barry's escapades were legendary and admiration for him rivaled that of celebrities and sports superstars such as Muhammad Ali. The devastation to Barry's image was dramatic. The circumstances under which he returned had to be equally grand, Wilson and the group concluded.

Besides, the planners wanted the white establishment to understand unequivocally that it could neither select nor eject the black community's leaders. African-Americans always agonized about whether whites were or weren't attempting to handpick their leaders. This fear dated back to the pre-Civil War era, when house slaves, rarely trusted by those in the field, often had a special status conferred on them by their masters. Even in 1997—six years after Barry's controversial trial—George Curry, editor of *Emerge* magazine, saw fit to write on the topic in an article entitled, "Handpicked Leaders." "We saw this when W.E.B. DuBois opposed Booker T. Washington's support of segregation in his 1895 'Atlanta Compromise' speech. We saw it when Dr. Martin Luther King Jr. was being pitted against the NAACP's Roy Wilkins to determine which leader should be deemed the most 'responsible Negro.' We saw it in the FBI's COINTELPRO activities, which were designed to disrupt legitimate civil rights organizations. And we've seen it in efforts to isolate Malcolm X and Minister Louis Farrakhan."

Curry blasted what he calls an effort by 1990s conservatives to "challenge the opinions of credible African-American leaders and propping up black conservatives...Despite all the dollars used to promote wannabe black leaders, we will not be fooled," Curry continued. "We'll pick our leaders and they won't be people who sound like [House Speaker] Newt Gingrich in blackface."

Not only were blacks in the District claiming their own leadership. They were determined to let Barry know—in what seemed a magnificent gesture—that the community he had served since 1965, especially his core base of supporters, had not abandoned him.

◆ ◆ ◆ ◆ ◆ ◆ ◆ ◆ ◆ ◆ ◆ ◆ ◆ ◆ ◆ ◆ ◆

Some of Barry's supporters, believing it would be better for his recovery, preferred a muffled return for him. The opposition, however, argued that a camouflaged reentry would have the effect of an alien invasion, and cause more talk and fright than his bold, confident arrival. "He was not sent out quietly. When he started his [prison] term, there was so much fanfare. Because he didn't go out quietly, he shouldn't come back that way," asserted the Reverend Wilson. "We wanted not to bring him in down and destroyed, but more to show the redemptive nature of the faith and to give him the opportunity to redeem himself."

Further, throughout his entire career both as an activist and as politician, Barry had refused to permit the perception that he ever lost a battle. He often reshaped results to conform to his own self-image as invincible. In the way he lived, Barry proclaimed that no one would take him down, at least not easily.

◆ ◆ ◆ ◆ ◆ ◆ ◆ ◆ ◆ ◆ ◆ ◆ ◆ ◆ ◆ ◆ ◆

The caravan stopped once in Breezewood, Pennsylvania. By late morning, it stopped again at the Days Inn at Johnstown, Pennsylvania—about 30 miles from Loretto. The original plan did not include Johnstown, recalls the Rev. Willie Wilson. The night before, prison officials suddenly decided to release Barry somewhere other than Loretto, to avoid the expected media bombardment. "Shortly before we made the trip, we became aware he wasn't even going to be at Loretto when he was released, so we decided to welcome him at the [Johnstown] motel."

As the passengers disembarked, carrying green and white balloons, a crew of young white waiters and waitresses gawked. They had never seen so many African-Americans in one setting, certainly not arriving to collect a man many considered a common criminal. Several Johnstown residents showed up with camcorders after learning that Marion Barry was in town. "I just came to see the excitement of all the television (cameras) and celebrities," Nancy Boes told the *Washington Times*. Her brother, Tom Buck, visiting from Rockville, Maryland, said he hoped Barry didn't see all the fanfare as a "hero's welcome." Buck was hoping in vain.

Preparing for the arrival of the caravan, Barry spent most of his time in a motel room, receiving visitors approved by the planning committee. Everything had been finely orchestrated to achieve the ultimate effect: Barry as hero—a man who had faced the system but not been destroyed by it; a man who had faced down and defeated his own demons; a man for the people and of the people. "It's only going to be a few minutes until we see the king," a woman in the crowd yelled to others waiting for Barry.

Not since the flamboyant Adam Clayton Powell's defiant stand against Congress did African-Americans have the opportunity to so brazenly thumb their noses at the white establishment. Powell, who had been elected to Congress in 1944 to represent Harlem in New York, had become quite powerful as chairman of the House Committee on Education and Labor. But he'd run into trouble chiefly because he dared to behave like some of his white counterparts. While he was indeed suave, sophisticated, and a natty dresser, with an arresting personality and powerful intellect, he was not white. But no one told Powell that.*

So he challenged the system, including President Lyndon Johnson. He took very public and very expensive jaunts with women who weren't his wife. And he kept his wife—the third one—on his government payroll, long after she'd stopped working for him. Powell experienced a very public fall when Congress voted not to seat him, forcing the state of New York to hold a special election to replace him. Ignoring the signals of a predominantly white Congress, Harlem voters once again elected Powell as their leader.

Marion Barry disgraced himself with a similarly defiant display, returning to his city as if he were triumphant. Some said the rally for Barry at the Days Inn—though smaller and more contained—resembled a scene outside the South African prison earlier in 1992, when African National Congress leader Nelson Mandela walked through the gates to freedom, released after spending twenty-seven years behind bars.

"When they brought him out [of the Days Inn], he looked good. He looked nervous at first. He didn't know what to expect," recalls Sandra Seegars, a Ward 8 activist who wrote Barry numerous letters she signed simply as "S.S." A medium tall, light-skinned African-American woman, Seegars fancied herself a sort of investigator. She had retired early and invested herself in civic activities. Barry became a special project. Although he never answered her letters, he acknowledged her as a supporter, expressing his appreciation to her when they met and informing her that he would need her support. In typical Barry fashion, he knew there would be time to cultivate her, an opportunity to weld her into his political machinery.

But in some ways, S.S. was like other women around Barry, particularly the ones from the 1960s. They were captives of his charisma, eager to attach themselves to him—mostly because of the indisputable power he possessed. Barry's own propensities, which sometimes made it difficult for him to keep his pants on, often were aided by women whose goal was to get him into bed, even for a single night. Some pursued their goal with consistency and vigor. Seegars agreed to join the caravan only after she exacted a promise from Allen that Barry would ride her bus on the trip back to D.C..

Standing around Barry as he greeted the crowd were mostly average citizens. Many privately bore the scars of the drug epidemic of the 1980s, which swept through nearly every major urban center in America. In the District, the drug scourge first announced itself in the mid 1980s, when a forty-something black woman, a mother of six on her way from the super-market, was found near 8th and H Street NE with a lead pipe stuck up her anus. The heinous nature of the murder shocked the entire city, but it was only the beginning of a crime wave that would ultimately see thousands of children and youth maimed or killed, and remains unbridled today. Whole families were rent asunder, leaving many homeless and without jobs. Neigh-borhoods began to look and feel like demilitarized zones. Barry became the drug epidemic's most famous victim.*

The members of the Johnstown caravan personally knew the ravages of addiction. Someone in their family, or a friend of their family, had battled substance abuse. They were there to find solace in Barry's story, to see if it were possible to rise again from the dead, for crack addiction, in truth, was worse than death. They were there to offer their own family members and friends a ray of hope in the name of Marion Barry.

The moment temporarily caught the normally glib Barry speechless. He had not imagined there would be so many people willing to pay fifteen dollars to ride hours in a bus, just to escort him home from prison. He bounded to the podium in a charcoal-gray suit, white shirt and burgundy tie, sporting an African Kente cloth scarf and kufi hat. The attire seemed a fitting symbol. Kente cloth, historically, was a fabric reserved for Ghanaian kings and royalty.

Back in the 1960s, the dashiki—the large, unshaped, African-style shirt—was Barry's uniform. But by 1984 he had only one or two of the relics in his closet. He had switched to pinstriped Christian Dior suits, and indulged himself with hundreds of silk ties. If he hadn't now gone all the way back to his dashiki days, he was close enough that District residents rec-ognized the return of an original. This Kente-cloth-wearing Marion Barry was the one they had known and loved a decade earlier, the one few of them would ever reject.

He had dyed his gray hair brown. His seventy-five-year-old mother, Mattie Cummings, stood at his side, as did an entourage of bodyguards. Days earlier, Barry had celebrated his mother's birthday. No son could have been blessed with a more stoic and supportive mother than Mattie Cum-mings. She'd seen her only son rise from student leader to national leader.

Each day for months in the federal courthouse, she watched his very public fall drag on. Never once did any observer see disappointment in Mattie Cummings' eyes, or hear her express anger over the way her son had lived his life. She went to visit Barry while he was in prison, and stood at his side when he was released. Barry must have considered his political resurrection a necessity for his mother as well as for himself.

The story of Mattie Cummings' relationship with her son is highly reminiscent of Langston Hughes' poem, "Mother to Son":

Life for me ain't been no crystal stair
It's had tacks in it
And splinters
And boards torn up, And places with no carpet on the floor
Bare
But all the time
I's been a-climbin...
So, boy, don't you turn back. Don't no set down on the steps
'Cause you finds it kinder hard
Don't you fall—now

"I am overwhelmed by the outpouring of love and concern for me," said Barry. "I was going to quietly reestablish myself in my community after I paid my debt for my mistakes. I hope this is the beginning of how we receive each one of our brothers and sisters after they've paid their debt." He called his past problems a "spiritual power outage in my life." And when asked what he intended to do, he coyly responded that his "immediate plan is to be with my son, mother and a few close friends, do some volunteer work, and relax. I don't have anything to say but that. I'll take one step at a time."

Barry ambled into the restaurant where tables had been arranged for lunch. "People were still standing around. He was escorted by Nation of Islam security to the head table, and treated like a king or something," recalls Sandra Seegars. "All he had to do was lift his fork. It was, 'What do you want? What do you need?' He just had to look around and people were making sure he was taken care of."

After lunch, Barry and Cora Masters boarded the lead bus. The caravan made only one rest stop. Seegars pulled Allen aside to complain that Barry had not yet ridden on her bus—the one where most of the passengers were from Ward 8. Just before the caravan pulled out, Barry boarded that bus.

◆ ◆ ◆ ◆ ◆ ◆ ◆ ◆ ◆ ◆ ◆ ◆ ◆ ◆ ◆ ◆

The group arrived back at Washington, D.C.'s Union Temple at about eight p.m. Another large crowd of supporters awaited them. When Barry stepped off the bus, he pulled out a line most often associated with civil rights leader Martin Luther King, Jr., shouting "Free at last, Free at last!"

Barry said very little at the night-time rally in Union Temple Church. In fact, he stole out of the building as the crowd continued its perfervid celebration. He refused to answer any questions about his political plans, although word had already begun to surface that he was looking for an office to claim. He said only that he'd reach a decision within two weeks.

But Mary Cox, one of his most ardent supporters, predicted that Barry would target Ward 8's D.C. council member Wilhelmina Rolark. It will be "one of the bloodiest [political] fights ever seen," she predicted.

That he would take on Rolark for her Ward 8 Council seat was anything but far-fetched. In 1990, when an arrested and charged Barry chose to run for the council's at-large seat instead of mayor, he captured only five thousand votes from Ward 8. It was certainly an embarrassing showing, but Rolark, the Ward 8 Councilperson, had never tallied more than five thousand votes herself. In Rolark, he correctly saw a weak opponent, and Barry—the consummate politician—was never above exploiting *anyone's* weaknesses.

CHAPTER THREE

BACK HOME FROM PRISON in April 1992, Barry tried to settle into ordinary life. But things for him were not what they had been. In some circles, he was now a pariah, and even his "friends" didn't bother to call him. "Nobody wanted to be near him," Sandra Allen recalls.

At the University of the District of Columbia, the city's only land-grant college, and the one created during Barry's second term, officials refused to allow him to sit on the dais during the May 1992 graduation. "I like the university, I supported it. I've only missed one commencement," Barry said after learning of the rejection. "What's the big deal anyway? The university ought to be glad to have strong support from people like me."

Technically, the request for Barry to participate in commencement ceremonies came first from Rosetta Bryson, president of UDC's Student Government Association.

Barry himself later sent a telegram to the university's president, Tilden LeMelle, seeking permission to march in the graduation procession wearing the cap and gown he had received several years before, when granted an honorary degree. He also asked to be introduced, stating that "protocol and tradition dictate that former mayors are seated on the platform." Although UDC President LeMelle was not a native Washingtonian, he knew a scam when he smelled one. He understood the former mayor wasn't interested in demonstrating support for the graduating class. Rather, Barry was searching desperately for legitimacy, for a way to return to the political glow, whether he used young people or not.

"Contrary to your opinion, it is not protocol or tradition to seat former mayors on the dais," LeMelle said in his written response to Barry. University officials then called Barry's probation officer asking that the former mayor be "counseled against disrupting graduation."

Barry was always gaming, figuring out angles, points of access. To regain his office, the pol knew he couldn't squirrel himself away. He needed to actively polish his tarnished reputation. If he were to be redeemed, he couldn't simply be redeemed in his own eyes. The entire city, actually the entire world, had to know that he had been forgiven, and once again possessed the people's love. The university's rejection provided him with an impetus for persevering.

Barry was now as isolated as he had been in Loretto. Just days after his return, he and Cora Masters called Sandra Allen and Bob Bethea, inviting them to a gospel concert at Constitution Hall. It was quite a turnabout. A man who had been a guest at the White House—a man who had officially welcomed heads of international government—was now entertaining his former employees. Life off center stage for someone who had known it most of his adult life was excruciating. Ever since his days with the Student Non-violent Coordinating Council, Barry had been "the man," the person consistently in the director's seat, casting characters, dictating the action.

Now he was on the sidelines, watching, agonizing. As much as he had been addicted to sex and alcohol, he also was addicted to power. What began as a desire to aid African-Americans in their quest to gain civil rights transformed into a self-absorbing relationship whose primary goal was maintaining power at all costs. Barry's quest to perform a public service had become almost pathological, as Norman Cousins accurately described the condition in his book, *Pathology of Power*.

Power, wrote Cousins, tends "to drive intelligence underground, to become a theology, admitting no other gods before it, to distort and damage the traditions and institutions it was designed to protect, to create a language of its own, making other forms of communication incoherent and irrelevant, to spawn imitators, leading to volatile competition, and to set the stage for its own use." Even before his destructive dance with drugs, Barry had grown imperious, Machiavellian.

But Barry is hardly the only American politician to have begun his career embracing good intentions, to take power as his mistress, and to be ultimately ravaged by her insatiable appetites. James Michael Curley, a famous Boston politician, fell from grace by committing fraud, convincing his brother to sit for someone else's civil service examination. And hadn't Dan Rostenkowski been caught running a de facto furniture store and offering special favors to his most ardent supporters? And how about Vice

President Spiro Agnew? Hadn't the IRS nailed him on tax evasion? The list is large. American political history is littered with stories of politicians making it into bed with power and still not finding satisfaction. Former D.C. Secretary Dwight Cropp and civil rights activist Lawrence Guyot, who understood Barry's power addiction, knew that, like Curley, Barry wouldn't just sit around twiddling his thumbs, acting like a victim, after leaving prison. They knew he would strike back.

"Marion Barry is a twenty-four-hour politician. While you're home asleep at night, he is awake and plotting," said Julius Hobson, a lobbyist who worked in the first Barry administration in the late 1970s and early 1980s.

◆ ◆ ◆ ◆ ◆ ◆ ◆ ◆ ◆ ◆ ◆ ◆ ◆ ◆ ◆ ◆ ◆

Hatching the strike-back—the resurrection, the redemption of Marion Barry—began in earnest in May 1992, just three weeks after he had been released from prison. As he sat in the backyard of his Suitland Road home in southeast Washington, he reveled in the magnificent weather. Spring, the most beautiful time of year in the nation's capital, had fully arrived. Cherry Blossoms on the Tidal Basin stimulated everyone's senses. Neighborhoods weighed down by the dreariness of winter came alive with people walking, hanging out on corners, laughing, telling jokes. Children skated and rode bicycles.

The idyllic scene in Barry's backyard that May day was reminiscent of days in the South, when everyone lazily rocked and chatted, oblivious to world events and bothered only by a few persistent mosquitoes. In another era, which must have seemed like another lifetime for Barry, the backyard had been the venue for his annual crab feast, attended by hordes of media, civic, and business leaders. It had been the place to get business done—to network and make contacts with those in a position to pass out favors or exact pain. Barry had neither invented nor perfected the art of political socializing, where every drink served came with a favor, and the exchange of business cards accompanied every introduction. Down South, everything was done over food. More than a few politicians there were made and destroyed over a plate of fried catfish, collard greens, and corn bread. The tradition was perhaps more prevalent with black politicians, who understood that crouching over a plate at someone's table told others that you didn't think you were better than they were. It was a non-verbal embrace that more than once sealed a vote. Just ask former Governor Douglass Wilder, who may well have won his long-shot election as Virginia's first black governor eating fish and talking trash as he toured parts of the Old Dominion.

◆ ◆ ◆ ◆ ◆ ◆ ◆ ◆ ◆ ◆ ◆ ◆ ◆ ◆ ◆ ◆ ◆

Barry's Southeast home had been all but deserted while he was away in prison. His third wife—Effi Cowell—left soon after his sentencing for a job at Hampton University in Hampton, Virginia. During his controversial trial on drug possession charges, she had stood at Barry's side each day, bombarded with testimony about his infidelities—testimony that most women are loath to hear even in private. A few years earlier, she'd heard the tale of Karen Johnson, the twenty-something government employee who lived at the Dorchester Apartments on 16th Street NW and who had befriended Barry, providing drugs and sexual favors.

On more than one occasion, the mayor had visited the young woman at her apartment, even writing his name in a guest book as required by apartment management. Like many women who became intimate with powerful men, Johnson couldn't contain her excitement. She told a former boyfriend that she had sold cocaine about twenty or thirty times to an important "individual." The U.S. Attorney's office figured that individual was Marion Barry. Using the information supplied by the former boyfriend, Johnson was charged with possession and sale of narcotics. Federal officials hoped to squeeze her into snitching on Barry. But she refused to testify, choosing instead to serve time in jail for contempt of court. The Karen Johnson story became big news during 1983.

Barry denied everything, a pattern he had found useful most of his life.

He bragged to *Washingtonian* magazine, "I don't need [drugs]. If I did, I couldn't function as well as I do. I'm too alert and too energetic and got too much sense and [am] too bright to have to be messing around with that stuff."

While he was denying his drug addiction to the *Washingtonian* magazine, Barry further deluded himself and lied to the public, making a cameo appearance on a Chuck Brown record that admonished listeners of "go-go" music not to participate in violence or drugs.

Johnson never revealed the nature of her relationship with Barry. For her silence, she received financial support. Regular contributions came from Barry cronies, including John Clyburn, and were characterized in the media as "hush money."

But while Barry had attempted to send Washingtonians on a dead-end hunt, the true story of his drug use and womanizing unfolded during his trial, as Effi Barry heard yet another tale from another woman—Hazel Diane "Rasheeda" Moore, the former model, turned drug addict, turned FBI snitch. By enduring this ordeal, Effi was not unlike the women who had come before her in Barry's life. Adherents of Eastern religions might say she was now suffering the consequences of bad karma.

When Barry was still married to Mary Treadwell, his second wife, he had begun a public and torrid affair with Effi. After a very violent argument, Barry and Treadwell split. Not much later, he started living with Effi. By the time he was elected to his first term as mayor in 1978, the two were married. Perhaps she foolishly believed she could convert him into a monogamous, attentive husband. But tens of thousands of people witnessed her failure. At trial, they learned of Barry's late night rendezvous with dozens of women during his twelve-year marriage to Effi. The city's first lady sat unflinchingly through what had to be her most demeaning experience, never revealing the emotional trauma she surely must have felt during the lengthy proceedings. After the trial ended, Effi escaped public attention, her personal dignity intact.

"Marion and his relationship with women...I'm not surprised he had several wives. He is a nice person. He is not always very responsible about some things," admits his friend Ivanhoe Donaldson. "Marion could be very disciplined about work. But his personal lifestyle—it's all over the map."

◆ ◆ ◆ ◆ ◆ ◆ ◆ ◆ ◆ ◆ ◆ ◆ ◆ ◆ ◆ ◆ ◆

Cora Masters, Barry's long-time friend, stepped in for Effi as if she had been Barry's lady-in-waiting, or some American rendition of a co-wife. Cora and Marion Barry met in the 1970s, when she sported what she called "an Angela-Davis-style Afro hairdo." A political scientist by training, Masters had come to the District ostensibly to earn her master's degree from Howard University. She was married to Moses Wilds and had two daughters when she pushed her way into the city's political circles, working as a volunteer in Barry's council campaign and later mayoral campaigns. When Barry married Effi Cowell, a former high school teacher, Cora Masters Wilds befriended her.

By the 1980s, Cora Masters Wilds had been named by Barry to the D.C. Boxing and Wrestling Commission. Later, she became its chairman and served as the focal point for the revival of big-ticket boxing in the city. But by the mid 1980s, she had divorced her husband and found herself in trouble after media reports that she had billed both the city government and the International Boxing Federation/United States Boxing Association for travel—a serious infraction of the rules. Masters, who by now had dropped her married name, faced stiff criminal charges, pleaded guilty to a lesser crime and later repaid the nearly three thousand dollars she owed the government. "She did some good while she was on the commission, but [that] case detracted from what people thought of her works," says D.C. Council member Frank Smith, whose committee had oversight of the boxing commission.

Barry, just beginning his third term, didn't turn away from Masters. Instead, he introduced her to his newest appointee to the boxing commission—Jeffrey Gildenhorn. "The mayor called me up and said he had this friend who wanted to meet me. He asked if I [would] mind meeting this person. I said I didn't. So they came to my place. And who do you think it was? Cora," recalls Gildenhorn. After the three had dinner at one of Gildenhorn's restaurants, Barry called again to say that Masters "liked you." Gildenhorn understood the nuance Barry intended: The mayor was making it clear he wanted Masters to receive special treatment from the commission despite the fact she was no longer a member.

By the time Barry was arrested, he and Masters were more than friends. Before leaving for Petersburg prison, the mayor asked Bob Bethea to "look out for Cora for me." It was the kind of statement men make about their girl-friends or their wives—not platonic friends. A friend of Masters and Barry characterized the relationship "as more physical than romantic. Effi knew about it. She and Marion fought all of the time. Sometimes, Effi and Cora argued about it. Sometimes, all three of them argued about it."

As Barry's relationship changed with his wife, it also changed with his mistress. Everyone in Barry's immediate circle says that Masters visited him frequently while he was in prison. She accepted all of his telephone calls. Using her wit and connections, she extracted cash and other assistance from Barry's friends so he could meet his financial obligations. "She loved the nigger's dirty drawers," says one Barry confidante.

"She has played an enormously important role in his life. She was available to him. She ran errands, she baby sat, she played governess, nurse maid. I think she really loved him," says James Gibson, head of the D.C. Agenda Project and one-time Barry cabinet member.

In spite of Masters' help, Barry knew he couldn't hold onto his southeast D.C. home—he had no job and his divorce was pending. He was spending his last days in the home, swallowing the freshness of spring, the blossoming magnolias. He knew he would never really know personal peace without somehow recovering his name, tainted as it was.

◆ ◆ ◆ ◆ ◆ ◆ ◆ ◆ ◆ ◆ ◆ ◆ ◆ ◆ ◆ ◆

Seated on his back porch next to Sandra Allen, Barry plotted his political comeback. Allen hadn't always been a faithful ally. Born into an old guard Washington family, she tended to look askance at newer arrival. Importance and prestige among black families in the nation's capital didn't derive merely from being a native, although that helped. A family was generally regarded as "old guard" if it met one or more criteria, established—unofficially, it seemed—almost by acclamation. First and foremost was complexion. A light-skinned black could go a long way in the District, even if the person had beans for brains. If the person were well placed in the government or academia, there were additional points to be tallied. And, if the person had money, coupled with etiquette, they could be as black as midnight and still garner a place at the table of Washington's elite. Allen's family parlayed position into political connections, and later power.

Much of Washington's old guard initially was unkind to Barry. With his decidedly Southern diction, he didn't speak like them. With his dashiki, he didn't dress like them. He didn't behave well in public or private. He often was rowdy and rude. Although he held a masters degree in chemistry, his failure to find a tenure-track teaching position at a prestigious university rendered him without any particular academic standing. But Allen, who had had an unfavorable early encounter with Barry, permitted the civil rights radical to politically seduce her, and she turned into a true "Barryite."

"I was converted when I saw the programs that were put in place for senior citizens, the youth, and the genuine interest for those two populations. When Carol Schwartz ran against him back in 1986, I went out and asked to be part of his team in Ward 8. I did not want to see a white Republican woman as mayor of this city," Allen remembers. "When I asked to be part of the team, there was some apprehension—I had not been active in politics. Once I got in, the first thing I did was have a party in my backyard to raise money for the mayor's campaign. People were afraid that I would not be able to bring others out. But I had about 150 people in my yard that day.

"The following year, in 1987, I got a call from the mayor's office, asking me if I wanted to be the Ward 8 coordinator [in the Office of Constituent Services]."

In 1992, Allen was getting another call. Barry had decided to run for the Ward 8 city council seat. "I knew he could win, but we would have to do a lot of work. He asked me if I would be his campaign manager. I said yes."

As a candidate, Barry could bring attention to a community that was literally and figuratively dying. Bordered by Morris Road, Southern Avenue and the Anacostia River, Ward 8 sported the highest number of teen pregnancies, the highest rate of infant mortality, and the highest number of unemployed residents in the city. In 1992, twenty-four percent of its households were below the poverty line. Median income was seventeen thousand dollars a year, though there were several small pockets of middle-class homeowners. When a community faces such intractable problems as those in Ward 8, it is ripe for the talents of a savvy organizer like Marion Barry.

Ward 8 was desperate for attention, services, and relief from the ills of urban blight. Gaining residents' support wouldn't be any more difficult than it had been in the past. Even with the twin albatrosses of prison and drug addiction around his neck, Barry's considerable political influence and the deep admiration for him in the District's low-income communities were sturdy springboards.

"I told him that, from my experience, you will be the best thing to happen to the ward and the people because I know you care," Allen said. But she added a word of caution. She promised to be the proverbial thorn in Barry's side if he "didn't do right."

Allen's biggest mistake that day was not asking Barry of his future political aspirations. From high school on, ambition had always been his driving force. He never attempted to camouflage his lust for status and power. It radiated from him. But Allen never broached the idea of a possible mayoral run. Maybe, like thousands of others in the city, she subconsciously believed he could never recapture the office. Residents had rejected him so resoundingly in 1990, when he ran for an at-large Council seat, that no one believed he would sacrifice his ego to another such defeat. Thinking about returning to the mayor's office was premature at best, and downright delusionary at worst.

Barry's decision to oppose Council member Wilhelmina Rolark, a one-time ally, seemed smart. Rolark's Ward 8 base was weak. She'd won the last three terms, mostly by default. A large field of candidates, splitting the vote, allowed her repeatedly to slip into office with less than one third of the vote. While Barry denies it, he smarted over what Rolark and her husband, Calvin, a cofounder of the Black United Fund and a newspaper publisher, did just after his drug arrest. The aging couple abandoned him, throwing their support behind the Rev. Walter Fauntroy, the former D.C. Delegate to Congress, for mayor. Now, it was payback time.

◆ ◆ ◆ ◆ ◆ ◆ ◆ ◆ ◆ ◆ ◆ ◆ ◆ ◆ ◆ ◆ ◆

Though Allen and the folks from the caravan may have sung Barry's praises, not everyone in Ward 8 loved him or wanted him to represent them on the council. When he announced his candidacy, some accused him of using the poor to advance his career, of making a Council seat a stepping stone to the office he believed was taken from him. Although he touted his concern for the poor, the record over his twelve-year tenure as mayor suggested otherwise: The District government under Barry had been sued by social services and prisoners rights advocates, and in nearly every case the government had lost, resulting in costly court-appointed monitors and receivers for correctional, mental health, and later foster care facilities. The public housing agency was declared one of the most troubled in the country.

"He ran through public-housing administrators faster than he ran through women," said Harry Jaffe, co-author of *Dream City: Race, Power, and the Decline of Washington, D.C.*

From 1984 through 1989, when the crack epidemic struck the District, the hardest-hit wards—7 and 8—were left unprotected. During 1987—the first year of massive crack-related violence—only 352 of the city's 3,880 police officers were assigned to Ward 8, and just 234 to the police district covering the territory east of the Anacostia River. Precincts with a preponderance of wealthy and middle-income communities, such as Georgetown and Dupont Circle, each had at least a hundred more officers than the poorer wards.

"You ask what precipitated the crime wave. It doesn't take a rocket scientist to figure that out. People had lousy places to live, terrible police protection, and nowhere to go if they needed drug treatment," Jaffe said.

◆ ◆ ◆ ◆ ◆ ◆ ◆ ◆ ◆ ◆ ◆ ◆ ◆ ◆ ◆ ◆ ◆

Despite Barry's abysmal mayoral record of delivering services to the poor, he understood that if people in Ward 8 had a choice between him and most anyone else, he would win hands down. He had composed a "Resurrection Suite" that began playing non-stop with his release from prison. He characterized himself as the Prodigal Son. African-Americans are raised on that Bible story and on the message of church spirituals. Both instructed that a great reckoning is coming, that the last shall be first, and the first shall be last. Barry knew these elements of black culture were his to exploit.

"African-American vernacular culture permits the redemption of a person both in religious and social terms and therefore permits it politically," Rev. A. Knighton Stanley once said. By adopting African-inspired clothing and embracing cultural nationalists like Rev. Willie Wilson, Barry also sought to manipulate the historical connection between slavery and the victim psychology that pervaded black communities in the 1990s more than at any other time in the race's history in the United States. The symbolic dimensions of his attire and rhetoric would prove a dangerous combination for Rolark. In previous political campaigns, Barry made mincemeat of opponents who reeked of the establishment and sometimes sounded like "handkerchief-head Negroes," who couldn't be trusted and would sell-out their mothers to protect the white man.

Casting his opposition in this light accentuated the traits most blacks, even those who had gained seats in mainstream corporate America, found poisonous. Raised in an ambience where obvious symbols divided "our Negroes" from "*their* Negroes," they still responded in adulthood to these symbols, sometimes failing to recognize that they concealed a lack of substance.

"Symbols have been the mainstay of blacks' faith that someday they will truly be free in this land of freedom," notes Derrick Bell in his book, *Faces at the Bottom of the Well*. "Not just holidays, but most of our civil rights statutes and court decisions have been more symbols than enforceable law. We hail and celebrate each of these laws, but none of them is...fully honored at the bank."

During his previous terms, Barry failed to deliver consistently valuable currency. But people in Ward 8, like Allen, deflected their attention from such factual data. And the symbolic potency of his resurrection permitted Barry to tap an unmeasured reservoir of goodwill in others who hadn't yet found reason to register to vote. The lemon man began preparing the largest batch of lemonade the District had ever seen or tasted.

◆ ◆ ◆ ◆ ◆ ◆ ◆ ◆ ◆ ◆ ◆ ◆ ◆ ◆ ◆ ◆ ◆ ◆

But even Barry couldn't shape a full campaign apparatus from nothing—despite the fact that some people did consider him God. He faced great difficulty finding supporters and funding for his revival. The search for an office highly visible to traffic wasn't nearly as challenging as putting together an election committee.

"Marion and I talked about who could be the treasurer. We came up with several names and finally settled on Carolena Key," says Sandra Allen. Key had worked with Barry before. He rewarded her service by appointing her to the first Commission on Women. When Barry called Carolena Key this time, she didn't hesitate, accepting the responsibility to oversee financial transactions, including the preparation of the very tedious campaign finance reports.

But while landing Key may have been easy, finding a chairman was an entirely different matter. Allen and Barry talked with nearly a half dozen prospects. When the conversations ended, each candidate said yes, only to call back the next day, expressing reservations and bowing out of the commitment. Robin James, president of the Ward 8 Business Council, was approached, then Al Smith, manager of the Southeast Farmer's Market. Finally, Mary Wolfe, a personal friend and neighbor of Allen's, accepted.

Allen, Barry, Masters, Wolfe, and her husband met to develop campaign strategy, although they still had no office, no money, and Barry wasn't yet an official resident of Ward 8 —his Suitland Road house was in Ward 7.

After weeks of searching, Allen finally found a place for campaign headquarters. But it would take a bunch of people working long hours together before it could become a suitable office. The building on South Capitol Street SW had been used by a dry cleaner for forty years, and the cleaning had been done on the premises. It was a horrible mess, but still was slightly too expensive for the Barry campaign. They bartered with the landlord to reduce the price of the rent. Allen called a friend who was an architect, and he agreed to provide gratis drawings for renovating the storefront. But the campaign still didn't have any sizable amount of money.

One of Barry's friends provided the building materials. Volunteers from a homeless shelter started by Mitch Snyder, head of the Community for Creative Nonviolence, actually performed the renovation. The mere possibility of a Barry victory was enough to motivate some people to lend a helping hand. They knew he had taken care of friends and supporters during his last term, even if he had forgotten his general constituent population.

Cora Masters once said that Barry couldn't carry a grudge across the street. But the evidence, including his Ward 8 council run, suggests otherwise. Like Chicago's Richard Daley, Barry didn't forget a slight, though he didn't react to every one. He was deliberate, private, and adept when exacting revenge.

With a committee and office now in place, the campaign's biggest missing ingredient was money. The man who had been out of work for six months, whose mortgage reportedly had been paid through the generosity of friends, decided to make a $7,000 personal loan to the committee.* Barry's ability to always pull a hundred bucks or more out of his pocket continually surprised everyone. As mayor, it was generally thought that he hadn't grown wealthy like some other politicians, who managed to develop a sizable investment portfolio prior to leaving office. And while fourteen of his political appointees from previous administrations, including the former deputy mayor for finance, Alphonse Hill, and longtime civil rights buddy Ivanhoe Donaldson, had been arrested for skimming taxpayer money, evidence of Barry taking such liberties had never surfaced.

Two U.S. Attorneys—Joseph Di Genova and Jay Stephens—had spent a great deal of time and money trying to snag Barry in contract fraud and kickbacks, but the investigations hadn't revealed any Barry financial wrongdoing. Rumors and innuendoes surfaced, and a weak drug bust was made, but a jury found Barry guilty of just one count of misdemeanor possession, deadlocking on twelve other, more serious charges.

The work of reviving Barry's torpedoed career couldn't be handled by the small cadre the former mayor had pulled together, regardless of their loyalty and commitment. Barry needed to broaden his base of workers. But it wasn't easy. Fishing for volunteers, the campaign called in more than two hundred people for an initial organizational meeting, but only fifteen took the bait.

The first crew of volunteers was largely from outside Ward 8. Audrey Conners, an elderly resident, sat at a chair and table on the sidewalk outside the campaign office, registering people to vote and encouraging them to volunteer. The registration drive took on a life of its own, with workers going anywhere people could be found, pressuring them to sign the red and white form, and then pressing them to practically pledge their souls to Barry. And pledge they did.

"A lot of unemployed people became part of our operation," Allen recalls about that initial crew of workers.

Barry also was his own best press agent, walking around the community, talking with people, urging them to join his movement. "He had a magnetism," said one resident. Allen and Barry mapped out his walking terrain every day, finding forgotten pockets of forgotten communities.

Allen mostly flew by the seat of her pants. She wasn't a trained political scientist, but she did make deep inroads into the ward. She had an extensive network, and people felt comfortable around her. "I just knew there were people who had not been involved in politics. We walked almost every night, in alleys, [in] hard-core, low-income housing areas to get supporters, and we would pick up two or three people every time we went out," recalls Allen. "The middle and upper class in our ward kind of frowned a little. We did have some right there with us, but, for every ten low income, we had one middle income. Everybody thought Marion had got a raw deal in his incarceration. A lot of people were upset the government spent the kind of money it did to lock him up on what we called a 'garbage beef.'"

"A lot of them had the same kind of thing happen in their families— only difference was the people didn't rebound. They were proud to see a brother [who had been] locked up and now he was going to do right."

♦ ♦ ♦ ♦ ♦ ♦ ♦ ♦ ♦ ♦ ♦ ♦ ♦ ♦ ♦ ♦ ♦ ♦

When the campaign officially kicked off in front of headquarters, Barry sounded like a blend of Baptist minister and politician, roles often played by one and the same person in the nation's black community. Buoyed by a crowd of about two hundred, including Ivanhoe Donaldson, the event closely resembled a spiritual revival. Barry, honing his redemption theme each day, frequently referred to God as if he were his personal friend, and to his own political resurrection as if he had been nailed to the cross and personally deserved the same adulation as Jesus Christ. This theme would strike the heart and soul of not only black Washington, but black America as well.

"Every one of you out here has made a mistake. You don't knock on a person because they made a mistake. You grab them by the hand and keep on going," Genevieve Simms told *The Washington Times'* Vincent McCraw. Tom Skinner, who like the Rev. Willie Wilson had become a sort of spiritual adviser to Barry, further bonded the community. He claimed the campaign wasn't merely about the election of Marion Barry, but "the restoration of Ward 8."

Linking the religious with the political seemed a stroke of genius. But the antecedents for such a mix can be found throughout American politics, especially black American politics. Hadn't Adam Clayton Powell been a minister before he was elected? Hadn't the civil rights movement been led by a group of black Southern Baptist ministers? Barry Passett, president until 1991 of the Greater Southeast Washington Community Hospital, commented that the "rhetoric of redemption is the life of [Ward 8]. You get people whose lives are completely caught up in the criminal justice system. Ward 8 was made to order for Barry. There are all the men who had been through the process and all the women who had watched the men go through the process…and he came out of it saying he had been through it and could serve them better. My God, what a story!"

◆ ◆ ◆ ◆ ◆ ◆ ◆ ◆ ◆ ◆ ◆ ◆ ◆ ◆ ◆ ◆ ◆

Barry's political comeback story also evoked a religious parable—that of David and Goliath. "We consider ourselves the underdogs in this country, so we fight for the underdog," says Eydie Whittington, a Ward 8 political activist and former city council member. "Marion Barry is the underdog who always out-slicks the establishment. We look at [him] as someone who won't bend for white folks...no matter how much you threaten him. So, we respect him. We respect a person able to withstand a whole lot of controversy and ridicule."

Former D.C. Secretary Dwight Cropp, putting it another way, captured the essential allure of Marion Barry: "What drew me to Marion was he was an intellectual. Folks have consistently under-estimated Marion's intellect. Deep down inside, we admire Marion, even though *I* know he's bad for the city. Even though *I* know he's dishonest. Even though I know he's corrupt. But I have to admire him, because he knows how to push [white folks'] buttons, and he *will* do it."

Ward 8, like Barry, often cast itself as a forgotten child, an underdog, the David among the city's economic Goliaths. D.C. Mayor Sharon Pratt Kelly, a former utility company executive with old-guard credentials—including light complexion, money, and a former D.C. judge for a father—sought to allay Ward 8 residents' fears that her mayoral election in 1990 meant their further disenfranchisement. But her message and actions never resonated. People east of the river still considered her much too "snooty" and too aloof.

Rolark, while a Ward 8 resident, possessed the same image as Kelly. Were it not for her husband, who affected a street-wise persona, Rolark probably would never have been given a second thought by voters.

Barry, in contrast, embodied the community's concept of itself as an ultimately victorious underdog. He was David, the Prodigal Son, and Anansi the Spider all rolled into one.

◆ ◆ ◆ ◆ ◆ ◆ ◆ ◆ ◆ ◆ ◆ ◆ ◆ ◆ ◆ ◆

Barry became such a hit in Ward 8 that residents and elected officials else-where in the city became alarmed about a possible Barry victory, and launched a counterattack. First, there was the residency challenge, mounted by Jepunneh Lawrence, another candidate for the city Council seat. Accord-ing to District law, Barry needed to have lived in the District for one year prior to running for office. Lawrence charged that because Barry had been in prison, he did not meet the residency requirement.

There also was the issue of how long Barry had actually lived in Ward 8. The former mayor had moved into the ward only eleven days prior to opening his campaign headquarters. He rented a two-bedroom unit in Washington Overlook Apartments, a once-deteriorating housing complex that had received a government redevelopment subsidy during his third mayoral term. Some candidates and their supporters argued that Barry was manipulating the system—that he was moving into Ward 8 just to run for office. The D.C. Board of Election ruled in Barry's favor. Lawrence took his challenge to D.C. Superior Court and later the Court of Appeals. But he hit a wall.

The court ruled that although Barry had gone to prison, the District remained as his permanent residence. "There is no evidence in the record to show that during this involuntary physical absence from the District, he expressed any intent not to return to the District...Likewise there is no evi-dence that he changed his voter registration or failed to pay District taxes," wrote the appeals panel on July 28, 1992, eight days after Lawrence filed his petition and weeks before the September Democratic primary.

The media praised and excoriated Barry, constantly raising questions about whether he had actually given up drugs and whether another foray into politics would re-ignite whatever demons had caused his disgrace. Barry was too busy making lemonade to bother about the headlines. After all, he knew he didn't have any friends in the media. *The Washington Post* had aban-doned him years before and *The Washington Times*, which began operation in the 1980s, had never embraced him. As expected, the black media, particu-larly the *Washington Afro-American* newspaper, one of the country's oldest black media organizations, steadfastly supported him.

The elected political establishment turned against him. Mayor Sharon Pratt Kelly endorsed Rolark, as did council members William Lightfoot and

John Ray. And Barry's former civil rights buddy, council chairman John Wilson, also opposed Barry's candidacy. Wilson once commented, "It's a bitch fighting someone with nine lives."

Barry ignored the criticisms and endorsements, gaining strength, it seemed, from the human wall of prominent city leaders which stood against his return to office. Throughout his career, Barry's intimates said that for him, confrontation was like an invitation to make love. And while most politicians spent time courting their supporters, Barry spent time trying to convert his enemies. In most instances, he succeeded.

In 1992, some were obtaining a perverse pleasure from seeing Barry squirm. The Rev. Willie Wilson, a drug treatment expert with years of experience in the field, had made every attempt to divert Barry's return to politics. "It was my original desire and intent to go to some people whom he had worked with, who as a result of working with him became financially well off, and ask them to pool some money to create some kind of job for him so in fact he would not have to go back into that arena," recalls Wilson. "The response I got was so overwhelmingly negative, I said, 'Well, there's little choice left for him but to go back to the kind of work to which he had committed and devoted himself all his life.'

"I thought the community owed him something. This man had given twenty plus years to public service. There were those who were very adamant about him not being involved [in politics]. I presented [the idea] as an either-or proposition," continues Wilson. "I said, 'If you all don't want to do that, then I am going to support him and do all that I can to see that he's able to function again in the political arena.'"

◆ ◆ ◆ ◆ ◆ ◆ ◆ ◆ ◆ ◆ ◆ ◆ ◆ ◆ ◆ ◆

David Watson, a young, savvy political operative who once worked for former council member Nadine Winters, decided to throw his support behind Barry. To a campaign that had few seasoned political strategists on staff, he was a godsend. Watson initially wanted to handle Barry's press, but

Cora Masters became the gatekeeper, deciding who actually got to interview Barry and the scope of those interviews. Watson became the campaign's statistician, computing the "polling" numbers almost daily.

Barry didn't have enough money to set up traditional phone banks, so Watson, pulling names and numbers from the voter registration rolls, prepared lists for volunteers who made the phone calls from home and then reported the results. Bob Bethea coordinated campaign special events and fundraising.

"It was really a team—Bob, David, myself—and Marion was very instrumental," says Allen. "He got right back into the rhythm. He knew so many things that I didn't know. We talked every night and every morning. If he had meetings to go to, I went to the meetings with him, just to hear what his responses would be or to buffer for him. It was a good campaign. We worked really hard, but Marion was an easy sell."

Sandra Seegars, the letter-writing activist Barry came to call S.S., volunteered to do campaign fundraising. She laughs at the notion that Barry was an easy sell to donors. Seegars usually received a list from Bethea of would-be contributors to call. After they squeezed the last dollar from one list, they moved to the next. The lists indicated the campaign's desperation, rising from unquestionable supporters to long time allies who had jumped ship after the drug arrest. Roy Littlejohn was on the third list Seegars received. Littlejohn was one of the cronies who allegedly helped finance Barry paramour Karen Johnson's silence.

When Seegars called the well-to-do Littlejohn for a campaign contribution, he insisted that he was broke. "I said to myself, 'Okay. I don't know who any of those people are.' But when Barry saw the list and the note I had made [next to Littlejohn's name], Bob told me, 'The Chief wants to see you.'" Barry asked Seegars to repeat the exchange she had had with Littlejohn. Barry, recalls Seegars, seemed shocked. "He told you *that*? Then he kept repeating, 'He don't have no money.'" Barry told Seegars not to worry, that he'd personally call Littlejohn.

The campaign also tapped some of the city's Korean and Chinese businessmen, who formed an unofficial alliance and often provided cash, says Seegars. The group included Yong Yun, who years later would find himself in trouble, pleading guilty to charges that he falsified a loan application and took kickbacks; Ho Kang, the owner of Martin's Cafe on Martin Luther King Jr. Avenue SE; and Tony Cheng, who owned a Chinatown restaurant.

"Tony Cheng would call and say, 'Tell the mayor I have some money for him. Tell him to come and get it himself,'" recalls Seegars.*

But mostly, Barry's former cronies and supporters failed to come to his aid in the Ward 8 race. The campaign was financed principally by car washes, in-office flea markets, and especially senior citizen bake sales. The District's elderly vote is extremely high and vitally important. Barry had held onto it by catering to their needs, creating an Office on Aging, hosting senior festivals and dances, and always, always, being willing to hear their grievances.

"Nobody wanted to give us any money because they didn't want to give money to Marion Barry. They didn't want their names listed on the funding reports we had to file with the Office of Campaign Finance. The very people around Barry today didn't want anything to do with him when he first ran," recalls Sandra Allen.

The enthusiasm and commitment of Barry's workers substituted for the campaign's dearth of money. While Rolark spent a quite considerable seventy-six thousand dollars on her campaign, Barry spent only thirty thousand, according to official campaign finance reports. Seegars says those documents may have been misleading because the Barry campaign "never deposited all its cash."

Primary day activities indicate that Barry may have violated campaign finance laws by under-reporting his contributions. Nine vans were used to ferry voters to the polls, and an air-conditioned bus picked up senior citizens, to whom his campaign served lunch on the way to polling stations.

Overall, 38.6 percent of the 23,551 registered Democrats in Ward 8 showed up at the polls for the 1992 primary election. The turnout was considered extraordinarily good in an area where voter apathy had reigned for decades. Barry received 6,512 of the 9,080 votes cast by Democrats that day. His opponent Wilhelmina Rolark, the incumbent, garnered only 1,908 votes, or 20.4 percent.

Most of those who punched their cards for the former mayor—thirty-eight percent of the ward's 68,869 residents in 1992 were under eighteen— were young, often first-time voters. "They see what the power of the vote can do," twenty-two-year-old Alphonza Clements declared that night, after the votes had been tallied. "It doesn't take violence to make a change. Just use the vote to change things."

Barry held his primary victory party at the Patricia Roberts Educational Center, a D.C. public school. Refreshments were skimpy, compared to lavish tables set during previous campaigns. But enthusiasm and satisfaction ran off the charts.

Barry and his entourage, which included the Rev. Willie Wilson and Cora Masters, arrived amid chants of "Barry, Barry, Barry." Television crews and reporters paced all night, waiting to see if history would deal Barry a miraculous hand. The ragtag band of campaign workers, mostly poor and working class, danced at the feat they had just pulled off.

"We're saying to the rest of the city, 'You're going to stop disrespecting us,'" Barry said during his victory speech, which was filled with "I told you so" rhetoric and threats to the establishment that the people in Ward 8 would not sit idly by. He called them the "sleeping giant."

Some members of Congress greeted news of Barry's victory with disdain for both the politician and the people who elected him. "It reinforces some of the worst assumptions people have made about the District," commented Rep. James P. Moran Jr., a Virginia Democrat. "I think Ward 8 is not representative of the rest of the city. It's composed of desperate people who feel shunted aside by the rest of the city, and they feel Marion Barry will be aggressive on their behalf."

James Stroud, a resident of the Valley Green public housing complex and a Rolark supporter in the primary, sounded somewhat conflicted: "I reconciled my soul [to backing Barry in the general election]. I never quite trusted him as mayor, so this was a hard decision for me to make." But Stroud knew that even without his vote, Barry was a shoo-in for the November election. Because the District is primarily a Democratic city, a win in the Democratic primary has long spelled indisputable victory in November. "He's got four years to prove me wrong," said Stroud. Barry, it turned out, wasn't on the same timetable.

◆ CHAPTER FOUR ◆

THE CROWD BEGAN GATHERING early on Saturday, January 1, 1993, again sending a message to the city and the nation that the man the federal government had sent to prison was no longer a pariah, that he had been redeemed, that he had made amends for the harm he had visited on himself and the city. They packed the D.C. Convention Center to watch as Barry took the oath of office, becoming the new D.C. council member from Ward 8. More than two hundred residents from east of the Anacostia River leapt to their feet the moment he strolled across the stage.

Their unwavering endorsement conjured up a similar scene—this one on a January day in 1967. Then it was Adam Clayton Powell Jr., who had incurred the wrath of the nation's political establishment. Powell's supporters arrived by buses and assembled on the steps of the Capitol, knowing that there would be trouble in Congress over the Harlemite's re-election. Inside the chambers, Lionel Van Deerlin, a Democrat from California, stood and objected to Powell's taking the oath of office, and without it, Powell couldn't be seated. The other 433 members of Congress were sworn in; Powell wasn't. Later, Rep. Morris K. Udall, an Arizona Democrat, made a motion that Powell be sworn in and then investigated. Gerald Ford, who as president later issued a pardon for then-President Richard Nixon, showed no sympathy for Powell. He offered a counter-motion that Powell not be sworn in, and that an investigating committee be appointed and required to submit within five weeks a report with recommendations about the New York Congressman's fate.

Two months later, in March 1967, the committee recommended that Powell be seated and then censured. But the House, ignoring this advice, instead voted 307-116 to banish Powell from the body. Later, it notified the state's governor that Powell's seat had been stripped from him, and urged him to schedule a special election to install a replacement. In April 1967, in that special election, Harlem voters repudiated Congress and re-elected Powell to the House. Then fifty-eight years old, he was given back his seat, but he never regained his previous influence in the House. His controversial two-decade career ended in 1970, when he was defeated by Charles Rangel in a Democratic primary.

Barry once said that of all the country's politicians, Powell was his model and the one he most admired. "Adam did remarkable things," Barry said. "He got a few steps from completing his journey. But they broke him in the end, when he went to Bimini. He didn't make it.

"I was on the Hill the day the House voted to deny Adam his seat. Afterward, we went to his office. Adam was standing tall on the Capitol steps, but when I got to his office, you could tell he was so distraught. Adam said, 'I played the game the way the white folks played it. I even outplayed them.' In his heart, he didn't understand. It was a 'Why me?' thing. Then he felt, 'I know the difference. I'm black.'

"I know better about being black and playing the game the same way," Barry continued. "They don't count the score the same way. Every black person knows that. It's just history. You have to know it, even [if you're] a nice guy like [Los Angeles mayor] Tom Bradley, or [Birmingham mayor] Dick Arrington. They're nothing but nice guys, and look at them. But you can't stop. You keep going."

If Congress in 1992 had had its druthers, it would have stopped the fifty-eight-year-old Barry dead in his tracks. It would have done a Powell to him. But unlike Powell, Barry, a local official, had only to answer to the voters of Ward 8, and he knew how to assuage their fears, just as Powell had known what to say to Harlemites. Barry understood the major tenets of black politics: Protect your own. If you can't spread the wealth to everyone, make sure it gets to enough, and always get as much as you can from the white man, beat him at his game, and never, never let him think he's beaten you.

Barry stood on the stage of the convention center sporting his famous Cheshire Cat grin. He had proved himself the rascal, and neither Congress nor the city's elite could stop him from reclaiming his place in District politics. His election had not been as dramatic as that of Powell or Boston's James Michael Curley. And Barry's triumphant return to politics didn't set a national precedent. But it certainly set one in the District's still-young government.

As he stood with his hand on the Bible, his mother Mattie Cummings and son Christopher at his side, one elderly woman commented that it "seems like old times." The city had not been without a Barry candidacy since the 1970s. And except for the previous two years, Barry had dominated the political landscape. He was the person before whom other politicians and wannabes genuflected or with whom they battled. He was the one many tried to emulate, but no one ever duplicated. Now he was back in the center of the city's action, ready to join a council where, except for its chairman John Wilson, he was destined to be supreme.

The Ward 8 seat was less glamorous terrain than what Barry had been accustomed to, but his political acumen compensated for his diminutive constituency. His council colleagues were unsure of how to handle him. Even before he was sworn in, there was speculation about what committee assignment he would accept. Technically, Barry was a freshman, and freshmen received committee dregs. But Council members couldn't and wouldn't treat a former mayor as a young upstart. He was the District's "Kingfish." The only question on most people's minds that January day was how long he'd willingly swim in the small pond of the city council.

"For too long," said Barry, "the citizens east of the [Anacostia] river have been neglected and disrespected. Today is the dawn of a new day in Washington and Ward 8. I pledge to do all in my power…to uplift the lives of all of us who live east of the river," Barry said during his swearing-in remarks. The sustained audience applause forced Wilson to ask the new council member to run interference: "Would you ask your supporters to allow us to continue?" Wilson asked dryly.

Ward 8 residents were tasting the victory they had long hoped for. They would get respect because they had the political equivalent of Muhammad Ali in their corner. But all the enthusiasm Barry's supporters felt that day soon diminished under the weight of scandal, his lackluster Council performance, and his betrayal of Sandra Allen.

◆ ◆ ◆ ◆ ◆ ◆ ◆ ◆ ◆ ◆ ◆ ◆ ◆ ◆ ◆ ◆ ◆

On the first day Council member Marion Barry officially showed up for work at the District Building, Tyrone Ford stole his 1991 maroon Chrysler New Yorker. The car had been a gift from Ward 7 and 8 residents whom former D.C. Council member and businessman H.R. Crawford had organized. The mayor's arrest had left him handicapped. Barry didn't own a car—he had always had a government vehicle at his disposal.

The car thief was no ordinary fellow. A musical child prodigy, he had been honored at the age of 12 by President Reagan during his 1986 State of the Union address—the same year Ford led three church choirs in the District. But in the seven years since, he'd traveled a long way from his auspicious beginnings. Prosecutors surmised that Barry arrived at his office on January 4, 1993 at about 9:45 a.m. He hung his overcoat on a rack, his key ring in a pocket. When he discovered his key ring missing, he went looking for his car and notified a building security guard of its disappearance. The car was recovered the same day, after Ford crashed into a junked refrigerator.

But the nineteen-year-old Ford disputed the prosecution's trial contentions: "Mr. Barry did not get to the District Building at 9:45. He was there a lot earlier. I did have permission to use the car but I didn't come back when I said I would," said Ford. "I did do drugs. They took over, and it was because of my drug use that I did not return."

Barry first denied knowing Ford, but later retracted the denial. When accused of misdeeds, Barry had always denied knowledge or culpability. In some instances, helpful aides provided sufficient cover, shielding certain information and events from his watchful eyes. In other instances, however, denial was essential to the style Barry employed. Often, he refused to accept any documents unless they had been sent through layers of people before reaching him.

During his election campaign, he refused to accept keys to the office, providing himself an escape hatch should questions arise about activities in the South Capitol Street building. And because he never handled the bank accounts, he could legitimately deny any charges regarding financial mismanagement. Only when the evidence prevented any wiggle room would he admit to knowing about any wrongdoing. During the four years when his drug and alcohol abuse reached addiction levels, he routinely denied the problem to aides and friends.

"He lied through his teeth," recalls Sandra Seegars, referring to the car incident and to Barry's professed non-involvement in it.

Barry had actually met Ford two years earlier during a support rally at Israel Baptist Church in northeast D.C. Barry had recently returned from a drug treatment center following his 1990 arrest. Ford was one of the featured musicians at the rally. And Seegars, seated next to Barry, says the mayor commented more than once about the young musician's virtuosity. "Tyrone was there playing the piano. Afterward, Barry told Effi to ride in another car. And then Tyrone got in the car and rode with [Barry]," says Seegars. Seegars' account adds credence to long-circulated rumors about Barry's sexuality, which first surfaced publicly during the FBI's investigation of the mayor and the discovery of his relationship with Charles Lewis, a resident of the Virgin Islands.

According to news accounts, Barry frequented Lewis's hotel room on numerous occasions during 1989. Lewis later was arrested on narcotics charges. But while his arrest partially resolved concerns about the Barry-Lewis connection, the press shied away from, and never answered, the question of whether Barry was bisexual. Although homosexuality, with the advent of an aggressive gay rights movement, may have become acceptable in certain parts of the country, it is generally frowned upon in African-American communities. Homosexuals there are still treated as outcasts, and their lifestyle considered sinful. The black community—and especially its senior citizens—tenaciously holds to traditional values. It forgave Barry for his womanizing, and his drug and alcohol abuse, but it would never forgive him for bisexual activity, even if it were induced by narcotics, as some of his friends suggested.

Government sources inside early Barry administrations recount instances when the mayor made sexual advances toward male staffers, including former D.C. Secretary Dwight Cropp. The story is told that Cropp ran into Julius Hobson's office one day to report a discussion with Barry filled with sexual overtones and innuendoes. Cropp felt the mayor was trying to "pick him up," and he was visibly shaken by the encounter. Later, Cropp received a telephone call inviting him to travel with a council member, the council member's aide, and Barry to Atlantic City, New Jersey for a weekend of "fun." Cropp repeatedly refused the offer, using school and other personal responsibilities as the excuse. These same sources say Barry frequently visited one of the male dormitories at Howard University. Tyrone Ford, who had repeatedly struggled with drug addiction, had been a Howard University student, but dropped out just months before stealing the Barry car. Seegars says Ford also attended a Halloween party Barry threw during his Ward 8 election campaign.

Ford pleaded guilty to theft of Barry's car and a video recorder that was in the car, which he pawned for one-hundred and fifty dollars. The recorder eventually was returned to Barry. As part of a plea bargain, the U.S. attorney's office agreed to dismiss six other charges against Ford, including possession of marijuana, possession of cocaine, a later, unauthorized unauthorized use of a car owned by Ford's uncle, and failure to appear in court November 4 on a burglary charge. In a statement released by his executive assistant Pamela Hillsman, Barry said, "I left it up to the criminal justice system and justice has been served." But when the car was returned to him, he refused to keep it, because, he said, drugs had been recovered from it. Clearly, he wanted to distance himself from any possible claims that he too could have been involved, yet again, with drugs. Barry's car eventually was auctioned off.

Later, Barry's image suffered from press reports surrounding his failure to file several campaign finance reports on his Constituent Services Fund. Under District of Columbia law, elected officials can maintain a fund not to exceed an annual limit of forty thousand dollars for the purpose of providing assistance to voters in their jurisdictions. Individual or corporate contributions to the fund cannot exceed four hundred dollars. Barry's fund count was in shambles. While the failure to file was a minor offense, it proved an embarrassment for a man who boasted that before he became mayor in 1979, the city didn't even know how much money it had in the bank, and that he came to its fiscal rescue. The report finally was filed to the satisfaction of officials at the Office of Campaign Finance, but the incident left serious questions about whether Barry's campaign had raised and used contributions that circumvented the law.

The greatest damage to Barry's image came as a result of strife within his organization's machinery, most notably between Cora Masters, whom Barry married just after taking his City Council seat, and Sandra Allen, his former campaign manager. The two women had developed a bond while Barry was in prison, riding together and chatting about fashion. But the camaraderie evaporated soon after his election.

Initially, Allen was appointed to head Barry's ward office of constituent services. The office fielded hundreds of calls daily, from people who still perceived Barry as mayor and not simply one of thirteen council members without power to deliver any significant services. Complaints from his wife inspired Barry to make changes in the office's operation. Allen was pushed out, landing a job at the East of the River Development Corporation. Roslind Styles, a personal friend of Barry's wife, was hired to replace Allen.

But the conflict persisted and Allen subsequently was pushed out of the development corporation. Two years later, the dispute between Allen and Barry left him grievously wounded in his home base.

Although Barry promised aggressive action to tackle the Ward's seemingly intractable ills—such as unemployment and teen pregnancy—by the end of his first year as a city council member, he had very few tangible achievements. Barry established a business and economic development council whose strategy was to push contractors to increase minority hiring, but a major development project eluded the ward. His office coordinated a summer enrichment program at a local elementary school. He co-sponsored a Council bill that imposed a three-year moratorium on certain liquor licenses in Wards 2, 7, and 8, where alcohol-serving establishments were proliferating. He introduced legislation that made it a felony to have a gun, and gave police authority to seize an automobile when a gun was found inside.

"His presence has been felt, but there have been no specific remedies to specific problems that have plagued the ward," said political activist Absalom Jordon. It was not terribly surprising. Barry's hands were no longer on the levers of power. He could not deliver services, couldn't extract favors from business leaders or others in the community with the promise of government contracts or prestigious appointments to boards and commissions. Few of his previous mayoral appointees were still in key management positions, ready to deliver favors when asked.

As mayor, Sharon Pratt Kelly had purged the government of many of Barry's cronies. These reductions in the work force had been as detrimental to her as to Barry. But she wanted to insure that none of Barry's people would be there to stab her from behind. Losing experienced government workers left Kelly managerially vulnerable, without expertise to either implement or evaluate the potential effectiveness of her programs. Now, despite some efforts at damage control, Kelly knew that having Barry back on the scene spelled trouble for her. When her administration launched a major effort to privatize various services, Barry, aided by John Ray, introduced a bill that forced the mayor to prove there would be a ten percent savings from such efforts. The move handicapped Kelly and signaled to labor unions and government workers that Barry was still a friend who could be counted on to defend their jobs.

On the Council, Barry could hold Kelly accountable for the poor delivery of services in his ward, hamstring her attempts at reforming the government he had assembled, hold hearings, and position himself as the savior of several strategic populations. Comparisons were constantly being made between the two, and in the male-dominated arena of politics, it heightened concerns about women's abilities.

Barry hurdled the obstacle of limited power by resorting to what he knew best—symbolism. While budget shortfalls were causing some council members to consider closing the city's only publicly subsidized hospital, D.C. General—and the one which served many of the city's poorest residents—Barry entered into a rhetorical war, blasting those who would deny the city's impoverished health services. He staved off the hospital closing, launching a study of how to preserve its mission.

Without a campaign or a major office, Barry was denied a vehicle for cultivating his resurrected image. So, he stole prayer, the way Anansi stole the sun. Charles Ballard, a local government employee and political wannabe, had launched a school prayer initiative, which was being opposed by the ACLU, a few members of the D.C. council, and others in the city. Barry attempted to snatch the momentum from Ballard, introducing into the council a bill that would have permitted voluntary prayer in the schools.

He told *The New Yorker*'s David Remnick: "I know the power of persistent prayer from a personal point of view. To pray out loud, it doesn't just affect the person praying. It affects all those around who hear it." But Barry knew his proposed legislation would travel a dead-end path. He knew, even as he introduced it, that a strong lobby of council members and the ACLU stood poised to prevent the legislation from ever being enacted. Yet, the bill counted immeasurably with the Bible-thumping community and guaranteed its support for his future efforts. Barry needed to re-ingratiate himself with that community, which was wrapped around his finger at one time. While many ministers and churchgoers endorsed his return, their numbers would have to swell for what he had in mind.

He also had to deliver to the newest part of his constituency—youth. During the campaign, he'd promised them jobs. If he was going to keep them loyal, he needed to act on that pledge. Although he knew he couldn't provide a single job, Barry made it appear that he was trying, while telegraphing to the astute observer his political intentions beyond Ward 8. He introduced legislation that required employment of all persons in the city from fourteen to twenty-one years of age. "I am here to fight for the future of our young people," Barry said at a District Building event. "The District government bears a profound responsibility to help young people help themselves."

The measure required the city to provide a minimum of thirty-eight weeks of employment for youths aged fourteen to twenty-one. It mandated a minimum of forty weeks of employment for people eighteen to twenty-one who were not enrolled in school. It created a special Office of Youth Employment and Training, established a trust fund, required automation of the program's records, and mandated an annual report from the mayor. The bill swiftly drew criticism from various members of the council: "[Creating entitlements] is something we did in the eighties and it got us in big trouble," said Ward 3 council member Jim Nathanson. "We're still paying for it." Even Council member Kevin Chavous, whose constituents were just like Barry's, called the cost of the program prohibitive.

The bill had no possibility of passage, but Barry rode the horse until it died. He spent the first seven months of his tenure promoting the measure, holding citywide public hearings and later special meetings in each ward. But while the bill was referred to the Labor committee, which Barry chaired, it never was voted out. Nor did Barry locate within the city's budget the $10 million needed to fund the program for its first year. Consequently, when his own bill died in his own committee, no one was surprised.

♦ ♦ ♦ ♦ ♦ ♦ ♦ ♦ ♦ ♦ ♦ ♦ ♦ ♦ ♦ ♦ ♦

Barry played a dangerous narcissistic game with Washington, D.C.'s low-income African-American community. It was a game he had begun perfecting the moment he stepped into the city in 1965. He knew this community better than any other. He'd come to it, worked it as a civil rights activist, and par-layed that knowledge into a vibrant political career. He maintained a psychological link with these people. He knew they dreamed of becoming a part of the American mainstream. But while they may have wanted to pull themselves up by the proverbial bootstrap, many didn't have boots or any other shoes. Barry entered their shoeless world and promised them Italian loafers. But his employment bill, while raising the hopes of thousands of young people in the city, never was intended to do anything except provide a platform for his forays into wards beyond his own. In that respect, he was successful. He'd opened a door through which he would step in the next few months. Al Pearsall, a civic activist, acknowledged Barry's underwhelming record on the Council, but countered that, "You measure a politician by the feel-good index of residents. People in the ward feel comfortable."

♦ ♦ ♦ ♦ ♦ ♦ ♦ ♦ ♦ ♦ ♦ ♦ ♦ ♦ ♦ ♦ ♦

Symbolism seemed to work well on Ward 8 residents. Like hungry animals, they were satisfied with crumbs brushed from the table. By the spring of 1994, though, Barry had had enough of monthly legislative council sessions and phone calls from citizens concerned only about trash collection. He called a meeting at Allen AME Church on Alabama Avenue SE to float the idea of a Barry mayoral candidacy to a band of supporters, including Sandra Allen, Bob Bethea, Sandra Seegars, and Eydie Whittington.

The draft movement had begun weeks earlier, when various District communities were queried about a Barry for Mayor campaign. While the idea caught on quickly with some people, others, like Seegars, were enraged. At the meeting, she presented to Barry nine reasons she believed he didn't deserve to be mayor.* Chief among her gripes was that he had been insensitive to the people in Ward 8, and that he had used them as a launching pad for higher office. So upset was she that she called him a "turncoat."

Allen felt personally betrayed. Earlier, she had convinced people Barry was serious about serving the ward, that it wasn't simply a prop for his next political move. Now, eighteen months in office, Barry was making her into a liar. "But then I had to stop and think, 'Is this the best thing for the city?' He would be a better mayor than Sharon [Pratt Kelly] and I never saw John [Ray] as mayor. I didn't think he wanted the job badly enough," Allen reflected.

Bethea still believed in Barry—still felt the man he called "chief" cared about children, about black people, particularly about the underclass. "He was like a crusader," says Bethea. "I came from West Virginia, I had seen the civil rights movement and the changes it brought for people. I said, 'More power to him.' If he wanted to run for mayor, let's rock and roll."

CHAPTER FIVE

A GROUP OF YOUNG AFRICAN-AMERICAN MEN and women, most between the ages of twenty and thirty, scattered themselves throughout Congress Heights and other communities east of the Anacostia River. *Their mission*: to register residents pledging to vote for Marion Barry in the 1994 mayoral race. *Their method*: invade and assault dangerous housing projects, drug dens, havens for alcoholics, camps of homeless vagrants, and the kitchens and living rooms of working class families.

The group called itself the Fighting 54th, in honor of the black Civil War regiment depicted in the movie "Glory." Every day, it staked out territory, maneuvered the landscape, racked up more voters, simultaneously angering and frightening Barry's opposition. Sometimes, the 54th retraced previously traversed terrain, hoping to pull along just one more reluctant registrant. During a two block, one-hour-blitz, the 54th signed up twenty new voters—quite an accomplishment in a community that usually ignored the electoral process completely. The strategy was brilliant. The registration drive could neutralize traditionally potent anti-Barry covens, especially Ward 3.

Bordered by Montgomery County on the west and 16th Street NW on the east, Ward 3 contained the largest contingent of white and wealthy residents. It also paid nearly forty-six percent of all the income tax revenues collected by the District. Blacks held the political edge in the city, but whites retained the economic power—and considerable political clout. In previous elections, Ward 3 often had the highest voter turnout. Consequently, capturing Ward 3, and its black middle-class counterparts, Wards 4 and 5, were key to victory for a mayor-to-be. Mayoral candidates aggressively courted Ward 3 residents, but found them an obstinate bunch, unpersuaded by political rhetoric, and concerned mostly with the minutiae of municipal government operation—public safety, road maintenance, and trash collection.

In his first mayoral race in 1978, Barry seduced Ward 3 voters into joining his campaign's alliance of gays, low-income blacks, and Hispanics. Middle class African-Americans remained a healthy distance away from the dashiki-wearing rabble-rouser. But liberal whites believed Barry could advance their program of good government while serving the needs of the city's poor. By his second term, which began in 1983, Barry had lost the majority of liberal whites who had initially embraced his candidacy. They never returned. For three mayoral campaigns, he retained the support of *The Washington Post*. But in his third term, documented evidence of corruption and rumors of his drug use forced the paper's editorial board to abandon him, becoming as passionate an enemy as it had been a friend.

In 1994, Barry and his advisers knew they couldn't woo Ward 3, and only half believed that they might finagle an endorsement from the *Post*. Thus, Barry targeted the city's disaffected—drunks, addicts, the unemployed and the disinterested—to augment his base and dilute the usually potent vote of whites and middle class blacks.

He had help. Rock Newman, a boxing promoter and manager of Riddick Bowe, had befriended Barry's wife while she chaired the D.C. Boxing and Wrestling Commission. Now, he supplemented the Fighting 54th's registration effort. Reportedly a millionaire, Newman offered Barry workers one dollar for each new person they registered. This represented a major source of much-needed cash for Barry's campaign at a time when his candidacy remained controversial and isolated from traditionally generous donors. Newman and other business leaders thus introduced big money that legally escaped the reach of the District's newly reformed campaign finance laws. Organizations not associated with a campaign could independently spend tens of thousands of dollars on advertisements, brochures, and other campaign vehicles to advance a candidate's cause. At least several PACs (Political Action Committees) made independent expenditures in support of Barry's campaign.*

A cultural nationalist who often dressed in African clothing, Newman passionately embraced Barry's mayoral campaign. He admitted to spending as much as $50,000 on it, and thereby earned a reputation for being one of Barry's closest friends. Newman's one-dollar-one-registrant plan enraged

Joseph Johnson, campaign manager for D.C. council member John Ray. Johnson called it a "thinly veiled way to pay campaign workers." But Barry had used a similar technique in 1992, though less audaciously. Certainly there wasn't the appearance then of vote buying. Newman wasn't the money spigot in that operation. There wasn't a Fighting 54th. And there wasn't anything illegal about the operation. Voter registration didn't fall within the category of independent expenditures, and reports were not required. In 1992, Barry had discovered a major loophole. In 1994, with Newman's help, he boldly stepped through it. It was a move reflective of his entire political career: play the angles, exploit the weaknesses, push the margins.

While the arrangement drew some verbal protests, no one filed a formal complaint against Barry's campaign. *The reason*: fear of being labeled an opponent of voter registration—a mantle traditionally shunned by any black candidate. For Barry's opponents, to object publicly under these circumstances was a lose-lose proposition.

The voter registration campaign provided one additional benefit: Before Barry filed the forms with the D.C. Board of Elections, his campaign skimmed names, addresses, and phone numbers. The data ballooned the campaign's phone bank, presenting a readily available pool of voters who could be lobbied. The information permitted Barry to conduct his own unscientific polls, crudely determining his likely position on election day. When other candidates attempted to keep pace, the voter registration drive produced unprecedented results citywide—nineteen thousand voters hit the rolls as new Democrats, signing up between May 1, 1994 and August 30, 1994. At least one third of them lived east of the Anacostia River. In Ward 8 alone, more than four thousand residents registered as new voters—a fourteen percent increase over those registered in April 1994. By comparison, Ward 3 reported a 5.5 percent increase during the same period. While some portion of the increase could be attributed to the federal new motor voter law, most came as a result of the Barry campaign.*

"The sleeping giants are coming on," Barry proclaimed to *The Washington Post* as his campaign unloaded stacks of registration forms at the elections office. "People can think all they want that these kind of voters aren't going to come out on election day. I know they'll be motivated because they have someone to vote for." Barry knew getting the new registrants to the polls was none too easy. Low-income African-Americans in Washington historically stayed home on election days for such insignificant reasons as bad weather. The culture of civic participation was relatively young in the District—not quite thirty years old. Until 1964, residents couldn't even vote in presidential elections.

In his campaign, Barry didn't rely solely on those he registered. He used every vehicle available to reach the public. He went to forums and small gatherings in people's homes. He participated in radio discussions, and sat for press interviews, including one with *The New Yorker*, which appeared under the amusing title, "The Situationist." Barry had described himself in those terms when a *Washingtonian* magazine reporter, after his 1971 election to the D.C. Board of Education, remarked on his transformation. Barry stopped using profanity, and switched from dashikis to Western-style suits. "I'm a situationist," he explained. "I do what is necessary for the situation."

The situation in which Barry found himself in 1994 was an extremely hostile campaign environment. "I had to fight every single day," recalls Eydie Whittington, who served as the campaign's Ward 1 coordinator. "The city was totally divided. I had never confronted so much hatred—hatred toward [Barry] and anybody who supported him." Many whites, including some of his strongest abettors from previous elections, now loathed him. His seasoned political operatives were scattered (some worked with John Ray, others with the incumbent), leaving him to manage his organization with novices— people who didn't fully understand the intensity of a campaign and didn't really know the candidate. Behind the scenes, Barry still had Ivanhoe Donaldson as strategist, but mostly, he was his own campaign manager. And he was good at it. He could be analytical, think objectively, and make reasonable decisions.

He trumped the other candidates in his understanding of the city, the psychology that drove District voters. He knew the whites and the blacks, the poor and the rich, the government workers and the private business people. They had all passed before his window, sat inside his office, shook his hand, and pleaded for his aid. He knew the effect each slogan would have on them, knew what to say in certain wards, and what could only be whispered in others.

Years later, joking with the local media, he would suffer a Freudian slip, declaring "I am the District of Columbia." Who could dispute that claim? Even in 1994, as the one-time crack addict fought external and internal forces to regain his reputation and his dignity, he personified the nation's capital. Certainly, he reflected the travails of large segments of black America, particularly their bout with drugs and crime. The National Center on Institutions and Alternatives found that in 1992, on any given day, forty-two percent of the District's black males, ages eighteen to thirty-five, were in prison, jail, on probation, on parole, awaiting trial, or had arrest warrants issued for them—mostly for drug charges.*

Marion Barry's recovery became symbolic of large numbers of black communities in recovery—both in the city and throughout the country. John Ray and Sharon Pratt Kelly couldn't compete with the compelling, expansive narrative of a redeemed Marion Barry. Many District voters had experienced falls similar to Barry's, and while some knew they were not of his socio-economic ilk, the experiences they shared with him created a strong sense of identification.

◆ ◆ ◆ ◆ ◆ ◆ ◆ ◆ ◆ ◆ ◆ ◆ ◆ ◆ ◆ ◆

As his campaign took root, Mayor Kelly's popularity dropped drastically. Weeks before the Democratic Primary, polls foreshadowed a one-two-three finish by Ray, Barry, and Kelly. Kelly had an abysmal fourteen percent of the vote. A GAO report released three months before the election became her *bete noir*. A scathing treatise on her administration, it confirmed what had become unofficial common knowledge: She had decimated the city government.

Barry shifted his focus exclusively to Ray, exploiting his council colleague's weaknesses, lambasting his fiscal acumen and his legislative record. He held himself out as the experienced politician-manager and Ray as the legislator who had never managed anything in his life. But Ray, a Georgia native, had a handicap to overcome, even if had had no opponents. He still had a Southern accent, and continued to use his Southern dialect. In some parts of the city, and especially in middle class African-American communities, people cringed when he fractured verbs. His campaign staff hadn't taken care to recognize his speech patterns and write to his strength.

In the early 1980s, the Mississippi-born and Tennessee-bred Marion Barry spouted a mush of black nationalism and slang few could understand. "I used to go around and say to people that substance is more important than form," recalls Ivanhoe Donaldson. "We have to get off being impressed by form and brand labels and look at the substance and quality of the goods." Later, Barry took elocution lessons from Linda Wharton Boyd, who held a doctorate in communications, and his speech improved.

Ray didn't receive such assistance and people still cared about packaging. The District's self-image had plummeted in 1990, in part because of the Barry arrest and trial. Sharon Pratt Kelly won the election partly because she promised to repair the image. Electing a mayor with Ray's speech problems, some believed, would be a step backward.

Ray himself saw in the polls some evidence he could win, and decided to target Kelly as his key opponent. He hoped to swipe her middle class votes and consolidate them behind his candidacy, a move that, if effective, could also beat Barry. Ray figured he could run even in four of the city's eight wards, overwhelm both candidates in Ward 3, take a loss in Ward 7, and not even compete in Barry's Ward 8 stronghold. There was support for the notion and the strategy. In 1990, when he ran against her for mayor, Ray had nearly matched Kelly's vote count.

Barry now had his opponents where he wanted them—fighting each other. He concentrated on fine-tuning his strategy, studying the numbers, playing the odds the way he did during Saturday night poker games with his friends Elijah Rogers, Ivanhoe Donaldson, Lawrence Guyot, and others. In general, the outline of the 1994 plan followed the 1978 blueprint. Then, Donaldson had concluded that in order for Barry to finish first, he had to campaign everywhere. "We were not going to get our butts beat," he says. "I targeted four wards I thought we could win, two wards I thought we'd finish second in, and two wards I thought we would get buried in. We organized the campaign around that strategy."

In 1994, Barry already had a voting bloc large enough to win Ward 8.

He went after Wards 5,6, and 7, disregarded Wards 2 and 3, and tried to break even in Wards 1 and 4. A superior campaigner, Barry displayed sheer, undiluted charisma. He worked the crowds, dispersing facts and tidbits of information, zooming in with his voice to convey sincerity and warmth, taking credit for successes in his previous administration, forgetting the litany of failures, half-starts, and no-starts. He was brutally effective.

Barry had long understood the psychological bondage in which blacks hold themselves, and he often used it to his political advantage. Throughout the summer, the wily Barry alternated wearing African-inspired clothing—replete with matching kufis—and tailored, traditional business suits. In poor neighborhoods where black nationalism ran high, he strutted in Dashiki. In middle class communities, where blacks strongly felt themselves to be insiders who were nonetheless victims of racism, he donned a suit. Casting himself as a seasoned professional, he touched a raw nerve about the arrogance of the white power establishment. Moreover, he continued to latch on to the theme of redemption. While Barry admitted he had done wrong—being addicted to alcohol and sex—he went to the heart of black America, using religion as his vehicle. Once again, Barry understood that religious themes were always powerful magnets in black America. In black America, there are few atheists or agnostics.

Meantime, because he could not disguise his genuine dislike of Barry, Ray came across in joint appearances as both stiff and hateful. For African-Americans, the public display of such an emotion indicated a weakness, a lack of discipline and control—risky business in a world where blacks were always being goaded, and where success often came only by projecting the illusion of being unfazed.

Barry exuded control, although he sometimes flinched or brusquely answered a question—an indication the questioner had penetrated his veneer. But these were rare occasions. He once said the reason he resorted to drugs was because he frequently suppressed his true feelings, choosing to push ahead calmly when he really wanted to explode.

◆ ◆ ◆ ◆ ◆ ◆ ◆ ◆ ◆ ◆ ◆ ◆ ◆ ◆ ◆ ◆

The Washington Post covered Barry's campaign with pervasiveness and intensity—like white on rice. Wherever he went, *Post* reporters were there. And what the news pages missed, the editorial pages picked up on. It was an awesome assault that only an omnipotent institution like the *Post* could mount. In 1990, when it decided Sharon Pratt Kelly was its candidate for mayor, the paper ran editorials favorable to her for three consecutive days. Her victory rested almost exclusively on the *Post*'s unwavering support. And throughout the first year of her term, the *Post* sang the new mayor's praises. But it soon became disenchanted, and by the 1994 election, it was clear Kelly wouldn't win the editorial board's endorsement. But who would?

It couldn't rally behind Barry. And Ray was at best a lackluster candidate who had failed during previous runs to catch fire. For weeks, the paper considered endorsing no one, which would have been a first for the institution. It had always played civic big brother, asserting interest in the District through editorials and endorsements. And when Philip Graham was publisher, the paper started the Federal City Council, an influential group of local and federal leaders. The council pushed through a major Urban Renewal Project in southwest D.C. during the late 1960s and 1970s. It assumed control of the renovation of Union Station when the project was floundering and Congress was threatening to take away funding. In the late 1980s, it sponsored a major study of D.C. public schools. The resulting series of recommendations drove reformist-minded changes in city schools throughout the 1990s. Failing to endorse a candidate in 1994 would be perceived as a cop-out.

Intense lobbying by all of the campaigns complicated the paper's ability to easily arrive at a decision. None of the candidates came without baggage. Some had advantages. Mayor Kelly and Editorial Page Editor Meg Greenfield were friends. Sources inside the paper confirmed, however, that Greenfield had difficulty listing the advantages of a Kelly re-election. She blamed Kelly's shortcomings on the spouse she took after winning election. "It all started after she married that man," Greenfield once said, suggesting that Mr. Kelly had adversely influenced his wife as the District's mayor.

Ray's campaign manager assiduously sought the newspaper's endorsement.

Barry played both sides of the street. While he railed against the paper's attempt to discredit him, and its apparent desire to do the selecting for the city's majority black population, he lobbied furiously.

On September 9, 1994 the long-awaited endorsement arrived. But it was hardly an orthodox statement of support for a single, superior candidate. Rather, it was a long, convoluted listing of each candidate's record, beginning with Kelly and ending with Ray, who, only by comparison, seemed the least flawed of the three. The *Post,* in effect, told voters, "You decide—we can't." Still, most readers assumed that the *Post* was weakly endorsing John Ray, and they were offended by the roundabout manner in which the support came. Unquestionably, the "endorsement" infuriated blacks and inflicted irreparable damage on Ray's campaign.

Barry's supporters held up the endorsement as another example of whites attempting to dictate District leadership, even when they backed candidates like Ray, whom they acknowledged to be inexperienced and ineffective.

So the *Post's* odd endorsement for mayor did not faze Barry. He hadn't counted the newspaper among his friends and admirers, and he didn't expect even its reluctant support. Besides, he was an expert at handling lemons.

CHAPTER SIX

SOMETIME BETWEEN THREE and four in the morning, Eydie Whittington's head finally hit the pillow. Exhaustion had sent her to sleep faster than usual. Earlier in the day, she'd hung posters, and checked and rechecked her Ward 1 precinct workers, making sure they knew their destinations and expected time of arrival. Everything had to work with precision the following day, or the campaign would suffer. Around eight o'clock that evening, she'd dashed out to the Up-Against-the-Wall clothing boutique on 18th Street in the Adams Morgan neighborhood. She'd convinced herself she needed a new outfit for election day—and wouldn't wear one of the dozen suits already lining her closet. She needed something more appropriate, she thought—something that fit the mood of the campaign, that sent a message of her attitude and that of voters. She picked out a military-style camouflage suit.

"That's how they had destroyed me," recalls Whittington. "It was such a war. I felt like I had to get ready to protect myself."

Just as she drifted off to sleep, the phone rang, slicing into her brief rest. Marion Barry was on the other end. "He said, 'Eydie, this is going to be a good day.' I knew he was nervous. I was looking at the clock and saying [to myself], 'Can't I get fifteen minutes' sleep?' Then he had me call other people—conference calls. He was really nervous. But he works like that. We tried a conference call with a white couple. The man was a supporter and the wife wasn't. She wouldn't put her husband on the line and cussed the mayor out."

For all his bravado, the telephone call to Whittington revealed something that few people knew: Barry was afraid. He had everything to lose—more than Kelly and Ray. He was attempting to restore his reputation, which neither of his opponents had lost. He had the Vista tape and a six-month prison term to live down, to expunge from people's memories. Because he'd lost badly in 1990, he couldn't afford another citywide defeat. It would seal his fate forever, relegating him to ward politics that he found demeaning and unexciting. If ever he needed a prayer vigil, it was election day. For eighteen months, he had plotted to arrive at the door of the mayor's office. He would have been crushed if voters refused to open it to him. But losing was a distinct possibility. D.C. Council member John Ray, despite his limitations, had been a formidable candidate. The question now came down to whether Barry could get his voters to the polls. If he could replicate his previous get-out-the-vote mastery, he would be hard to beat.

◆ ◆ ◆ ◆ ◆ ◆ ◆ ◆ ◆ ◆ ◆ ◆ ◆ ◆ ◆ ◆

Several hours after the polls opened at seven in the morning, Whittington heard Barry "screaming" on the walkie talkie, checking the activity in each of the wards. Riding around, Barry could see that his "people"—the ones he'd targeted—hadn't made it to the polls. By midday, things hadn't changed much. If he didn't get them out, he would lose badly.

His operation shifted into masterful high gear, disturbingly demonstrating the level to which Barry would stoop to win. He deployed vans, cars, and even taxis throughout the city, ferrying voters to polls, particularly senior citizens. "They were really on the ball," seventy-six-year-old Edith Brooks told *The Washington Post.* "Every time you looked, there was a Barry man out there. Anybody who needed a ride, got a ride." Vans also were stationed at homeless shelters, especially the huge Community for Creative Nonviolence building at 2nd and D Streets NW., which held more than a thousand potential voters. But Barry's campaign didn't stop at providing rides. Just as he had in the 1992, Ward 8 election, Barry offered meals, and for some voters, cash contributions.

"Walking around money" is a common feature of most elections in the U.S.. The campaign normally sets aside a specified sum from its petty cash account to feed campaign workers and to handle emergencies or incidentals that may arise. Joseph Johnson said Ray's campaign spent about five hundred dollars on election day in 1994. "But we didn't have anywhere near the money Marion's people had." Workers in Barry's campaign admit the operation was "flush with cash," and attributed most of it to the generosity of Rock Newman. Barry's campaign reports did not reveal exactly how much was spent, but workers say the practice begun in 1992 of not reporting all cash raised and spent by the organization continued in 1994.*

The defining moment in Barry's get-out-the-vote effort may have come when his campaign workers raided drug dens. "I was pulling people out of crack houses, taking needles out of people's arms," recalls Whittington, who coordinated Ward 1 for the campaign. "When we conducted our registration drive, we went all over. My assistant was an ex-offender, so I wasn't afraid.

"But at noon, nary a black person had voted. White people had voted, ate breakfast and lunch. [Our supporters] hadn't gotten out of bed. I was devastated. When I saw the stats, I could not believe it. I had to do something," continues Whittington.

"A photographer from The Washington Times was traveling with me. This guy [in a drug den] said, 'Bitch, if you take another picture of us, I'm going to kill you.' It was clear we had just run up on 'New Jack City' [a drug-related movie]," Whittington says. "All I wanted for them to do was vote. So I told the photographer, 'Don't take any more pictures.' We got them out to vote and that was that."

When the reports came in from the early morning voting, Ray and Barry were nearly tied. But by late evening, Barry had pulled off the most stunning victory of his career, shocking the entire world, but most especially District whites.*

Barry puzzled over the hodgepodge of dissimilar voters—the homeless, drug addicts, criminals, senior citizens, youths, and middle class blacks. All had identified a single enemy—the white establishment—and one savior, Marion Barry. "It was a curious thing," admits former city secretary Dwight Cropp. "A lot of middle class black folks were completely turned off, repulsed by The Washington Post's heavy hand in that whole thing.

"I had no intention of voting for Marion Barry," says Cropp. "I was disillusioned with John Ray, but I was going to go ahead and vote for him until…" The Washington Post put Karen Shook, a decidedly second tier candidate, on the same level as Cropp's wife, Linda. For an at-large Council seat, the Post endorsed Shook. Linda Cropp easily won the race, despite the Post's opposition.

"I said, 'Wait one minute now'…I was so absolutely angry at The Wash-

ington Post, the only way I could show them was to vote for Marion. A lot of our friends did that. A lot of us thought the *Post* was heavy handed, and even the way they endorsed John Ray was a back handed kind of thing."

The next day, stunned political pundits analyzed how Barry had pulled off his win. Political scientist Ron Walters admitted to being caught with his pants down. "I didn't think the black middle class would vote for him. It turns out they did. It was a shock to me. My argument at the time was that Washington is image conscious. But that was a particular trait of old Washington. There has been a change in the nature of the black middle class. There are a lot more young people, and they are more pragmatic. They are about money. They are upwardly mobile. They are about the things politics can bring. Barry has never connected with old Washington. I just missed that altogether."

National newspapers, including *The Los Angeles Times* and *The Boston Globe,* led their roundup national election coverage with reports that Barry had won the Democratic primary. It was the kind of underdog, come-from-behind victory average people love, even if the victor is a crack-addicted, womanizing politician who would do and say almost anything to win, including playing the race and class cards.

◆ ◆ ◆ ◆ ◆ ◆ ◆ ◆ ◆ ◆ ◆ ◆ ◆ ◆ ◆ ◆

The campaign wasn't over, however. Barry couldn't claim complete victory. He still faced strong opposition in the November general election. "The hardest time in [1994] wasn't between John Ray, Sharon Pratt Kelly, and the mayor, but with [Carol] Schwartz," recalled Whittington.

Initially, William Lightfoot, an at-large D.C. council member with political sensibility, acumen, and arrogance matching Barry's, had promised to run as an independent in the November election if his colleague, Ray, lost the primary. Many blacks, like Cropp, who voted for Barry wanted to thumb their nose at *The Washington Post,* but had every intention of voting for Lightfoot in November. Barry's victory in the September primary, however, shocked Lightfoot and his supporters. They had not foreseen two things: first, that Barry could win in so many wards, and second, that race, in an election where all the Democratic candidates were black, would have such a profound effect.

The primary left the city racially divided. Lightfoot knew that if he challenged Barry, the racial and class divisions would only increase. What's more, Barry wouldn't hesitate to brand Lightfoot a "water carrier" for the white establishment. The man who played the race card better than Johnnie Cochran or David Duke would plaster Lightfoot with an "Uncle Tom" label, the way *Emerge* magazine and other black institutions had characterized Clarence Thomas during his confirmation hearings for Supreme Court justice.

After Barry's primary victory, the Rev. Jesse Jackson called Joseph Koonz, senior partner at Koonz, McKenney, Johnson, DiPaoli, and Light-foot, where Lightfoot worked as an attorney. Jackson asked Koonz to talk with Lightfoot. "Bill's time will come," Jackson reportedly told Koonz. "But if he runs now, he'll be known as the honky candidate." Rather than advising Lightfoot to quit the race, Koonz encouraged his candidacy. But pressure came from other quarters of the black community, even inside his own camp. Lightfoot eventually acquiesced to his advisers and pulled out of the race, leaving the Republican nominee Carol Schwartz to face Barry head-to-head.

An independently wealthy, white, Jewish woman, Schwartz was no pushover—something people knew from the raspy sound of her voice, and from her defiant stance against her party's more conservative policies. She and Barry had faced off in 1986; she lost by a two to one margin, but garnered considerable support from African-American voters. In a town where Republicans account for only about eight percent of the registered voters, she pulled in thirty-three percent of the vote. In November 1994, even with Barry's popularity ascending, her odds were better than they had been in 1986, or so most thought.

But Barry, the twenty-four-hour-a-day politician, could never be underestimated. He manipulates his friends and enemies equally, and exacts fear on both, whenever appropriate. Barry might say he didn't force the business community to start holding fundraisers, breakfasts, and luncheons for him immediately after his September win. But most business leaders knew that if they withheld their support, there would be hell to pay if Barry returned to office. They could make excuses for why they couldn't support him in the primary. There wasn't any excuse for ducking the November election. Robert Linowes, a real estate lawyer who had been a Barry supporter long before the Vista Hotel sting operation, rebuffed him after the arrest. But after September 1994, he donated the maximum allowed by law to Barry's campaign—one hundred dollars. Robert Johnson, who owed Barry more than most businessmen in the city, had jumped ship before the mayor's drug sentencing and lobbed his support to former D.C. Delegate Walter Fauntroy, also gave Barry the maximum. The D.C. Board of Trade's Political Action Committee returned to the Barry fold in 1994, making its financial resources available to his campaign. "It's a bunch of businessmen voting with their pocketbooks instead of their minds," magazine publisher Bill Regardie told *The Washington Times*.

But Marion Barry didn't care who voted, what condition they were in, or what their motivation was, so long as they voted for him. The return of his former business allies-turned-enemies-turned-allies meant much needed cash for the financially strapped campaign. It also shrunk the base from which Schwartz could pull financial support. She'd begun her primary campaign late, to conserve cash, and ran a virtually all-volunteer operation. When business lined up behind Barry in the general election, her campaign correctly smelled trouble.

But even if the businessmen hadn't been so effusive, knocking themselves out to place money in Barry's campaign, he would have gone to them. Barry had never been shy about meeting his enemies. In an Anansi-like strategy, he trotted right up to them. If he proved unable to corral his adversary, his attempt disproved all claims that Marion Barry was the problem, shifting the attention to the antagonist. If he happened to ingratiate himself, he won additional support. With this win-win logic, Barry forged into Ward 3 just days before the November election, to take part in a "Unity Walk."

The ward, a predominantly white area, had roundly rejected Barry in the democratic primary a few weeks earlier. Now, audaciously coming to opposition territory, he began his stroll at the American City Diner on

Connecticut Avenue Northwest, a restaurant owned by Jeffrey Gildenhorn, Barry's one-time appointee to the boxing commission.

The mayor and Gildenhorn were no longer friends. Gildenhorn had been one of Barry's advisors to his aborted 1990 mayoral campaign. The day before the FBI arrested Barry at the Vista Hotel, Gildenhorn and other advisers, including Robert Johnson, met with the mayor to come up with the campaign's fundraising plan. The money-advisors were increasingly concerned about talk that Barry's drug use had gone from recreational to addictive. "And he [Barry] said, 'No, no. That's just talk.' He swore to us. The next day he gets arrested." After the arrest, says Gildenhorn, the advisers talked Barry out of continuing his 1990 campaign because he needed to focus his attention on the upcoming trial. Gildenhorn went on to raise and donate thirty-five thousand dollars for Barry's legal defense fund.

In late October 1994, D.C. Council member James Nathanson stood outside Gildenhorn's diner, greeting Barry, smiling, and urging residents to support the Democratic nominee for mayor. "If you are a Democrat and you believe in the way the system works, you vote for the Democratic nominee," Nathanson said, skirting the issue of Barry's record, or the September primary. Playing the scene for all it was worth, Barry said: "Who says Ward 3 does not support me? Look at all the people here." About 125 residents and curiosity seekers crowded the sidewalk in the front of the diner. "We have to come together as a city regardless of race, religion, or whatever." Yet, Barry secretly hoped Ward 3 would continue to isolate him. When whites excessively criticized blacks, especially black males, African-Americans became enraged. Even if the person attacked had a prison record, and a demonstrated lack of integrity, blacks invariably circled the wagons.

Three weeks before Barry's disingenuous effort to unite the community and the District's Democrats, *The Washington Post*, on October 3, 1994, released the results of a survey it had conducted, which revealed the racial and class fault lines in the city. Eight out of 10 blacks surveyed said they "were confident Barry would be good for the city." A majority of whites, however, called his primary victory an embarrassment. Three out of four blacks believed Barry was a good role model for youths. Three out of four whites said he wasn't. Asked about the general election, eighty-one percent of the blacks said they would vote for Barry, while seventy-four percent of the whites said they'd punch their card for Schwartz. Schwartz had a strong black following in the city, and she hoped they would see through Barry's game-plan. But the survey portended a Schwartz defeat, while exposing dramatic divisions in the District.

Annette Samuels, a former press secretary for Barry, who never forgave the mayor for his drug arrest and his dishonesty, blasted him in a long op-ed article that appeared in *The Washington Post*. "Religious redemption, in a democracy that separates the right to practice one's religious beliefs from the role of government and those we choose to govern, must not and should not be the issue in the District's mayoral race. Nor should pleas by the former mayor for a second chance to correct the devastation he chose to wreak upon this city, especially the poor, during the last four years of his twelve years in office be an issue. After all, Mr. Barry quit his job, we did not fire him." She urged Democrats to cross party lines and vote Republican.

Barry didn't offer a single retort. *The Washington Post*, perceived by most to be a Democratic newspaper, endorsed Republican challenger Schwartz for mayor, stirring the flames, re-igniting the anger of some blacks. There was enough residual animosity from the September primary for Barry to coast. He didn't overtly play the race card, but alluded to it in the subtle, coded language that African-Americans have long cultivated, whether on plantations or in corporate board rooms.

Whittington said she and others in the campaign were concerned because some of their black middle class voters, like Cropp, had transferred their political loyalties, voting for Schwartz after the alternative black, Lightfoot, got cold feet. But there was never really any doubt Barry would prevail—not in his mind, and not in the District's mind.

In November, Barry defeated Schwartz by fifteen percentage points.* "A narrow victory" some called it. But when Barry started on his journey, most believed such a victory impossible, whatever the margin. He had come a long way from the Vista Hotel sting and the Loretto jail.

The day after the election, when asked about the racial division, Barry acknowledged the racial split. He told the whites in Ward 3 to "get over it." Marion Barry, like Lazarus, was back. Pundits once again attempted to point to various reasons for the victory. But Barry had done nothing new or spectacular in the eighteen months since coming out of Loretto prison. He had merely practiced black politics, the way he had all his life—the way he had learned down South and from other politicians. Barry was only a conduit for a dying tradition, one that nonetheless still caused some to marvel at its power to persuade the electorate.

MARION BARRY and mother, MATTIE CUMMINGS

REV. WILLIE WILSON, the black cultural nationalist at
Barry's side since 1990

MARION BARRY on the campaign trail in April 1992

Barry-ite SANDRA ALLEN, whom Barry betrayed after winning a council seat in 1992 and then vacating it two years later for a mayoral bid

· PART TWO ·

IF THERE IS A THEME SONG that captures the essence of Marion Barry's life, and the road that led him to the nation's capital, it might be Nina Simone's "Mississippi Goddam":

> *Hound dogs on my trail*
> *school children sitting in jail*
> *black cat across my path*
> *I think every day's going to be my last.*

While blessed with breathtaking deltas, Mississippi's history of intense racial hatred and strife often overshadows everything else about it, becoming embedded in the state's residents like soot under the fingernails of a miner, never fully disappearing despite a lifetime of hand washing.

"It was in Mississippi, the dark heart of the frontier of the South, that the most fundamental statement of white supremacist vision was expressed," notes historian Vincent Harding, author of *There Is A River: The Black Struggle for Freedom in America*.

Mississippi was a major depot during the country's slave-trading and slave-holding era. The state was infamous for its brutal treatment of slaves. Slave insurrections elsewhere in the country prompted state officials to make it "unlawful for any slave, free Negro, or mulatto to preach the gospel upon pain of receiving thirty-nine lashes upon the naked back of the preacher." By the end of Summer 1861, forty black men had been hanged in the Natchez, Mississippi area for their part in slave liberation movements.

Even after the Emancipation Proclamation and the end of the Civil War, conditions didn't get much better for Mississippi's blacks. "No two dissimilar races could live together on a basis of equality anywhere," wrote the editor of the Natchez *Courier*. "One must be superior—one must be dominant. If the Negro should be the master, the white must either abandon the territory or there would be another Civil War in the South—a war of races—

the whites against the blacks. And that would be a war of extermination."

With the passage of various laws, and untethered vigilanteism by white supremacists, aggressive attempts to oppress and exterminate African-Americans began in earnest. The Black Codes in Mississippi prohibited blacks from renting or leasing land outside the towns and cities. Officials wanted to contain African-Americans, preventing them from achieving any measure of economic freedom or power, especially acquiring land.

In 1890, the Mississippi constitution, like those in most Southern states, established three conditions for voting: residency, payment of a poll tax — about one dollar, but far outside the budgets of many blacks—and the ability to read or interpret sections of the state constitution. These criteria gave election officials tremendous authority over who exercised the right to vote.*

Mississippi's white leaders also deliberately impeded the educational advancement of its black population. Throughout the slavery era, it had been unlawful to educate slaves. While small schools, mostly church-run operations, cropped up after the Civil War, hundreds of thousands of Mississippi's African-Americans went without an education. And those who did receive one were purposely cheated. In 1930, Mississippi spent five times more money to educate a white student than a black one.

There were transitory intervals where blacks fared well in the South, most notably during Reconstruction, when dozens were elected to state legislatures, and a few, like New Orleans' Thomy Lafon, prospered. A merchant, moneylender, and real estate dealer, Lafon left an estate of half a million dollars when he died in the 1880s.

In general, however, African-Americans remained in a centuries-old chokehold. And while the race war discussed in the Natchez *Courier* never quite came to pass, racial tension continued uninterrupted well into the twentieth century, leaving scars on both whites and blacks, some imperceptible to the naked eye, but nonetheless deep and festering.

Race, hatred, and poverty became Barry's crucible, as it had been for tens of thousands of African-Americans before him, shaping his early foundation and remaining the critical elements in the formulation of his personal philosophy and political career. Psychologists have long acknowledged the dominant role early childhood experiences play in the formation of adults.

Sometimes the effects of these experiences, undiagnosed and untreated, yield neurotic or psychotic grownups. Their adult lives are forever colored by one defining moment, or by a blinding sharp image, flashing forever before their eyes, too bright to dismiss or see around, or by a word spoken—softly or loudly—that it could not be tuned out. Just as the South made George Wallace a passionate advocate of segregation, standing before presidential emissaries and the National Guard, refusing to permit blacks to enter the University of Alabama, it also imbued men like Mississippian Marion Barry with an equally stark racial consciousness.

◆ ◆ ◆ ◆ ◆ ◆ ◆ ◆ ◆ ◆ ◆ ◆ ◆ ◆ ◆ ◆

Born in 1936 in Itta Bena, Mississippi, Barry smelled the malodorous properties of race, hatred, and poverty before he knew his name. "I was born with nothing," Barry once said. He was not exaggerating. A small town in the state's northwestern section, Itta Bena and the surrounding area consisted mostly of former plantations—some with as much as five thousand acres. Mattie Cummings, Barry's mother, was only eighteen when she gave birth to Marion—her third child and only son. Her husband, Marion Sr., was forty-six. The disparity in their ages was common during that period, when youthful wives not only provided older husbands with the possibility of children, but also a strong hand to help out in the fields. Moreover, families were willing to give their young daughters to such unions, believing older men offered greater stability. Both Marion Sr. and Mattie, uneducated and from impoverished backgrounds, exemplified average Mississippi blacks of their time.

In 1936, the year Marion Barry was born, the average per family income for Southern rural blacks was $566, while for whites it was $1,535. Most blacks didn't have indoor plumbing or heat. Their disenfranchisement was similarly evident in the political realm: At the 1936 Democratic National Convention, the South Carolina delegation protested the presence of blacks, walking out of the proceedings.

And, of course, the advent of the twentieth century didn't prevent blacks from being victims of racially motivated violence, either. Eight lynchings were recorded in 1936 alone.

Mattie and Marion Sr. worked as sharecroppers, living like most of the state's black population in rickety shacks that lacked any semblance of modernity. Some didn't even have outhouses, leaving families to find places in the fields to relieve themselves. Then as now, Mississippi was one of the poorest states in the nation. The sharecropping system required that families rent from the plantation owners the land they lived and worked on. As compensation, the farming families provided the landowners a share of the proceeds from their harvest sales. The "nickel and dime" nature of sharecropping often left families without enough to make it through the following planting season. Forced to buy provisions on credit from the county store, the Barrys, like most blacks, owed their soul and their earnings when harvest time arrived. Share cropping, which was nothing more than a de facto system of slavery, was vicious. Only with a bushel of children was there any likelihood of scratching out a small profit.

"My parents were sharecroppers. They had twenty children. I was the twentieth," wrote Fannie Lou Hamer in her autobiography, *To Praise Our Bridges*. "All of us worked in the fields, of course, but we never did get anything out of sharecropping. We'd make fifty and sixty bales [of cotton] and end up with nothing…I was about six years old when I first went to the fields to pick cotton. By the time I was thirteen, I was picking two and three hundred pounds [a day]."

◆ ◆ ◆ ◆ ◆ ◆ ◆ ◆ ◆ ◆ ◆ ◆ ◆ ◆ ◆ ◆

Barry didn't stay in Mississippi long enough to develop his cotton-picking skills. Mattie moved her children from Itta Bena while her son Marion was still young. Initially, Barry thought his Daddy's death prompted the family's move from Mississippi. Actually, Marion Sr. died several years after that departure. Barry later learned that his mother left the family's home because she simply had grown tired of a husband who beat her and who had begun to use alcohol to anesthetize himself, hoping to smother the humiliation of Southern segregation and poverty.

Mattie ran away to Memphis, Tennessee. A port city with a population of nearly three hundred thousand—forty percent of which was black—Memphis came with its own history of segregation and race hate. In the spring of 1866, forty blacks were killed, seventy severely wounded, and more than a dozen schools and churches burned during an outbreak of racial violence. In the 1940s, Memphis—not unlike most Southern cities—maintained a system of Jim Crow laws that forced African-Americans to use public bathrooms and water fountains separate from whites. Most African-Americans were barred from various restaurants and hotels. And few department stores catered to their retail needs. As in Mississippi, whites in Memphis controlled the political and economic machinery, and the imposition of a one dollar poll tax created tangible barriers to changing that equation.

Despite the discrimination (or because of it), small black businesses flourished nationally. According to the National Negro Business League, there were twenty thousand such businesses in 1900 and forty thousand in 1914. Black banks grew from four to fifty-one; undertakers from 450 to one thousand; drugstores from 250 to 695; and retail merchants from ten thousand to twenty-five thousand. But while these establishments provided good quality goods and services, they weren't always conveniently located, and because acquiring inventory was sometimes hard, their prices sometimes were high.

A deeply religious woman, Mattie Barry did what most Southern blacks did when arriving in a new town. She joined the church—Martin Temple Christian Methodist Episcopal Church. Black churches served simultaneously as economic, social, and educational institutions. The church and community were like Siamese twins. Ministers in black communities often served as arbiters with whites, protecting their congregants from needless attack, or spurring them to fight against white incursion.

Although not a raving beauty, Mattie Cummings was pretty enough to attract a fairly upstanding man in Memphis. She married Dave Cummings,* a butcher who hailed from rural Tennessee. Dave Cummings had a steady job, but the living wasn't easy. A shotgun shack, the standard architectural design in Southern black urban communities, served as the family's living quarters. Entering the door of a shotgun shack, a visitor met the living room, followed by bedrooms—never more than one or two—and then the kitchen. The expression "shotgun shack" developed because of the narrowness of the houses, and the clean view they offered from the living room to the kitchen. If a shotgun were fired, people joked, the bullet would speed through the shack without touching anything.

Mattie had two daughters by Dave, bringing her brood to five, and putting Marion, the only boy, in the dreaded position of middle child. Psychologists have found that middle children often become either a super-achiever or a major delinquent. In many families, the greatest amount of affection is accorded to the first born or the last born, while middle children are left to fight desperately for their parents' attention.

Barry slept on the sofa while the girls bundled up in one bedroom. He awoke early to cut wood for the stove before leaving for Florida Avenue Elementary School.

There were days when the family's income forced Barry to use cardboard to fill the holes in his shoes. A budding capitalist, he sold to classmates the sandwiches his mother made him for his lunch, choosing finance over food. He even joined the choir to advance his financial standing. The pastor of the church had promised to pay choir members' bus fare to and from rehearsals. Barry pocketed the coins, walked home, and sang off key.

By the time Barry entered Booker T. Washington High School in Memphis, he had begun to blossom, securing the attention middle children tend to covet through remarkable feats. He was inducted into the National Honor Society, became the first black Eagle Scout in Memphis, played basketball, joined the boxing club, and worked a variety of odd jobs: He delivered newspapers, bagged groceries, collected empty soda bottles, and worked as a carhop at a drive-in restaurant. He stayed connected to his home state when his mother took him and the other children on cotton-picking trips. They earned thirty cents an hour picking in Mississippi (and Arkansas).

◆ ◆ ◆ ◆ ◆ ◆ ◆ ◆ ◆ ◆ ◆ ◆ ◆ ◆ ◆

Conditions for blacks in Barry's native state of Mississippi didn't change much during the years he lived in Memphis. "In the 1950s, trying to organize for civil rights in Mississippi was like trying to pick a plantation's entire cotton crop single-handedly—one boll at a time, in the middle of the night, with a gun pointed at your head," said Juan Williams, author of *Eyes on the Prize.*

Yet, several groups tried. Chief among them was the National Association for the Advancement of Colored People, an interracial group founded just after the turn of the twentieth century. Moorfield Storey, a white Boston lawyer, served as the organization's first president. Initially, everyone—blacks included—regarded the NAACP as a Communist organization. But with its aggressive defense of Southern blacks against racial discrimination, the NAACP shifted, and its membership became predominantly black, though its financial base remained largely white.

In 1954, the NAACP argued before the Supreme Court a lawsuit against school desegregation. The case was known as *Brown versus the Board of Education of Topeka, Kansas.* Oliver Brown had been sending his seven-year-old daughter, Linda Brown, across the tracks to an all-black school because Jim Crow laws prohibited her from attending the closer white school. It was a dangerous walk. The local branch of the NAACP decided to test the state law that required it. Throughout the country, the NAACP, with the aid of daring local residents, began testing school segregation laws. Finally, in 1953, faced with several such cases, the U.S. Supreme Court consolidated them, referring to all as *Brown versus Board of Education.* In 1954, the court ruled that separate educational facilities were inherently unequal, and thus ended legal school segregation in the United States.

Reaction to the Supreme Court ruling was swift and decisive. Mississippi changed its constitution to permit schools to close to avoid desegregation. And by outlawing common law marriages, notes Juan Williams, Mississippi increased the state's number of illegitimate children, who were ineligible to attend public schools. In July 1954, whites in Indianola, Mississippi created the first White Citizens Council, aimed at preventing desegregation and black advancement. Mississippi held the dubious distinction of leading the nation in beatings, lynchings, and mysterious disappearances. The following year, in the summer of 1955, Emmett Till, a fourteen-year-old black from Chicago, was visiting relatives in Mississippi, when he talked briefly with a white girl. When Till's body was found, one eye had been gouged out and the side of his skull smashed in.*

◆ ◆ ◆ ◆ ◆ ◆ ◆ ◆ ◆ ◆ ◆ ◆ ◆ ◆ ◆ ◆

By 1958, Barry was already entrenched at LeMoyne College, a small co-ed school in Memphis founded by the American Missionary Society in 1862 for the education of blacks. Because the school lacked dormitory facilities, he was forced to remain at home, locking him inside an environment of racial hatred and poverty even as he struggled to escape it. Concluding that too many blacks were becoming teachers or social workers, Barry targeted chemistry as his area of interest. He maintained a B-plus average and pledged the Alpha Phi Alpha fraternity. Later, he became the vice president of the campus chapter. He also was elected to the student council and joined the NAACP.

During his senior year, the once-shy, reserved boy from Itta Bena, Mississippi broke out of his cocoon. As president of the LeMoyne College Chapter of the NAACP, he issued a public challenge to Walter Chandler. The former mayor of Memphis and a U.S. Congressman, Chandler held the post of chairman of LeMoyne's Board of Trustees. "The problem of the Negro," Chandler argued, "will not be eliminated by permitting him to be seated alongside white passengers on the buses in the city. If the NAACP would spend more of its efforts in trying to elevate the Negro morally, mentally, educationally and health-wise, it would be of far more benefit to the race...The Negro is our brother, but he should be treated as a younger brother, and not as an adult."

The statement enraged Barry, who fired off a letter to LeMoyne President Dr. Hollis Price, calling Chandler a demagogue and demanding his resignation from the college's board. The letter appeared in the school newspaper and in the dailies. The NAACP's national director, Roy Wilkins, also attacked the board chairman, and during a large rally in Memphis, recognized Barry for his contribution to racial pride. Barry used the episode to catapult himself to prominence in a growing civil rights movement. Chandler didn't resign, however, and the school's trustees initially sought to expel Barry. But they decided merely to reprimand him. It didn't matter to Barry. His racial stance had already been established.

◆ ◆ ◆ ◆ ◆ ◆ ◆ ◆ ◆ ◆ ◆ ◆ ◆ ◆ ◆ ◆

When Barry arrived in the fall of 1958 as a graduate student at historically black Fisk University in Nashville, Tennessee, he was determined to receive a master's degree in chemistry. However, he was just as determined to continue the civil rights activity he had begun at LeMoyne. Despite signs that Nashville had begun to desegregate, including the election seven years earlier of two blacks to its city council, Barry found a black community eager to more dramatically engage white authority, forcing businesses and government to enforce the Constitution. Among those he met were Mary Treadwell— later to become Barry's wife and partner—and James Lawson.

A divinity student from Vanderbilt University, Lawson had refused to fight in the Korean War, and, like the Rev. Martin Luther King Jr., was much influenced by Mahatma Gandhi's philosophy of nonviolent resistance. It was Lawson who offered Barry and other Fisk students insight into the power of Gandhi's philosophy and how it, over time, won India its independence from British rule.

In fact, Lawson had enormous and immediate impact on Barry, Fisk student leader Diane Nash, and John Lewis. In practically applying Lawson's lessons, the three-some began conducting sit-ins at various lunch counters around the city. They arrived at a restaurant, took seats, and waited to be refused service. But in February 1960, believing they were ready for more vigorous engagement, the students staged a city-wide boycott, spending an entire day sitting at the counters, and preventing anyone else from being served. At the Woolworth store, a rowdy bunch of whites spat on them, poured condiments onto their heads, dragged them from their seats, and beat the hell out of them. Police looked on for a time before deciding to arrest Barry, Nash, Lewis, and about seventy other demonstrators, and to charge them with disorderly conduct. Eventually, the arrested protesters opted for jail time rather than pay the fine.

"I took a chance on losing a scholarship," Barry once said about the incident. "But, if I had received my scholarship and master's degree and still was not a free man, I was not a man at all." Even then he tended to exaggerate the circumstances in which he found himself. In fact, Fisk College's president, like many other African-Americans, lent support to the students' efforts to integrate public facilities in Nashville.

Shortly after their citywide sit-in, Barry and other student organizers around the country traveled, by invitation, to Shaw University in Raleigh, North Carolina. Ella Baker, a senior member of the Southern Christian Leadership Conference, which staged the successful boycott in Montgomery that launched the modern Southern civil rights movement, had the idea that recruiting young people into her organization could infuse its protests with greater energy and guarantee the movement's future. At the North Carolina meeting, the strongest contingent came from Nashville and from Atlanta, Georgia. Others, like Ivanhoe Donaldson, arrived from Michigan. Wherever they originated, they looked to Barry, Nash, and the others for direction.

"I went down to meet all these heroes—people I'd been reading about," explains Ivanhoe Donaldson. "I was in the audience while Marion Barry was one of the leaders. This guy was with Diane Nash, and Diane Nash was a superstar. I was a grunt, glad to be there, impressed by all the happenings. I didn't know them. It was like going to a reception and shaking the hand of the president." Barry, who maneuvered behind the scenes at the meeting, was elected chairman of the Temporary Student Nonviolent Coordinating Committee. He plunged into the position with abandon—and without sacred cows. He attacked presidents with the same vigor as he attacked racist white waitresses at lunch counters. In the summer of 1960, he attended the Democratic National Convention, where he addressed the platform committee, calling for federal aid to school districts, support for civil rights lawsuits, and creation of a Fair Employment Practices Commission. That same year, the apparently nonpartisan Barry traveled to the Republican National Convention, where he made a similar appeal.*

By the fall, however, academia beckoned and Barry accepted a teaching post at the University of Kansas, where he met once more the ugly face of racism. The demands of teaching in an integrated environment took a heavy toll on Barry, and in November he resigned as SNCC's chairman, a position which he had held for just seven months, although he remained on the executive coordinating and finance committees. Leaving Kansas, he enrolled at Tennessee State University at Knoxville and, as his top priority, began studies for a doctoral degree in chemistry. Within a year, he reversed himself, and again decided to make his movement activity the most important thing in his life.

◆ ◆ ◆ ◆ ◆ ◆ ◆ ◆ ◆ ◆ ◆ ◆ ◆ ◆ ◆ ◆

In the summer of 1961, after more than twenty years away from his home state, Barry went to McComb, Mississippi, to which SNCC had been invited by the NAACP to conduct a voter registration drive. While the NAACP had attempted to organize the black citizenry, it was having very little noticeable impact. The young bucks of SNCC, the NAACP hoped, could shake things up a bit. Robert Moses, a teacher from New York and a SNCC member, was charged with recruiting persons for a fall conference. He also conducted weekly voter education classes with workers from the NAACP. Reginald Robinson and John Hardy came to McComb later that summer. They went door to door, hoping to recruit blacks willing to take voter registration tests.

Barry came with a different, more radical strategy. He believed in direct confrontation. He, Diane Nash, and others in Nashville had learned the effectiveness of confronting the enemy, of waging an unrelenting war against him face-to-face. Barry took this knowledge to McComb and began unapologetically to organize protests.

"He started the first public demonstration," remembers Lawrence Guyot, who worked in Mississippi with SNCC. "We knew some people were going to go to jail, but that didn't stop him. He was fearless."

Wanting to involve teenagers in SNCC's efforts, Barry began workshops to teach another generation of young people the fine art of nonviolent protest. Curtis Hayes and Hollis Watkins, who attended the workshops, eventually staged a sit-in at the Woolworth lunch counter in McComb. They were arrested and sent to jail for thirty days after Barry, acting as their attorney, failed to make a credible case for their release. In all fairness, there wasn't much Barry could have said to convince the white judge to keep the two protesters out of jail. Later, other teenagers became active in the protest, drawing jail time for their involvement. Throughout the South, more and more young people began to resist segregation actively. Barry had succeeded in his goal of increasing youth involvement.

That summer was a tumultuous time in Mississippi. Herbert Lee, a SNCC supporter, was killed in cold blood. SNCC workers were harassed through constant arrests. And James Meredith, aided by the NAACP, tried to integrate Mississippi State University, popularly known as Ole Miss.

Barry, while continuing with SNCC, seemed, by contrast, to be settling down in his private life. Now nearly 30, he married Blantie Evans. But the two parted ways in less than two years. Evans became a feature of the past Barry rarely revisited.

In the summer of 1964, SNCC launched an ambitious voter registration project in Mississippi, busing in college students from other regions of the U.S., especially from the North. Most were white, and that created some tension within the organization.

"When SNCC was having all the conniptions about Freedom Summer, Marion Barry introduced a resolution that said SNCC supported Freedom Summer and that [organizers] should use any number of [white] students they felt necessary," recalls Guyot. The resolution circumvented the problem of numbers without directly addressing the issue of race.

When the bodies of three civil rights workers—Michael Schwerner, Andrew Goodman, and James Chaney—were reported missing in Mississippi that same summer, Barry was in Chicago hustling money for the movement. Organizing efforts might have been focused on the South, but funds came mainly from Northern wallets. Additionally, racial hatred was flaring around the country. In Harlem, the killing of a fifteen-year-old black boy by an off-duty policeman ignited violence that resulted in one dead, 140 injured, and five hundred arrested. Later, Jersey City, Paterson, Chicago, and Philadelphia all went up in flames.

By the fall, Barry was in New York. Using the deaths of the three civil rights workers to dramatize the seriousness of the struggle and the dangers he and others faced, he raked in tens of thousands of dollars from entertainers, politicians, and social activists. The poor boy from Itta Bena now found himself rubbing shoulders with the rich and famous. They liked him and he liked them—especially their money.

◆ ◆ ◆ ◆ ◆ ◆ ◆ ◆ ◆ ◆ ◆ ◆ ◆ ◆ ◆ ◆

The recognition that black achievement carried a price tag of blood and unwavering commitment imprinted itself in Barry's mind. Like other African-Americans, he was developing a view of politics and human advancement built around notions of race and culture. There could be no improvement of black lives without confrontation, without demands and threats. Blacks couldn't expect whites to offer anything voluntarily. Everything had to be taken—by force if necessary. What's more, the white rich had to be made to feel guilty for the prejudiced in their ranks. They would have to pay to assuage their guilt. And blacks who had achieved any measure of success were obligated, with their physical presence or their wealth, to support the struggle of African-Americans less fortunate than themselves. To turn a blind eye to the suffering of their brothers and sisters was considered sacrilegious. The political and cultural tenets Barry and others learned during the 1960s demanded distinct boundaries between friends and enemies. Absolutely essential was a clear understanding that blacks must always consider those of their race first—before all others.

Politically, young African-Americans like Barry shifted further left than their older civil rights counterparts. They, too, wanted to become part of the American mainstream, but they weren't willing to compromise their "blackness" and their "cultural heritage" to make that voyage. Additionally, they saw nothing wrong with the pervasive "self-preservation" dictum. They reflected on what whites had done: How they ran schools in the interest of whites; business in the express interest of whites; political parties that bolstered white needs and interests through lopsided public policy. African-Americans found comfort and reassurance in these actions, instigating their own budding brand of black politics.

Marion Barry, a leader in this movement, was both benefactor and beneficiary. He created Barry-land, which in later years became a developed political terrain supported by a fully engaged racial doctrine. Because it anchored itself in the African-American Church, moved through the social milieu of black communities, and invested in the frayed but advancing school of black businesses, Barryland was not much different from Powell-land, or Conyers-land, or later Dellums-land.

This was the frontier of black politics, although it was nearly a decade before political scientists began to describe it that way. No one was yet articulating clearly defined principles and actions, but black politics had taken on a definite shape of its own, becoming a presence on the American political scene like that of the Irish or Polish in some U.S. cities. Powell was the first national hero in black politics, setting the stage for his successors, including Barry, Gary's Richard Hatcher, Detroit's Coleman Young, and Cleveland's Carl Stokes.

On the terrain on which many black politicians operated, African-Americans played tough—talking and acting black. Cultural nuances were important, because they established authenticity and garnered trust. There could be no doubt about priority: If it was for and about blacks, then it had to be number one. If a black person was in charge, then it was okay. If it advanced blacks at the expense of whites, so much the better. Race was the prism through which everything was first viewed. Class came next. Blacks saw American society as clearly divided into poor and rich. Because of Jim Crow suppression, they knew they were part of the former.

Yet, African-Americans also knew that in an environment where black politics were supported, they could walk upright, proud, and strong. And for this measure of dignity and heightened self-worth, they were more than willing—after years of oppression and subjugation under white rule—to ignore flamboyancy, missteps, and mild forms of corruption. White leaders, after all, were guilty of the same, and the system was inherently flawed. In Barryland, and the brand of black politics espoused therein, what mattered most was that African-Americans were protected from whites and the terror of white supremacy.

As roving rabble-rouser and money-collector for SNCC, Barry spread the doctrine and principles of black politics in general and Barryland in particular. In every community he touched, including that of rich whites, he merged his personal narrative with that of all blacks. Like an African griot (storyteller), he recounted their hardscrabble life in the deep South, calling out names, ticking off dates, invoking the name of the Lord. He described the blood- spattered streets, the sad sight and wretched smell of a lynched body like Emmett Till's. He talked about old black people who could neither read nor write, and were prevented from voting because they couldn't come up with the one dollar poll tax.

What black hearing this story would not fall in love with the teller, would not blend the storyteller and story until they were inseparable, would not develop immense respect for, become in awe, of the storyteller, and perceive him as invincible, as touched by some magical power? And what storyteller, repeating these tales each day, would not begin to perceive himself and his story as one?

Liberal whites enthusiastically embraced Barry and his brand of politics. After all, they supported people of other ethnicities in their political development. Like African-Americans, whites became mesmerized by Barry's courage and that of other civil rights workers. They were impressed by his seeming invincibility, his charisma. They trusted him to express their guilt without abusing them, without publicly embarrassing them, without lynching them, as whites had lynched African-Americans down South. "My God," they thought, "if these blacks have had all this done to them at the hands of white people, why shouldn't they want to kill us? Maybe they *will* kill us." Their hope for survival lay with Barry and his brand of politics, which at once gave voice to African-American anger but tempered it with the promise of change.

But Barry himself was not completely healed. The lines between reality and fiction, between past, present, and future often were blurred. Like Americans who lived during the Depression, and decades later still found it difficult to trust any bank—secured by the federal government or not—Barry could not shed his formative years' legacy of poverty and racism. It remained a complex, multifaceted presence in his adult life with an unfortunate propensity for rearing its head at the most inopportune of moments. A psychological burden too heavy to remove, Barry's childhood in the deep South was also like a clouded crystal ball through which he attempted to prognosticate about African-Americans' future. Predictably, it also generated a sometimes overpowering fear of whites, making it nearly impossible for him to ever fully trust them—even those whom he grew to like. In consequence, Barry was never able to fully liberate either himself or his people.

◆ CHAPTER EIGHT ◆

In JUNE 1965, Barry received a call that changed his life. By phone, SNCC field secretary James Forman transferred him to Washington, D.C.

There was a logic to the order. The District, though long integrated, possessed its own brand of racial problems. Back in 1948, the National Committee on Segregation in the National Capital criticized the District government practice of corralling black residents into deteriorating sections of the center-city. And while the District lacked the White Citizens Councils of the South, it had its all-white Federation of Citizens Association, which urged its members not to sell homes to African-Americans. Most houses retained strict racial covenants prohibiting lease or sale to blacks. Although the Supreme Court in May 1948 ruled the covenants illegal, they still existed in 1959, particularly in communities west of Rock Creek Park. The result was that even in 1965, the city maintained strict segregated housing patterns that reserved the area west of the park for whites, Capitol Hill for whites, and the rest for blacks. Most low-income and working class residents were squeezed into far northeast and southeast D.C.—the areas frequently called East of the River.

Compounding the racial discrimination was the District's colonial-like status. Residents lacked a locally elected representative government. The Constitution gave the Congress ultimate power and control of the District, and, since 1874, a commission appointed by Congress and the President had operated the city, adhering to the wishes and desires of representatives who lacked any native interest in the District. The political climate of the nation's capital was thus characterized by covert racial segregation and a sense of oppression from without.

As a matter of strategy, SNCC's top officials figured that, if they could make major advances in the District, like winning the right of local citizens to elect their own mayor, city council, and Congressperson, SNCC itself would move easily and prominently into the national arena. Already it had played a strategic role in the signing of the National Civil Rights Act of

1964, whose passage came shortly after the 1963 March on Washington, attended by more than 250,000 citizens of all races, classes, and religious affiliations.

The same year the act passed, Fannie Lou Hamer and a contingent of civil rights workers from Mississippi challenged the seating of the official state delegation at the Democratic convention. While unsuccessful, the group set the stage for the 1968 convention, when an integrated group was seated in Chicago.

Barry's transfer to the District came as the country awaited passage of the Voters' Rights Act of 1965, which promised to change the character and complexion of electoral politics. It—and the Civil Rights Act of 1964—forecast great political influence and clout for African-Americans, and SNCC's brash young leaders wanted to be in the vanguard.

Much like a big fish in a little pond, Barry discovered that he could sparkle in the District. He arrived with an arsenal of techniques for fighting racial discrimination, poverty, and political oppression. His battle scars gave him legitimacy in Washington's black communities. At thirty, he knew how to organize and mobilize large numbers of people—young and old—to take direct action. He understood the country's political and economic system and had been successful in raising large sums of money. He was comfortable with poverty and wealth, fame and anonymity.

During his first two years in the District, Barry did three things that shaped his future in the nation's capital, virtually guaranteeing his prominence in its history, while seeding a political machine that would serve him for almost twenty years: He cut his ties with SNCC, organized a bus boycott, and created Pride, Inc.

◆ ◆ ◆ ◆ ◆ ◆ ◆ ◆ ◆ ◆ ◆ ◆ ◆ ◆ ◆ ◆ ◆

In 1992, it seemed ironic that a bus caravan would come to collect Barry from prison. Buses had always played a starring role in the lives of poor and working class African-Americans. Certainly they did during the civil rights movement, when the tactic of integrating public transportation took center stage. Boycotts became the primary means for changing the policies of private companies throughout the South.

The famous Montgomery Bus Boycott began in December 1955, just after Rosa Parks refused to relinquish her seat at the request of a white bus driver. It continued a full year. An elaborate transportation network of private cars and trucks helped sustain the Montgomery boycott, badly damaging the bus company's bottom line. Earlier in 1955, blacks in Tallahassee, Florida began a boycott of that city's bus company; it continued right through March 1958. By 1960, when SNCC was founded, bus boycotts were routine strategies used throughout the South to call attention to the segregation of public transportation facilities.

The District of Columbia, however, had never been a site of such protests. A strange detente existed in the city between blacks and whites. Not unlike blacks in the South, those in the District knew the discrimination of public and private facilities. They had been followed around in department stores as if common thieves. They had been denied the opportunity to try on apparel before purchasing it. They had been chased out of neighborhoods, threatened with arrest and abused by police. But organizing in an urban environment up north was infinitely more difficult than in the rural South.

"The poorest urban blacks, who were the focus of their efforts, were more alienated, antisocial, and angrier than their counterparts in the rural South," noted former SNCC member and author Clayborne Carson. "Lacking the sharply defined target of southern racism, SNCC workers in urban areas began the formidable task of building a social movement among blacks filled with undirected hostility and generalized distrust. They soon realized that their previous victories in the deep South had exaggerated their sense of power to confront the entrenched...social problems of urban industrial society."

Blacks in the District were even more difficult to harness and direct. The working and middle classes flaunted a polished veneer. They struggled against casting themselves in the same conflicting molds of their Southern relatives. In a sense, they were throwbacks to the days of slavery, and equal to the "house niggers" who had close proximity to the master, and a more sympathetic relationship existed between them. Working and middle class blacks inside government—the District's primary industry—believed that by quietly affecting a rational, sophisticated demeanor, they could destroy the vestiges of racism in their communities.

Because he understood the effectiveness of bus boycotts in uniting a community and garnering press coverage, Barry bolted ahead in his strategy to organize the difficult-to-organize District.

As in other cities of the country, the District's bus company was operated by a private businessman—O. Roy Chalk. A crude New Yorker, Chalk decided in 1966 to raise bus fares by a nickel. Many Washingtonians thought the increase too much. They also saw the bus company as insensitive—it lacked facilities for the handicapped and had routes that were inconvenient for many working-class people. Barry understood the adverse impact even an extra nickel could have on poor and working class families. From personal experience, he knew the importance of a good inexpensive public transportation system. In Memphis, he had traveled to his jobs and school by bus. His mother and sisters had used buses as their primary means of transportation. Barry planned the District bus boycott for January 24, 1966. He knew that if he could get enough people to refuse to ride the bus in the dead of winter, he could authenticate his own power and influence.

Most African-Americans cooperated. They commuted to work using cars and vans provided by private drivers, and left the Chalk buses largely empty. Sam Smith, editor of *The Progressive Review* newsletter and author of *The Captive Capital*, volunteered to drive during the boycott. "People were sticking together that Monday. I carried seventy-one people, only five of them white," he said. By Barry's estimate, the company that day lost 150,000 fares. Anything else he did in the city could only expand his influence, affluence, and power.

While the boycott tapped into the protest legacy of the civil rights movement, it also provided Barry invaluable information that, years later, gave him leverage in nearly every political election he entered. He learned the geography of the city, and developed contacts in each of the wards. He could map a traffic pattern based on the movement of people in their communities, and knew, for example, when the largest number left for work or came home. This rudimentary data proved highly useful as he and others plotted strategy for getting African-Americans to the polls in upcoming political elections.

◆ ◆ ◆ ◆ ◆ ◆ ◆ ◆ ◆ ◆ ◆ ◆ ◆ ◆ ◆ ◆

Barry became so impressed with his own organizing efforts that when new SNCC chairman Stokely Carmichael ordered him from the District to Atlanta, he refused to return. Carmichael, elected SNCC chairman in 1966, moved the organization to a more secular and militant posture—he coined the phrase "Black Power"—alienating some of its long time supporters in the process. Even before Carmichael defeated incumbent John Lewis (Barry's old colleague from Fisk) to the SNCC presidency, some SNCC members began to push for the expulsion of white staffers and members.

Carson notes that a position paper by SNCC's Atlanta Project equated the subordination of blacks to that of colonized people in the Third World. White civil rights workers were compared to "the white servants and missionaries in colonial countries who have worked with colonial people for a long period of time and have developed a paternalistic attitude toward them." The authors of the position paper called on SNCC to adopt a strict policy that only blacks staff, control, and finance the organization. It was a formalization of black politics already being practiced by newly elected officials such as John Conyers of Michigan and by older leaders like Adam Clayton Powell.

Additionally, SNCC members battled over whether race or class conflict should be the dominant feature of the organization's platform. Some SNCC staffers wanted to form stronger coalitions with white and leftist organizations, including those involved in the anti-war movement. They did not prevail. While Carmichael did not advocate black separatism, he wanted the group to remain focused on race relations, and it ended up reversing course, forming closer ties with more radical organizations such as the Black Panther Party. Carmichael also was willing to venture into international waters, connecting with Third World countries, many of which had socialist leanings. He even visited Fidel Castro in Cuba. Needless to say, the once respected, church-connected group began to be seen as excessively radical and thus lost its prominence as an agent for the achievement of integration.

The group's actions were even too extreme for Marion Barry, who saw himself, oddly enough, as a moderate, and his seemingly "namby pamby" positions ran him afoul of many in SNCC. So, when he resigned rather than go to Atlanta, his resignation was warmly received. But the image his resignation cast in the larger, public arena, was of Barry as integrationist, willing to work with non-blacks to improve America, rather than abandon it or further segregate its African-American population.

Barry himself threw down the gauntlet to SNCC. He told Carmichael not to expect one dime from the funds he'd raised in the city. He intended to use them for the Free D.C. Movement he'd begun since his arrival: "We want to free D.C. from our enemies, the people who make it impossible for us to do anything about lousy schools, brutal cops, slum lords, welfare investigators who go on midnight raids, employers who discriminate in hiring, and a host of other ills that run rampant through our city," Barry said in explaining his departure. It was time for SNCC and others involved in the civil rights struggles to shift gears, Barry said. "We must concentrate on control—economic and political power."

The Free D.C. Movement contained all the aspects of the voter registration and education drives Barry conducted down South. He tapped into the frustrations of young African-Americans growing weary of leaders whose accommodationist rhetoric only prolonged residents' fight for self-determination and local representation. He used small block club parties and group meetings as a way to get his message across. He and his supporters disrupted the city's annual Cherry Blossom Festival. They were arrested. Barry urged black businesses to display "Free D.C." signs in their store windows and threatened a boycott of other businesses. "Southern white segregationists have gotten together with the moneylord merchants of this city to oppose our right to vote," Barry said.

But the District's accommodationists stepped in, calling his measures too extreme. Coming from the South, where blacks had been shot down in broad daylight, where taxpayer dollars were diverted to White Citizens Councils, Barry saw little that was too radical. For him, there were no limits and no barriers. He subscribed to the "by any means necessary" theory of political action.

The bus boycott and the Free D.C. Movement brought Barry to the attention of the city's white power establishment, who viewed him as both sinner and savior—the trouble in the city and the answer to the city's troubles. Barry sculpted those sentiments into a public persona of the "daring champion of the people." Sixteen months after his arrival, he ranked fifth in a survey of residents who had "done the most for Negroes in the area." In 1967, President Johnson, responding to the pressure of the Free D.C. Movement, reorganized the local-commissioner form of government, and created an elected school board, securing Barry's future as District leader. It would be six years before the city won the right to elect a mayor and city council. But Barry well-leveraged his first few years in the nation's capital, and, by 1972, already had abandoned his street organizing career and re-packaged himself as part of the establishment.

◆ ◆ ◆ ◆ ◆ ◆ ◆ ◆ ◆ ◆ ◆ ◆ ◆ ◆ ◆

President Johnson's reorganization of the District government was very much a compromise. He had sought full home rule, but Congress, reacting in part to the Free D.C. Movement, rejected his proposal.

Like many whites in urban centers, Johnson was afraid. Two years earlier, the country had become a towering inferno, fueled by African-American dissatisfaction. In 1964, racial violence rocked Harlem, resulting in one dead, 140 injured, and five hundred arrested. In 1965, Watts—a largely black community near Los Angeles—went up in smoke during widespread rioting. Philadelphia and Chicago similarly combusted.

In 1967, the entire country was in upheaval, with war protesters actively demonstrating in the streets and on normally pastoral college campuses. Blacks were not the only population venting rage, though at times the spectacles they created took center stage. Urban centers were being torched by rebel youths dissatisfied with their economic lot in the country, the persistent racism they faced, and the slow, almost timid, pace of the civil rights movement. The year before, Stokely Carmichael had yelled "Black Power." He thus incited thousands of young African-Americans, especially males, to abandon the nonviolent philosophy then fueling the civil rights movement and guiding the Rev. Martin Luther King Jr., the Southern Christian Leadership Conference, and originally the Student Nonviolent Coordinating Committee. Whites feared that the hand of every black teenager would soon hold a Molotov cocktail.

Hoping to placate Barry and other frustrated D.C. residents, President Johnson proposed an elected school board for the District. But Secretary of Labor Willard Wirtz knew electing a few people to run the city's schools wasn't nearly enough to douse the flames of dissatisfaction among African-Americans. Residents, especially those following Barry, needed jobs, Wirtz argued. If the nation's capital were to be safe from potential riots, the government had to provide employment, he said.

Barry had come to the same conclusion after asking *the* obvious question: "How can you interest people in voting when they don't have money to buy food for their families?" As he moved through the District in 1967, he scouted an appropriate strategy for building his movement.

In the wings was Rufus "Catfish" Mayfield, a young radical from a public housing complex in northeast D.C. On paper, Mayfield roughly outlined the proper mixture of jobs and political justice. But, lacking credentials, and possessing a police record, he couldn't find any funds or government support. Mayfield and Barry connected out of mutual interest: Barry needed Mayfield's deeper access into the District's disenfranchised communities, and Mayfield needed Barry's organizing and fundraising skills.

Wirtz's concern that a police shooting might ignite tensions in the District brought frustrated residents—Mayfield and Barry among them—to a meeting at a local church. The labor secretary met an angry group of tough, unpolished African-American men whom some would have regarded as thugs. To Barry, they would become his army and the beginning of his political base.

Wirtz accomplished nothing during his first meeting. He made progress later, however, in a private session with Barry, Mary Treadwell, Carroll Harvey—head of community renewal—and Mayfield. The team wanted Wirtz to support a program that could reach the kind of guys he had seen at the first meeting—the unemployed, uneducated, and unruly. Using Mayfield's sketchy program, Barry proposed an employment program. Wirtz funded the five-week summer project, which came to be called Pride, Inc. to the tune of three hundred thousand dollars.

Mayfield became the organization's chairman, albeit with limited authority. Harvey served as Pride's first executive director, handling day-to-day operations. Treadwell oversaw the fundraising operation. And Barry played politics, schmoozing with those in the streets, in government, corporations and foundations. Even then, Barry's follow-through on details left a lot to be desired. But there wasn't a single riot in the District that summer.

Pride, Inc. was a natural extension of the work Barry had begun in McComb, Mississippi. He easily related to young people, even delinquents. He talked their language and understood their desires to shape their own destinies and to develop their own communities. Reflecting on his days in Memphis, Barry knew how important a job could be to a young person's self-image. And with poor families, every paycheck counted. In McComb, he had organized teenagers to join the nonviolent civil rights movement, training them in techniques and then directing them to points of contact. While the caliber of young people Barry contacted at Pride was different, training was training and he could hone any group of people into a razor sharp instrument of social change.

As in McComb, where his youthful followers developed an allegiance to him, the young people of Pride and their progeny would develop a similar loyalty. From the corner of 16th and U Streets, where Pride would subsequently locate its offices, Barry could build an empire, using his subjects whenever and wherever he wished, exacting from the establishment whatever price he demanded.

But some in Congress objected to thousands of dollars being funneled to Barry and his band of misfits. Even if they didn't articulate it, they understood their own vulnerable position, and the lethal weapon they had placed in the hands of an unpredictable radical. In September 1967, when funding ran out, it was doubtful that Pride, Inc., despite its success, would receive any additional funds. In an exercise of political muscle-flexing, Wirtz successfully lobbied for a full year's funding of Pride—$1.5 million.

Interestingly, the additional money did not protect the nation's capital from rioting that spring. The assassination of the Rev. Martin Luther King, Jr., as it did in major urban centers throughout the nation, ignited riots in the District, and the entire city seemed to be on fire. Stokely Carmichael exacerbated the situation, providing rioters instructions on points of attack. The aim was to inflict great harm on whites, especially those businesses which many blacks felt had leeched off the black community and returned very little to its development. The National Guard was eventually called in to restore peace. By the time it was all over, seventy-six hundred people had been arrested, twelve hundred buildings had burned, and property damage was estimated at twenty-five million dollars.

While Carmichael served as instigator, Barry attempted to calm the disturbance, to control the random destruction. He won praise from *The Washington Post,* which credited him with acting as the community's voice of reason. An unsatisfied Barry warned the District's appointed council that all was still not right in the nation's capital.

"There's a black culture, there's a black psychology, there's black value. There's white psychology, and there's a white value," Barry said. "You can't plan for black people like you can for white people, because there is a difference. If this city is rebuilt the same way it was, it is going to be burned down again."

While Barry wasn't a native Washingtonian, he became—with that statement—the translator and guide for white Washington no less than he had become a leader of the District's blacks. Whites and government officials reasoned that his civil rights background and his roots in the District's poor communities gave him greater insight. And they began to rely on him, becoming more comfortable with his ability to chart a course and get them more safely through troublesome terrain. In fact, they were more comfortable with him than with people like Walter Washington—the District's presidentially-appointed mayor.

When Pride's big money came, Harvey, Treadwell, and Barry pushed Mayfield out of the picture, assuming full control and operation of an organization based on the former street thug's idea. In the five years of its existence, Pride, Inc. created several spin-off operations. One was Youth Pride Economic Enterprises, which by 1970 owned and operated six gas stations, a landscaping company, and a painting and maintenance company. The group also owned a southeast D.C. apartment complex.

Although it achieved dramatic and measurable successes, the organization suffered a pattern of corruption almost from its inception. First, there was the power struggle between Barry, Harvey, Treadwell, and Mayfield, which nearly resulted in the firing of weapons. In 1969, two years after the organization was established, seventeen employees were indicted on charges of misappropriating ten thousand dollars in federal funds. Only three people were convicted. But by the 1970s, with massive, swift expansion, and the mishandling of funds, Pride, Inc. was in the red. Barry and Treadwell mounted a massive fundraising campaign. District residents donated fifty thousand dollars, giving the organization a few more days to live.*

Barry floated through the civil rights movement amassing skills and a network of contacts to aid him in what he knew was inevitable: increasing black participation in the political life of America. Better than most in SNCC and other civil rights organizations, Barry measured each step he took. By 1971, he had it all together: He knew how to appeal for money from blacks as well as whites. He knew how to work the government, using the threat of black violence to extract ransom and booty. Six years after his arrival, his name was a household word because the media came running whenever he called. He perpetually served up interesting sound bites and copy. Using Pride, he had built a base—a constituency of people who owed him for their livelihood. Some believed that without Marion Barry, they would have been just a number at Lorton correctional facility, or some other prison. When the time was right, he intended to knock on the doors or ring the telephones of those who owed him and they would be expected to punch their ballot next to his name, regardless of the office being sought.

Two years later, Barry called in some of his chits. President Richard Nixon signed legislation giving the District limited Home Rule, which included the right to elect its own mayor and city council. Barry decided to run for the office one step down from the mayor—at-large Council member. His supporters, especially from the poor and working class, acknowledged their debt to him, electing him to the position in 1974. With that electoral success, Barry's political career started its ascent.

CHAPTER NINE

Two YEARS BEFORE THE DISTRICT received Home Rule, and six years before Marion Barry became the second mayor of the nation's capital, thousands of African-American leaders and organizers converged on Gary, Indiana for the country's first black political convention. The 1972 National Black Political Convention left little room for doubt: Blacks were announcing to the country and to the world that they would be major players in mainstream politics.

The convention was organized and promoted by Richard Hatcher. In 1967, Hatcher, hoping to claim the title of first black mayor of Gary, made a telephone call to Ivanhoe Donaldson, who had left his SNCC assignment in New York for one in the District's quasi-public section—a position at a liberal thank tank called the Institute for Policy Studies. Donaldson had organized several successful political campaigns, including Julian Bond's bid for the Georgia state legislature. The guy who once talked about Barry as a star was by the late 1960s a hired political gun with several impressive notches in his belt and stories in black media publications that bolstered his reputation. Donaldson told Hatcher his political organizing was "just luck."

"[Hatcher] said we need some of that [luck] up here. So I went to Gary," Donaldson recalls. Hatcher won.

With assistance from Amiri Baraka—then a black cultural nationalist whose political base was Newark—and Ron Daniels and Ronald Walters, both political scientists—Hatcher sought to forge from the 1972 convention a National Black Political Party to rival the Democratic and Republican parties.

"The '72 convention was a meeting of people who were doing grass-roots mobilization and an eclectic group of Marxists, civil rights leaders, [and] black nationalists, together with a new class of black professionals," recalls Walters, who admits to helping plan the event out of his Howard University office.

The convention culminated a promising two-year period that saw several African-Americans elected to run significant cities, where blacks had concentrated and would remain the dominant population for nearly a decade. Kenneth Gibson, aligning with Baraka, won election as mayor of Newark. Also in 1970, James McGee became mayor of Dayton, Ohio. Ron Dellums, then a psychiatric social worker who had served on the city council of Berkeley, California, was elected to the U.S. House of Representatives from that state's seventh congressional district. Interestingly, Dellums, a dove who opposed the Vietnam War, won election in a area whose population was less than thirty percent black.* Parren Mitchell, a human rights and civil rights activist who oversaw the implementation of Maryland's public accommodation law, also won a seat that same year in Congress.

Were the early 1970s to be a repeat of the Reconstruction Era? Some blacks worried this latest period of political progress could end just as badly as it had with Reconstruction. Hoping to prevent a tragic end to what appeared to be newly budding political clout, more than eight thousand black delegates converged on Gary, Indiana.

While providing fertile political soil for black politicians, the country seemed at a crossroads. Urban centers were still reeling from the damage of riots associated with Dr. King's assassination. White liberals were not only shocked, but somewhat ashamed of the ongoing violence—more than one significant black leader was murdered, not to mention Robert and John F. Kennedy. Whites seemed more willing to make concessions to blacks. Arthur Fletcher, a black Republican from Philadelphia, got Richard Nixon's attention long enough to win support for affirmative action legislation that set in motion a quota system, forcing the private and public sectors to more aggressively integrate their work force. Television stations sought out "articulate" blacks to train as news anchors. And federal money flowed through black communities in the form of anti-poverty programs. Still, the two major political parties continued to largely ignore African-Americans.

The Gary convention, says Charles Christian, author of *Black Saga*, "signaled to black people across the country that black leaders were aware of their plight and frustrated with the American political system."

And while blacks had made significant gains from the Montgomery Bus Boycott and SNCC's summer campaigns in Mississippi, evidence of the deep-seeded hatred and devastating effects of racism continued to surface. For example, the same year of the Gary convention, news reports exposed the Tuskegee syphilis experiment, where medical personnel with government approval permitted dozens of black men and their progeny to contract the disease. Doctors had wanted to explore the effects of syphilis—an incredible subject of scrutiny given the fact that the Tuskegee Experiment began *after* a syphilis vaccine had been developed. Worse, the experiment was allowed to continue for nearly three decades. Worst of all, the doctors deliberately neglected to treat some of the program subjects.

There were other, more devastating problems. "Our cities are crime-haunted dying grounds. Huge sectors of our youth face permanent unemployment," leaders wrote in their *National Black Political Agenda.* "The schools are unable—or unwilling—to educate our children for the real world of our struggles. Meanwhile, the officially approved epidemic of drugs threatens to wipe out the minds and strengths of our best young warriors. Economic, cultural, and spiritual depression stalk Black America, and the price for survival appears to be more than we are able to pay."

The 8,000 conventioneers in Gary, Indiana drafted and approved their "black manifesto," which was considered a radical document. The following year saw the continued election of African-Americans in record number. By 1984, black mayors would be elected in 255 U.S. cities.

◆ ◆ ◆ ◆ ◆ ◆ ◆ ◆ ◆ ◆ ◆ ◆ ◆ ◆ ◆ ◆

In this rich black political environment, Barry flourished and was inspired. He was part of that first wave of civil rights activists and black professionals determined to find a place in the American political arena. And, like the others, his tactics for leadership followed a civil rights tradition steeped in religious overtones, but also wrapped in the rhetoric of racial pride and empowerment. The target of discontent, of course, was the mainly white establishment.

Barry himself had served as president of the District school board, but he hungered for greater power. In 1972, he remained as determined to gain control as he had been when he first warned Stokely Carmichael that it was time to shift strategy, and targeted the District as a place to converge. Other SNCC activists obviously agreed. By the early 1970s, Frank Smith, John Wilson, Charlie Cobb, Reginald Robinson, Lawrence Guyot, and other black political luminaries were all calling the District of Columbia home.

When Barry won a seat on the District's first elected city council in 1974, he carried out precisely what had been articulated in 1972 in Gary, where black leaders set out to imprint both their physical presence and style on American politics. The campaigns of many black leaders, notes Donaldson, were similar. "The difference between Hatcher's campaign and Andrew Young's was the emotional level. They had the same agenda. It was multiracial politics that pushed the right of black people to have opportunities to come into public office and the right of black people to run agencies of government."

But despite efforts at multiracial politics on the D.C. Council, there was little Barry and his civil rights associates could do to effect change. The Council's role appeared far less decisive than that of the executive. Barry and his colleagues could develop programs and policies all night, but without an agreeable executive, they would languish. After one term under Mayor Walter Washington, Barry knew that he wanted to control the levers of power much more directly. He needed to rise in the chain of command.

◆ ◆ ◆ ◆ ◆ ◆ ◆ ◆ ◆ ◆ ◆ ◆ ◆ ◆ ◆

As Barry was deciding whether to take on Walter Washington, the incumbent mayor, and Sterling Tucker, the incumbent Council chairman—both of them declared candidates for mayor—some in the local Democratic Party urged him to wait his turn. He was too eager, they told him. The two mayoral candidates were heavyweights, they said. But Barry never had much patience, and, so far as Barry was concerned, the civil rights agenda had stalled under Walter Washington, whom he saw as nothing more than a tool of the white establishment.

With Washington and Tucker both targeting the black middle class, Barry was left to create a base from a multi-racial, multi-class coalition that included gays, whites, Asians, Hispanics, poor and working class blacks. "He was adopted by everyone, " Albert "Butch" Hopkins Jr., president of the Anacostia Economic Development Corporation, once said.

The political chameleon, or "situationist," became full grown during his first mayoral campaign. He donned a dashiki, capturing the approval of the poor while casting Mayor Washington as a "handkerchief head," an incompetent manager who had failed to make any tangible changes to the city during his tenures as appointed and elected mayor. He painted Tucker in the same frame. He played on the feelings of the poor, arguing that because of his long association with civil rights and poverty issues, he could effect real change to improve the lives of the disadvantaged and disenfranchised in the District. He also sought the support of whites, asserting the superiority of his leadership over that of the sitting government. Members of the District's growing gay community understood that Washington and Tucker represented the old, conservative black school when it came to gay rights, and were accordingly supportive of Barry, who spoke to them in more sympathetic terms.

In 1978, all the pieces of the puzzle came together for Barry—the puzzle he'd been working on since his days at LeMoyne, through SNCC, Free D.C., Pride, the school board, and the city council. All the techniques he'd mastered as well as those amassed by his political strategist, Ivanhoe Donaldson, were employed. Using what they'd learned about organizing small groups, the campaign held sessions at supporters' houses, providing Barry with intimate audiences for presenting his message. The private transportation network he had created for the D.C. bus boycott was resurrected when the campaign pushed to get the maximum number of Barry voters to the polls. Barry's work with young, working class blacks at Pride, Inc., and with others during his Free D.C. Movement, offered a reliable base. To these, Barry preached the message of black politics: blacks took care of their own, providing jobs and creating a new balance of political power.

Sterling Tucker and Walter Washington wound up splitting the black middle class vote, and, Barry, by a surprising margin, won the election with a mandate. Still, he worried about the indisputable opposition of middle class blacks. If he intended to go any farther in a predominantly black city, he knew he couldn't always depend on the poor to rally behind him. He needed taxpayers, property owners, people with money to enter his circle. Before his first term was over, Barry, in a return to his roots, was courting the entire gamut of black voters, especially the African-American middle class.

With Barry as mayor, Washington's community of liberal whites demonstrated its willingness to coalesce around important issues. Yet, Barry couldn't break away from his Mississippi past. He couldn't escape the image of the battered Emmett Till or the assassinated Medgar Evers. He couldn't escape the paternalism of LeMoyne College's Chandler, or the poverty of his youth. The history of racial and economic discrimination gave him no peace.

What's more, the presence of his civil rights buddies, who carefully followed their agenda of uplifting the race, prevented him from standing in the middle of the road. Whenever there was a choice between black or white, poor or rich, Barry's buddies always supported the underdog. Tradition, and the past, demanded loyalty to the cause. It would have been construed as an act of self-mutilation, a brand of self-hate, if they abandoned "black politics." African-Americans had nurtured and chosen Barry—a poor boy from Itta Bena—as their leader. He still wanted their warm support. He wasn't ready to sacrifice it—his political career wasn't yet secure.

In 1982, during his second run as mayor, whites deserted Barry, leaving him standing as he began: the radical rabble-rouser who talked black, even if he no longer dressed black, and who saw everything through the prism of race. And though he vehemently disagreed with those who accused him of "playing the race card," Barry had returned to his original locus—black politics. He had temporarily traded in the '72 Gary, Indiana agenda to gain the foothold he sought, achieving that goal well enough to rival nearly every other black mayor in the U.S. at the time.

With political power firmly in their hands, elected African-American officials hoped to shift the economic balance, to pour dollars into the hands of more black business leaders, to improve the quality of urban education, and to reduce the despair that permeated urban centers. And while the early 1980s were fueled by a booming national economy, the mayors' success was fleeting.

In 1990—the year of Barry's drug bust—Richard Hatcher, Kenneth Gibson, and other black mayors had been kicked out of office, were seeing the writing on the wall, or had chosen not to run for re-election. None had been effective in fully shifting economic power to African-Americans, and the plight of the hardcore poor in their cities remained unchanged. The District stood as testament to the unrealized goal of the National Black Political Agenda of 1972: Schools were in sharp decline, crime was on a steep *in*cline, drugs had ravaged black communities, and the price of survival was still too high to pay.

Yet, many African-Americans in the District, including Barry, held tenaciously to the tenets of black politics. Barry's failure to achieve their loftiest goals had been caused, he thought, by the refusal of a "white dominated" Congress to provide the predominantly black government with the funding it deserved and needed. His 1990 arrest, in his view, stemmed from his unwavering commitment to the black political tradition, which effectively required him to paint the white power establishment as the culprit of all the black community's ills.

But even as blacks in the nation's capital clung, somewhat desperately, to traditional black politics, another breed of African-Americans was assuming control of major urban centers. Their new style of leadership, coupled with the District's downward spiral, would begin the final chapter for Barry and the brand of politics he advanced in the District. But that end would not come without a fight, without the political equivalent of the "Rumble in the Jungle."

Young MARION BARRY, with fellow D.C. organizers
RUFUS "CATFISH" MAYFIELD and CARROLL HARVEY,
during their days with Pride, Inc.

© Bill Rice

Barry with political strategist IVANHOE DONALDSON,
who made a comeback less public than Barry's after being
convicted of stealing District funds

Nation of Islam Leader LOUIS FARRAKAN created quite a stir at Barry's trial by seeking—and initially being denied—a seat in the courtroom.

EFFI BARRY, the mayor's third
wife, was at Marion's side
each day during his trial.

With JESSE JACKSON at Barry's 1995 inaugural.
After the Vista sting, Barry hoped his erstwhile civil rights ally would occupy the mayor's
office while serving his six-month prison term, then support him in his comeback bid.
Jackson at first said yes, then quickly bowed out.

"Let's All Say Amen"

or

The End of an Era

·PART THREE·

CHAPTER TEN

ON THE FROSTY MORNING of January 2, 1995, Maya Angelou, the statuesque African-American poet, looked out at an audience of more than two thousand, gathered in the gymnasium of the University of the District of Columbia, to see Marion Barry inaugurated as mayor. Most of the crowd was relegated to bleachers, but VIPs sat on metal folding chairs in the center of the room, roped off from the others. Normally frumpy Washingtonians displayed their more flamboyant side, wrapping themselves in furs and fancy silk suits. Even the media came appropriately dressed.

During the 1980s and 1990s, Angelou had acquired an impressive reputation for her literary and dramatic contributions to American culture. In a series of critically acclaimed, autobiographical books, she exposed her life's story for all to read, gaining status alongside Toni Morrison and Alice Walker as one of the country's best, and best-known black women writers. In her poetry, she exalted black culture, with clean, unimposing rhymes, and verses that, to the average reader, were simple, lyrical, and memorable and that, to her critics, were deceptively simplistic.*

In 1993, President Clinton plucked Angelou from a list of far more accomplished poets, commissioning an original poem to commemorate his inaugural. She was the first black writer so honored. Barry's use of the nationally recognized figure for his own inaugural two years later seemed a stratagem by which he hoped to place himself on a par with the president of the United States.

The connection between Clinton and Barry went beyond their taste in literary ornaments for inaugural ceremonies. Both master politicians hailed from the South. Both were progenies of strong women who endured abusive husbands. Both married forceful women. Both ran for office and won against the odds. Both were charismatic and articulate—capable, like jazz musicians, of riffing on a theme. Someone said "hit it," and they blew. Both were libertine when it came to their relationships with women. Both possessed political acumen and political credibility, which the public strangely disconnected from their personal integrity. But while Clinton realized his dream—becoming governor of his home state and president of the country—Barry hit the political equivalent of the glass ceiling. And while Clinton was credited with bringing good times to the nation, Barry was excoriated for presiding over a wasteful, ineffectual government that failed to perform its municipal duties well.

Barry's 1995 inaugural wasn't graced with Angelou's specially commissioned verses—as Clinton's had been. Instead, Angelou reached for a previously published classic, whose lines, by *another* poet, always won commendations and whose message touched the collective emotional chord of black America. Always one to savor the theatrical, Angelou paused at the microphone, breathing deeply as if sucking in the triumphant energy contained in the spacious room. Buoyed by her audience's anticipation, she intoned in her rich, Southern voice:

> *They dragged you from your homeland*
> *They chained you in coffles*
> *They huddled you spoon-fashion in filthy hatches*
> *They sold you to give a few gentlemen ease...*
> *They cooped you in their kitchens*
> *They penned you in their factories*
> *They gave you the jobs that they were too good for*
> *They tried to guarantee happiness to themselves*
> *By shunting dirt and misery to you*
> *You sang: Me an' muh baby gonna' shine, shine*
> *Me an' muh baby gonna' shine.*
> *The strong men keep a-comin' on*
> *The strong men git stronger...*

When she ended, the crowd leapt to its feet, applauding and shouting wildly. The poem encapsulated the story of their ordeal in America. It recapitulated the tale of Barry's woes—from the 1990 Vista FBI sting, or "set-up" as syndicated columnist Clarence Page called it, through his stunning return, first as Ward 8 D.C. Council member, and now, once more, as mayor of the city. "To restore him back to power was triumphant. It was the victory of black people," explains political scientist Ron Walters. "It wasn't just the religious aspect of this. One has to see Marion in cultural and symbolic terms."

"Strong Men," the poem Angelou recited, linked all African-Americans by history and suffering, casting each as the victim of a racist, unjust system that never could be forgiven fully for its sins. It depicted blacks' perception of themselves, as forever the underdog, but always masterfully surviving the persecution and discrimination that confronted them. It justified Barry's often defiant image, projecting the recovering drug addict cum politician as freedom fighter, boldly resisting efforts by the white establishment to emasculate him as it had countless of his brethren during and after the slavery era.

Barry himself had been whipped by the system, and tainted by personal trials, but returned triumphant by sheer will and the uncompromising support of people throughout the world, especially African-Americans. Many blacks counted Barry as a phenomenal character, the kind of which myths and legends are made. He, like Muhammad Ali, was their champion.

The selection of "Strong Men" for the inaugural offered one of many ironies that filled the day. Sterling Brown, the native Washingtonian and Howard University professor who penned the poem, had been the city's first and only Poet Laureate. While he represented Washington's old guard, he rebelled against its elitist and therefore exclusionary expression. His poetry sang the praises, painted portraits, and told the stories of the common black person.*

During Barry's second term as mayor, Effi Cowell, Barry's third wife, and a group of cultural activists, including award-winning poet and Howard University employee E. Ethelbert Miller and Smithsonian Institution executive James Early, decided to create the Poet Laureate post. Like Joan Mondale during the Carter years, Effi chose the arts as one of her primary areas of interest while serving as the District's First Lady. She began a rotating gallery of art exhibitions in her husband's office, making it possible for works by many of the city's lesser known visual artists to be seen by national and international dignitaries. And, she gathered around her a circle of writers, sometimes holding meetings at the couple's southeast D.C. home.

Interestingly, when Barry came to the podium to take the oath of office, he didn't mention the correlation between his own history and the Brown poem. He also didn't bring up the rebuff he had experienced only months earlier from the leadership at the University of the District of Columbia, which refused to seat him on the dais during graduation ceremonies. But UDC President Tilden LeMelle and the others were receiving their comeuppance now. Barry sat on center stage, no longer needing their permission or validation. Undoubtedly, this private act of vengeance fueled the selection of the school as the location for the inaugural ceremonies instead of the larger and more comfortable D.C. Convention Center.

In true Richard Daley style, Barry, as mayor, struck back at his enemies without commentary—one-by-one. He refused to run interference for Black Entertainment Television President Robert Johnson. One of Barry's advisers in his failed 1990 mayoral campaign, Johnson had quickly retreated after the Vista raid, turning to the Rev. Fauntroy as his candidate. When the cable television executive found himself entangled in 1994 with the city's Redevelopment Land Authority and Abe Pollin, a powerful sports team owner, over the downtown sports arena, Barry smiled from the sidelines. What might be seen as karmic retribution against Barry's former allies was not widely noted.

The mayor-elect stood on UDC's stage next to his fourth wife, Cora Masters Barry; his mother, Mattie Cummings; and his only child—son Christopher—who had come to live with his father shortly after Barry and Effi were divorced. Accounts of Barry's relationship with his son are mixed. Some suggested that Barry was inattentive to his child's needs—too often, they said, Barry left the care of the boy to various female friends. Both Sandra Allen and Sandra Seegars tell stories of their caring for Christopher, taking him for haircuts and preparing meals for him. But most people say Barry has doted on his son. At public appearances, certainly, Barry's fatherly pride shines through.

On inauguration day, Barry's family beamed with reciprocal pride, as he stood holding the Bible that belonged to a dead friend. Tom Skinner had consoled Barry during those early days just after his arrest, when self-doubt overwhelmed him and humiliation became a constant companion.*

In the 1960s, Barry sought to forge a moderate image, and used his dress to make the point. Now, at his 1995 inaugural, he abandoned the African-inspired clothing of kufi hats, Kente cloth scarves, and Nehru jackets that he had worn like a costume since leaving prison. Instead, he wore a pinstripe suit and white shirt. The nonchalance with which he continued to switch clothing telegraphed a deeper message—that he couldn't be consistent. Time and circumstance dictated his style, not a set of unmoveable principles.

In 1992, after Barry got out of prison, the Rev. Willie Wilson thought that one way to establish the former mayor's new identity was to give him a new name. He crowned him Anwar Amal—Arabic for Bright Hope. But Barry felt uncomfortable with the moniker. For his inaugural, he needed another disguise, so he dumped that persona, and went back to calling himself Marion Barry again. In his book, *What Black People Should Do Now: Dispatches from Near the Vanguard*, author Ralph Wiley talks about the practice of many African-Americans to change their birth names. Wiley himself admits that, in some circles, he himself is known as Malik al Din, "and I am about as much Muslim as Chuck Berry. I know I'm in a war and it's a question of identity, stripes, and rank."

The whole notion of name-changing peaked during the 1970s, when blacks, claiming Africa as their ancestral home, sought to identify in tangible ways with their pre-slavery roots. They took African-sounding names, wore African-inspired clothing, adopted African religions, and began to master the cuisines of East and West Africa. Barry's name change put him squarely inside this trend. Later, in 1995, a trip to West Africa brought him yet another African name. It didn't stick, either.

At his 1995 inaugural, Barry chose to present himself as the accommodationist political insider he had always been at his core.* Like many civil rights activists, Barry never fully intended a revolution to upend the American political system. He simply wanted access to the authority, power, influence, and affluence that his white counterparts possessed. Despite the message of his social programs, Barry always dreamed of being part of the mainstream team. While he may have used the city's poor and working class as a step ladder, he never wanted to remain in their world. He liked being able to buy expensive suits, drink imported cognac, and hear adulation wherever he walked. Having achieved that lifestyle during his earlier administrations, he wasn't going to completely repudiate it now.

Like most African-Americans, Barry wanted to be in both places— inside *and* outside. Consequently, he switched roles, depending on the situation. Most often, he simultaneously rode two horses—a grueling, if not impossible, task.

As she watched her husband taking the oath, a tear inched down Cora Barry's cheek. She brushed it away with a grand gesture, making it difficult for the moment of sentimentality to go unnoticed. Certainly, she understood the historic drama in which she had played a leading role. No one had worked harder than she to restore Barry to the throne, becoming both famous and infamous for her tactics and her fierce protection of her husband. In the nearly two decades since they met, they had crossed a large swath of treacherous territory together, and each learned to depend on the other. Despite the flying arrows and cannon fire of the previous eighteen months, they now stood victorious.

Barry's victory celebration had begun days earlier, mimicking, in aura and trappings, a coronation. In some senses, it seemed inappropriate. For more than a decade, Barry held the reins of the District's political development—sometimes choking them tightly, other times slackening his grip. He was the signpost by which everyone measured his worth.

Yet, in 1995, the degree to which he was worshipped was hard to fathom. Here, after all, was a man of markedly limited territorial command, a recovering drug addict, and a vastly overrated executive, to whom another class of voters would be loath to impute such potency.

◆ ◆ ◆ ◆ ◆ ◆ ◆ ◆ ◆ ◆ ◆ ◆ ◆ ◆ ◆ ◆

Still, the prison-to-election path was not wholly unprecedented. In the early 1900s, Massachusetts legislator Tom Curley and his brother James Michael both were elected to office, though both had been convicted of "defrauding" the government, and both were serving time in jail. James Michael Curley became alderman, finishing third in a field of twenty-six candidates—Tom was elected mayor. "The Curleys rested easy in jail," writes their biographer Jack Beatty. "They were leading Democratic politicians. The Sheriff gave them cells twice the size of regular cells and allowed them to see numerous visitors each week, though jail rules limited ordinary prisoners to just one. They took saltwater baths every morning, sent out for baskets of fruits, exercised, wrote letters and speeches, and read lots of books."

Barry wasn't treated so well while in either of the two federal prisons where he resided in 1990. In fact, he was forced to pay his room and board, and he was made to pull kitchen duty.

And Barry, unlike the Curleys, wasn't restored to power after prison simply by an overwhelming love for the fallen one. Rather, it reflected citizens' frustrations and his exquisite manipulation of their anxieties. "I feel I have to give Barry every chance to redeem himself—not because I fear what he might be able to do to my political career," wrote author Wiley, "[because] I don't have one. And not that I fear what he might be able to do to my access as a political writer—I rarely write about politics. I have to give him a chance because I never know when I may need redemption myself, as a fallible human being and a black man in America."

Other blacks were repulsed by Barry's continued exploitation of African-American history and culture, but they muffled their criticism, fearing that publicly rebuking the "beloved one" would label them "race-traitors." Just as all Americans cringe at being called "Benedict Arnold," blacks recoil at the mantle of "race-traitor." Throughout the 1990s, the phrase grew fashionable and ballooned with venom. Bearing such a stigma was far worse than being dubbed an Uncle Tom.

On the Sunday before Barry's swearing-in, sixteen hundred people gathered at Union Temple church, ostensibly to observe the last day of Kwanzaa, an African-American holiday that begins December 26 and continues through January 1. A 1970s creation of Ron Karenga, the holiday includes prayer, fasting, and nationalistic sermonizing. The seventh day, known as Imani or Faith, resembles Christmas in spiritual significance and feasting. After a high religious ceremony, families gather for huge, banquet-type meals and gift giving.

Barry strolled into Union Temple around three o'clock that Sunday afternoon, wearing a gray suit, accented with Kente cloth. The congregation cheered his arrival. Speaking in a cadence reminiscent of evangelical ministers, Barry talked from the pulpit of his redemption, and assured the gathered that he had not forgotten who helped him win a second chance. "There's no way, with all I've been through, I could still have joy without God's power. I'm going to use the same prayers, the same vision, to help the city overcome," he said, auditioning the theme he would use the next day in his inaugural speech. "Sometimes, when you get out of the valley...we forget who got us out of it. I want you to know I know who helped me get out of my valley. It was God.

"We talk about each other," Barry continued. "We criticize each other, and I just say to people, 'Give me a chance to be successful.' I say to *The Washington Post*, 'Just give me the chance to be successful.' I say to Congress, 'Just give me a chance to be successful.'"

Barry was preaching to the choir: Union Temple had been the vehicle of his resurrection. His success was the people's success, his failure their failure. But if congregants had been keenly perceptive, they would have heard a tinge of insincerity in his voice. They would have seen that he did not fully own the script from which he was reading. A new convert ushered to the altar, not by any spiritual awakening but by the FBI and a troubled former lover, Barry seemed timid in his speech. The intuitive in the congregation may have heard his self-doubt and simply ignored it, hoping that time might solidify Barry's faith in God and himself.

Later that Sunday, Barry traveled with his wife to the Omni Shoreham Hotel on Calvert Street NW. There, hundreds of senior citizens were attending a salute in the Barrys' honor, held as part of the official schedule of inaugural events. Anyone sixty-five and older was admitted free of charge. The young forked over twenty dollars each. Although he'd already been elected, Barry's future still depended on his ability to hold together his base of supporters, and senior citizens were a critical bloc. He had created an Office of Aging. For years, he capitalized on senior power.

He purchased buses to transport them to various events, especially political battles where he needed to demonstrate the backing of large numbers of District residents. When all else failed, seniors were his sure thing, the ace up his sleeve. They were bused to prayer breakfasts, to "State of the District" events, to community meetings, to budget hearings. They always helped to swell the crowd, sending signals to his enemies that he could galvanize "the people" with a moment's notice. In fact, they were carted around with or without their permission and led to believe that without Barry, their lot in life would be far worse.

An affinity for the old was also present in Dick Daley's administration in Chicago. According to columnist Mike Royko, the Chicago mayor "likes old people, keeps them in key jobs, and reslates them for office when they can barely walk, or even when they can't."

The District's senior citizens were anchored in the black church and the belief that every person deserves a second chance, especially one who sounded as if he had felt "the hand of the Lord" on his shoulder. They welcomed Barry back into their lives as they would a grandson stepping briefly outside of God's light.

Barry arrived at the seniors' inaugural ball ready for a good time. There was little talk about the campaign or even the next day's festivities. He and Cora danced the electric slide, or as some called it the "Barry Slide," thrilling those in attendance with their rhythm and agility.

Someone once said that James Michael Curley "had a capacity to project an infectious enjoyment of the fun and fakery of politics; a penchant for warming the abstract workings of government such that ordinary people felt it was on their side, and a habit of being indomitable—of not giving up in the face of political defeats and personal desolation." Certainly the same held true for Barry, whose genuine love of people and his ability to mingle with ordinary citizens endeared him to them. African-Americans like their leadership sophisticated, but they never want them to be elitist.

The actual day of the inaugural, many of those two-stepping, gray-haired men and women from the Omni arrived at the Sheraton Hotel for an ecumenical breakfast, where rabbis, imams, priests and Baptist ministers offered words of prayer for the new administration. Such religious events were hallmarks of previous Barry inaugurals, driven as much by the need for cash as the clear understanding that even in a hybrid town like the District of Columbia, African-American clerics still have clout.

◆ ◆ ◆ ◆ ◆ ◆ ◆ ◆ ◆ ◆ ◆ ◆ ◆ ◆ ◆ ◆ ◆

The morning of the inauguration, Nathaniel Clevenger arrived at Barry's hotel to find him still wearing his bathrobe. A Georgetown resident, Clevenger was a top executive with a Maryland-based mortgage company whose wife originally came to the nation's capital to work for Virginia Senator Paul Trible. That Nathaniel Clevenger was now acting as a Barry inauguration coordinator surprised even him. When recruited by Marilyn Funderburk to join the coordinating team, Clevenger knew about Barry only from the newspapers, and to say those reports were unflattering would be a gross understatement. So he hesitated when Funderburk asked for his help. He and his wife had lived in tony Georgetown for seven years, largely removed from the world of local politics. "Never in a million years did I think I would find myself sitting next to Mayor Barry," he said, reflecting on their association.

Although Nathaniel Clevenger and Barry's wife, Cora Barry, were novices in organizing inaugurals, Marilyn Funderburk, the former deputy social secretary in the Carter administration, was an old hand. Just four years earlier, she had coordinated the inaugural gala for Barry's predecessor, Sharon Pratt Kelly, pulling off a classy and sophisticated ball at Union Station. It surprised few that Funderbunk was able to move from Kelly to Barry with such aplomb. Political cross-dressing is performed frequently in the District. Republicans cross over to the Democratic Party; Democratic rhetoric sounds Republican. And political operatives do whatever is necessary so long as the money keeps coming in.

Funderburk, Cora Barry, and Clevenger struggled to reduce the racial, class, and gender divisions that the newly elected mayor had stirred up during his campaign. They decided on "Everyone Matters" as Barry's inaugural theme, and developed a schedule of activities, including a parade, a youth dance, and the official inaugural ball. Clevenger, a former lobbyist with the powerful public relations firm of Hill & Knowlton, pulled double duty, serving as both the committee's spokesperson and as Barry's speech writer. That Sunday night, he worked late, honing and polishing Barry's speech.

When Clevenger arrived that Monday morning at the hotel, Barry took a look and decided he wanted other changes made. The text was lackluster, even bland, for a man who had just accomplished one of the outstanding political feats of the decade. While the mayor-elect went off to the prayer breakfast, Clevenger remained at the hotel, making the requested fixes. Fifteen minutes before his swearing-in was scheduled to begin, Barry, notorious for being late, returned to his hotel room to retrieve his edited speech, and to leave with the day's entourage of security, aides, and boxing promoter Rock Newman. Clevenger had the speech in his left hand, a raincoat thrown across his arm, and his briefcase in his right hand. He was ready to join the group. "Everyone got on the elevator and there was no room left," remembered Clevenger. "The doors just closed on me. There I was, standing in the hall, alone."

◆ ◆ ◆ ◆ ◆ ◆ ◆ ◆ ◆ ◆ ◆ ◆ ◆ ◆ ◆ ◆

Despite the finality of the moment, many in the District and around the world still were stunned and greatly perplexed by Barry's victory. They couldn't understand how it had happened. In fact, three factors, in descending order of importance, seemed to explain it:

- the adept use of seemingly ancient but foolproof organizing tactics;
- an astute understanding of the city's deep-seated racial divide;
- and lots of money.

There hadn't been anything complicated about Barry's approach to the campaign. African-Americans of all social classes in the District were steeped in the tradition of black politics, and, despite new-found affluence, loyal to it. In the thirty years since the passage of the 1964 Civil Rights Act, thousands of African-Americans had risen to the middle and upper classes, but most still responded predictably to cultural buzz words.

Understandably, some suffered from feelings of guilt over their success, their ability to live beyond the boundaries of previous generations, evacuating the ghettos they once called home, resettling in formerly all-white suburbs or more upscale communities like those of Wards 4 and 3, where housing prices can start at $200,000. During the days of Jim Crow, African-Americans had no choice but to live in the black community. Consequently, they were more attentive to the needs of their neighbors. With many living in the suburbs, the poor and working class became isolated, leading to social stratification and destruction in African-American communities.

But the black middle class isn't the only group feeling the pangs of guilt. Liberal whites experience a similar ache when they recollect slavery, Jim Crow laws, and this country's long history of racial discrimination. Their guilt drives the debilitating paternalism suffusing many of the social programs they sponsor.

Like their white counterparts, wealthy African-Americans have often overcompensated for their good fortune, donning a strident black nationalism designed to protect them against accusations that they deserted their race and became too distant from their own people, unable to empathize with their anguish. Although whites frequently were afforded the luxury of traveling from their roots, blacks were held hostage by them. Their complete departure from the traditional community would never be forgiven by other blacks.

Long before many of these guilt-ridden blacks and liberals were born, Barry had expertly massaged their woes and employed explosive, culturally-coded phrases intended to exaggerate their angst. He possessed a conductor's timing.

But he dispensed with racial divisiveness on an august occasion like his inauguration. Completing his redemption, he dressed his speech in religious motifs and metaphors, while grabbing for memorable lines uttered by the legitimately famous, including allusions to Martin Luther King's "I Have a Dream" and "Mountaintop" speeches: "[The] hopes and dreams must not be mine alone. Hopes and dreams must be on the lips and in the minds of every D.C. resident. This is not my city. It's all of our city," Barry said, warning the public to anticipate trouble. They had gone against orthodox wisdom and Congress, re-electing him in spite of his habits and his spotty record for aiding the poor. And the city stood at the precipice of fiscal collapse. "As we move down this journey, we have some difficult days ahead of us, we have some difficult decisions to make. We have some walls to tear down—walls of distrust and regionalism."

In true Anansi tradition, Barry dexterously recast his entire campaign, depicting himself more generously as a coalition-builder, straining to close the chasm between dissimilar races, classes, and ideologies. He hinted at a keen understanding of the hazardous path on which he had embarked. And like Martin Luther King, he concluded he could meet any challenge. While King had been to the mountaintop, Barry had slid to the deepest gutter, and risen from it.

During the campaign, he had frequently confronted his past, reading media recaps of his less than stellar record in his last mayoral term, and watching as his opponents ran Vista Hotel repeats that featured Rasheeda Moore and him as her defenseless paramour. The *Washington City Paper*'s Michael Dolan called Barry a "living testimony to the Nixonian axiom that the press cannot kill a politician. A politician is not susceptible to murder, only suicide." In 1990, Barry had committed political suicide. But District residents resuscitated him in 1994—the way Bostonians did with James Michael Curley, and Harlemites did with Adam Clayton Powell. District voters failed to understand that their lifelines were inexorably linked with a politician who had never understood limits, and never met a boundary he wasn't compelled to violate.

Barry entered the job with the aplomb of a man, who, like King, had seen his possible end, and no longer feared his present or future. If he could rise to political office after his crack-smoking, what bogeyman could harm him?

Moments after the inaugural, everyone marveled at the talent of the city's marching bands and its youth. A three-hour parade made its way down Pennsylvania Avenue—the street newly inaugurated presidents walk down between the Capitol and the White House. Later that Monday night, thousands danced to Ashford & Simpson during an "alcohol-free" inaugural ball at the D.C. Armory. Actually, alcohol was served at a private ball also held at the Armory. The mayor and his wife spent more time at the private affair. Since coming out of prison, Barry made a point of telling everyone, especially the press, the number of days he was drug- and alcohol-free. Initially, he attended Twelve-Step meetings, but he claimed the media invaded his privacy, and he could not comfortably follow his recovery program like other former addicts. So he abandoned the meetings and developed his own strategy, using selected individuals as counselors. Prior to his inauguration, he named Johnny Allem as his communications director and a member of his cabinet. Allem, a white businessman and recovering alcoholic, understood perhaps better than most that Barry's resurrection remained both incomplete and untested.

◆ ◆ ◆ ◆ ◆ ◆ ◆ ◆ ◆ ◆ ◆ ◆ ◆ ◆ ◆ ◆

When the past and future mayor arrived at his ultimate destination, he strutted with a confidence that had eluded him when his first term began. In 1979, despite a short tenure on the D.C. Board of Education and a term on the D.C. City Council, he was an arrogant, unproven administrator. He was the Afroed, civil rights/street activist/rabble-rouser-turned establishment, guided more by instinct than wisdom, ad libbing in a city too young politically to know the difference. A brilliant organizer who knew how to transform the micro into the macro, Barry touted the incremental growth of his administration as if he had overpowered enemy forces at Normandy. And residents, including the media, extolled the accomplishments of Marion Barry in his pre-Vista incarnation as if he were a miracle-worker.

But the District was another land then. In the four years since he left center court, things had changed dramatically. Barry himself witnessed aspects of the shift while serving as Ward 8 council member. Then, a group of young Council members advanced an agenda of reducing taxes and social programs, increasing funding for police and corrections, and delivering municipal services in a better fashion.

The mood of the early 1990s replicated that found in Atlanta, Detroit, and Cleveland, where pragmatic management technicians, willing to join with former enemies of black America to improve the overall living and economic environment, took over mayors' offices, replacing more fiery rhetoricians like Detroit's mayor, Coleman Young. "The ideology of this newer, younger generation has been to deliberately break [with the tradition of black politics] and to say in some way that that tradition is a liability," says political scientist Walters.

"I think we are lulled, deceived into a negative or pejorative interpretation of the operational style, management style, governance style of people like Marion, because there are so many challenges to them based on who they are, where they are, and where they came from," explains Yvonne Scruggs, civil rights leadership director.

"They perforce have to be louder and protest more vigorously than their white counterparts because they have been taught to right injustices when they encounter them rather than wait for an appropriate moment and take propitious action. They are more visible and more apparently combative than their colleagues."

In the District, an assault on the left, where Barry had lived most of his political life, was taking shape nationally, too. A shift of political views resulted in the Republicans' 1994 takeover of the House of Representatives. Conservatives promulgated, through a "Contract With America," an austere program of welfare reform, a balanced federal budget, tax cuts, tough penalties for criminals, significantly less intrusion by the federal government, and returning various programs to local or state elected officials to manage. Moreover, they advocated school choice and the dismantling of affirmative action. The Republicans termed it a response to the competitive global economy, which brought with it wholesale personnel reductions, and downsizing, in both the public and private sectors. Fear struck the core of American families and communities. It was every man for himself, and black America wasn't exempted from this narcissistic mood.

Like their white conservative counterparts, many blacks publicly advocated fiscal restraints and self-sufficiency. The old bootstrap philosophy had been revived. In the mid to late 1990s, many of those blacks who once labored under the weight of guilt for leaving their former inner-city neighborhoods now felt comfortable voicing their weariness with subsidized homeless shelters, teen pregnancy, troubled youths, and adults who sat at home never attempting to find work. Like corporate stockholders, they were most interested in bottom lines, profit margins, and maximizing their investments.

On the other hand, Barry hadn't cleanly divested himself of his rural, deep South beginnings, although he tried desperately. He knew poverty far too intimately—the kind of shoeless, growling-stomach days that remain in the subconscious, never permitting the victim to completely escape. When he saw others aching, bruised by similar privations, he traveled back to his own pain. Once, during a visit to Soweto, South Africa, he witnessed firsthand the deplorable conditions in which people were forced to live, and he cried.

Like many civil rights activists, Barry became wedded to a wealth redistribution ideology, although he would never purposely describe it that way. Failing to instigate a revolution, many radicals either reverted to socialism, as did Stokely Carmichael (a.k.a. Kwame Ture, who left the country during the 1970s for West Africa), or they became unabashedly capitalist, fashioning schemes for ensuring that as many African-Americans as possible entered corporations, won government contracts, and generally made it up the economic ladder.

All his life, Barry sought to make the rich pay for their discriminatory sins and to ensure that blacks were the beneficiaries. As a political organizer, as a community development director, and later as an elected official, he retained that perspective. It endeared him to people like the Rev. Sam McPherson, pastor of Hope Church of God and a native Washingtonian. "Before Marion came in my neighborhood, there were no sidewalks, no senior citizen centers, no recreation centers for kids, no jobs for the youth of this city," remembers McPherson, who grew up in the District's northeast quadrant—in public housing. "He taught us we didn't have to take certain treatment, that we deserved better. You hear all the negatives, but if people only understood the dilemma we were in before he came…"

During the 1980s, Barry used his government as the primary vehicle for implementing his wealth redistribution program, handing out jobs and contracts like cocktails to businesspeople who had been passed over by the predominantly white—or elite black—establishment. He fervently believed every person deserved meaningful employment or some means of earning a living, even if it meant the government had to provide it. It wasn't by accident that the original language of the District's Home Rule governing charter contained a clause mandating full employment. While the clause was deleted, Barry, as mayor, revived the concept, creating a massive summer jobs programs and throwing open the doors to the government's office of personnel.

Two things happened as a result. Sections of the District's black population, previously feeling powerless, became empowered, connecting to the political system for the first time in their history. And the black business community as a whole began to flourish. Following the federal model for affirmative action policies, District law required that a minimum of thirty-five percent of government contracts went to black businesses and District-based businesses.

Barry's "we-take-care-of-our-own" philosophy replicated what many ethnic and white politicians had practiced unofficially throughout the history of American politics. The District ran into problems with various sections of the business community because it aggressively enforced the law.

"When you live in a city where most of the people are African-American and the economic structure is predominantly white…to make political decisions, you set up a natural tension between the people, their aspirations, and the power structure," says Ronald Walters.

"Every minority contractor that got business under Marion Barry took business from somebody white," explains Ivanhoe Donaldson. "Of the black mayors in America, the hardest ass was Coleman Young. He would give you business only if you were born and raised and died in Detroit. And then came Marion and then Maynard Jackson [in Atlanta]. Maynard's reputation was [built] around the Atlanta airport, which allowed blacks to win major building contracts."

For a time, the District maintained a strong, politically active black community, and its middle class expanded, making it one of the largest in the country. Barry's policies helped finance and subsidize successful business leaders like Black Entertainment Television's Robert Johnson, and R. Donahue Peebles, who in 1997 was a leading contender for developing the first black beachfront hotel in Miami. But Barry's generous policies caused the city's fiscal health to slip. He attempted to effect cuts in the bureaucracy, but shifted gears.

"Marion and Ivanhoe quickly understood that when you go after D.C. government employees, for the most part, you're going after the black middle class. From that point on, Barry had a no RIF (Reduction In Force) policy. Whites wanted to disassemble the bureaucracy and Marion realized to go to that extreme would mean an all-out attack on the black middle class, which he was not prepared to do," remembers Dwight Cropp.

"Who," asks Lawrence Guyot, "created the middle class in Prince George's County [a Maryland county south of the District]? I will concede some started before Marion, but Marion intensified it, accelerated it, and protected it in its economic growth." It was hardly in the District's best interest that the Barry-created middle class fled to the "milk and honey" of the suburbs, leaving the city a Mecca for the disenfranchised. By 1997, Prince George's County had grown to sixty-two percent African-American. According to a study conducted by Washington demographer George Grier, the average household income in Prince George's was more than fifty thousand dollars a year.

While the District didn't have a Statue of Liberty beckoning the poor to the banks of its rivers, it did offer a generous and ever-evolving body of social service programs, with few strings attached. The government's benevolence exposed it to attack. When the city's revenues took a dive, handicapping its ability to fully satisfy the requirements of programs and laws it created, aggressive advocates pushed the envelope, filing multimillion dollar lawsuits demanding services. Homeless advocates won citizens' approval of an initiative called the "Right to Shelter" law, which forced the city to provide overnight shelter on demand. Five years after its implementation, and before its repeal, the District government spent more than $100 million on homeless shelters, contracts, and lawsuits filed by advocates who accused it of intentionally withholding such amenities as towels and toothpaste.

Barry's good intentions further soured when he became more of a political boss, concerned about his own future, feeding the machinery and the friends who pumped cash into his re-election campaigns: friends who introduced him to available women; friends who greased his palms with land deals; friends who provided drugs and an otherwise good time.

The politician's practice of rewarding friends with business wasn't new in the District. Between 1868 and 1874, Alexander "Boss" Shepherd nearly bankrupted the capital by issuing an excessive number of public works contracts to friends. Congress responded in 1874 by repealing local self-government.

"We were not looking to run businesses or government the way white folks did," argues Kojo Nnamdi, host of Howard University's public television show "Evening Exchange." "We were looking for the opportunity to run [government] at a higher level of integrity and morality."

But Nnamdi and other civil rights activists may have been naive in believing their representatives would not be corrupted by the system. After all, black politics is a subculture of American politics. And though it maintains certain unique features, as it has matured, it has adopted—consciously or unconsciously—the morés and methods of mainstream politics, largely operated and promoted by whites. Former Michigan Congressman Charles Diggs and former Illinois Congressman Mel Reynolds stand as examples of blacks adapting to the patronage system, pork barrel legislation, and lobbyists courting power in national political circles.

Black political acculturation took on a more perverse expression in the District. With close proximity to Congress and the White House, and many residents working in these institutions, blacks saw up close the warts and pimples of the American political system. They and their leaders, including Barry, comfortably wore corruption like a fine silk suit. District residents accepted with ease the legacy of poor or non-existent service delivery, political excesses, corruption, waste and abuse passed on by the federal government. For its rewards, Chicago's Richard Daley insisted that his city machinery provide consistently high quality performance—and it delivered. Barry, by contrast, didn't agonize over shabby or delayed service delivered by his machine. His failure to follow the Daley lead—and his city's "monkey see, monkey do" attitude—meant that in the end, a minority set-aside program that had created thousands of African-American businesses is remembered only for its abuses and not its successes. Thousands of African-Americans would never have made it to the first rung of the middle class without the opening Barry and his wealth-redistribution policies created.

In 1995, none of that history mattered. The national and local environments were hostile to wealth-redistribution policies. The District, parroting the rest of the nation, focused on fiscal, programmatic, and service accountability. Unadulterated capitalist greed motivated even the poorest ghetto resident, sending many to the streets to sell drugs. A fast buck could always be made there, although it wasn't always guaranteed the person would live long enough to spend it.

At Union Temple, Barry had promised the congregants an exceptional inauguration because Washington was no ordinary city and he no ordinary mayor. No one could deny his extraordinariness. What many wondered was whether Barry had been redeemed, and whether he had reinvented himself sufficiently to survive the times. By mid-term, there wasn't any doubt about the answers to those questions.

CHAPTER ELEVEN

As HE BEGAN SETTING UP HIS NEW ADMINISTRATION, Barry's royal swagger grew more exaggerated. In announcing his transition team and the first of his cabinet appointments, he talked of his magnet-like ability to attract qualified professionals, whom many thought would snub Barry's new government. He aggressively insinuated himself into negotiations for a multi-million dollar downtown sports arena. His predecessor, Sharon Pratt Kelly, botched efforts to keep the Washington Redskins in the city, and without a group of influential business leaders on her side, she would have fouled out on Abe Pollin's offer to build a sports arena for his Washington Wizards (then the Bullets) basketball team and his Capitals hockey team.

Amid criticism about the city's inability to finance such a facility, Barry pulled off a coup of sorts. He convinced Pollin to build the arena using only private financing. The city agreed to cover infrastructure costs such as road maintenance and lighting. Barry also traveled with lame-duck Mayor Sharon Pratt Kelly and council Chairman David Clarke to Wall Street, meeting with investment bankers to discuss borrowing the sums necessary to pull the District government out of its financial woes. The trio left the Big Apple victorious, having convinced investors that buying bonds and short term notes from the city would not leave them exposed. The District, they said, had always paid its debts.

This swirl of activity was vintage Barry. Confidently grappling with pressing issues, but never really showing the pressure, he adeptly fielded media inquiries, leaping tight squeezes and finessing Powell-esque controversy. His enemies predicted disaster. He gloated over his apparent invincibility. But Barry either had a powerful mojo or a whole bunch of people praying for him. Somehow, he had often eluded difficult predicaments. When the feds snagged his second wife, Mary Treadwell, for fraud, sending her to the penitentiary, he escaped. When his cabinet members Alphonse Hill and Ivanhoe Donaldson were carted away to prison, Barry continued to wave his Merlinesque wand, running the city imperiously and imperviously. When Karen Johnson and Charles Lewis' drug dealing and use landed them behind cell bars, Barry remained on the outside snorting and sucking until he was trapped by the seduction of an old lover at the Vista Hotel. In 1995, he grabbed the reins of power unhesitatingly. It had been a long time since "Barry the master politician" had been on display before the entire city.

The last time he had surfaced was in the early 1980s. In 1993, as council member, Barry seemed reluctant to jump boldly into the fray. As he plotted his return to the mayorship, he missed council sessions and demonstrated a flagrant disregard for his constituents But, by his inaugural, he hinted at his 1979 fighting weight and style. In Zaire, a dancing Muhammad Ali looked into the stern, unyielding face of George Foreman and proclaimed himself "the greatest." As he began his new term, Barry struck a similarly cool pose.

"[The] cool pose is a ritualized form of masculinity that entails behaviors, scripts, physical posturing, impression management, and carefully crafted performances that deliver a single, critical message: pride, strength and control," write Richard Majors and Janet Mancini Billson, authors of *Cool Pose: The Dilemmas of Black Manhood in America.*

But like most men practicing the art of the cool pose, Barry used bravado in 1995 mainly to mask his fear. If he didn't get it right this time, he knew he might not have another chance. Some were excited about the possibilities Barry's return presented, especially the ex-convicts, homeless, and unemployed who carried him to the finish line, unscarred and unscathed. But others in the city reserved comment and evaluation for "later." They didn't have to wait long.

◆ ◆ ◆ ◆ ◆ ◆ ◆ ◆ ◆ ◆ ◆ ◆ ◆ ◆ ◆ ◆

Shortly after he won the September primary, Barry sent in a reconnaissance team of James Gibson, Elijah Rogers, and Ivanhoe Donaldson to determine how much damage had been done to the bureaucracy by the Kelly administration. Gibson had served as Barry's first director of the office of planning.

An intense man whose civic passion did not wane after his work with the civil rights movement, Gibson took Barry's fall personally. In his view, Barry's drug use was a betrayal of the movement. He remained angry, even after his old buddy came out of prison: "I never heard an apology from Marion for what he did to the city, and there was no sense of guilt." Gibson considered the stakes high. Barry, he, and other black professionals were engaged in a battle. Action either built upon, or chipped away from, previous success. Nothing was insignificant—everything had to be aimed toward the ultimate goal. "We were Southerners. We were changing a freaking culture that was absolutely formally and legally racist. And the very idea that you get so self-indulgent you lose your goddam way, when we still have people in those neighborhoods, that's where my anger comes from!"

Equally personal was Ralph Wiley's anger. His mother had come from Tennessee and moved into Ward 8. "My mother, Marion, and I always had home in common," wrote Wiley. "There are indelible lessons that the Delta teaches you. You have to be twice as good to go half as far. But, of course, we all know that, don't we? But more than most, black people from the Delta know what many white people are capable of and are not surprised by anything they might do in the way of holding up the progress of black people. So when Barry was videotaped, he hurt me, not because he was the black mayor of Washington, D.C., but because he was mayor of Washington, D.C.. A black man who had come up out of the Delta, who had been twice as good, was now gutted in public because he'd forgotten who he was, what he represented, how he'd gotten there, where he'd come from. He'd been foolish and inexcusably naive about the lengths to which some white folks will go to discredit you if you are black and independent and good at what you do."

Barry's closest cohorts remained in Washington after their service to the government, landing jobs with impressive local corporations and firms, all except for Gibson. He left, working from 1983 through 1985 as executive director of the Eugene and Agnes Meyer Foundation. The Meyers owned *The Washington Post* before giving it as a wedding gift to Philip Graham, their daughter Katharine's husband. In the beginning, the *Post* was a struggling stepsister compared with the powerful *Washington Star*, but with Watergate, it gained a national reputation. Gibson subsequently went to work for the Rockefeller Foundation, where he led efforts to both study and change declining conditions in the nation's cities. In 1992, he returned to the District as a senior fellow at the Urban Institute, a liberal think tank. Later, he became director of the D.C. Agenda, which at first operated as an affiliate of the powerful Federal City Council. An influential group comprised of the city's top business, civic, political, and federal leaders, the Federal City Council had been created back in the 1950s by the Washington Post's Philip Graham.*

Elijah Rogers was Barry's first city administrator. Rogers, a short man and a natty dresser, had a discriminating and finicky personality that demanded punctuality and indisputable excellence from his labor force. He had forged a personal friendship with Barry during those early years, and it remained intact even after he left the government. Residents and business leaders continued to laud Rogers' management skills.

Ivanhoe Donaldson, a short, edgy man, seemed perpetually restless. Though he had gone to prison, he was nonetheless roundly respected as the city's most brilliant political strategist and the person who could get Barry's ear when everyone else failed.

All three men—Gibson, Rogers, and Donaldson—quietly operated behind the scenes. All were considered ruthless when crossed. And all were more expert at manipulating processes and events than Barry, their former boss. The trio tried to determine for Barry if he needed to substantially rebuild the District's bureaucracy, if he knew where the land mines were and how to avoid them. He campaigned for office knowing that the whole truth about the state of the District government hadn't been told.

Barry and his team were methodical, competent, and intellectually superior—all the characteristics of Barry's first administration. By the late 1970s, after years of political and economic segregation, blacks were beginning to gain access to the executive suites in government. The going salary of $50,000 was considered a plum for many fresh out of law school or holding degrees in public administration. Their influx into government management compared with blacks' increased involvement in teaching during the 1940s and 1950s. In the 1970s and early 1980s, the District, like other city governments, had its choice of highly skilled professionals with graduate and postgraduate degrees from the nation's best universities. But as corporate America and international markets warmed to the idea of blacks in the board rooms, offering lucrative salaries and posh offices, the brightest and most talented candidates rejected public service careers. After his first administration, Barry had an increasingly difficult time locating qualified African-Americans willing to work for comparatively low pay in a highly volatile environment, and with an unpredictable executive. This may explain why Gibson, Rogers, and Donaldson retain the community's esteem long after their formal departures from government.

"We arranged to have him briefed by the McKinsey folks, who had done a study," says Gibson. "As he was absorbing it, he began to reorient his rhetoric [in the campaign] to the growing reality that the structural problems of the city were significant. But he still believed he could handle the problems." But that was before the three men began meeting privately with Kelly's city administrator, Robert Mallett, and the District's chief financial officer, Ellen O'Connor. "We realized the city had been in free-fall throughout most of Sharon's administration. People said Sharon didn't like bad news, so they didn't tell her any," said Gibson.

Evidence of the District government's rudderlessness became apparent with Kelly's revolving-door personnel policy. The former PEPCO executive promised to "clean house," and did just that, but she spent much of her time sweeping out her own people. In four years, she went through three housing directors, two city administrators, two chiefs of staff, three deputy mayors for economic development, and two heads of the city's Department of Finance. The management instability wreaked havoc on a city already reeling in 1990 from three years of an absent executive. City administrator Carol Thompson, who "held" the city together during Barry's drug years, came to her post with only District government service in her management portfolio.

As the city staggered from a recession, declining real estate revenues, escalating unemployment, and diving tax revenues, Thompson lacked the requisite experience to pull the District from its slump and grow its revenues. She also didn't have her hands fully on the levers of control, so that even if she had been inclined—which she wasn't—to reduce the size and cost of government, Barry would have prevented her. He always saw personnel reductions in complex, human, and political terms. Without knowledge and resources to produce real change, Thompson's chief job became an old one: ensuring that citizens did not witness their highest elected office holder in the throes of a drug stupor.

Unquestionably, the fiscal decline that overwhelmed the District in 1994 emanated from its leaders' delayed response. But the nation's capital also had been sorely under-funded by Congress. Moreover, when the District accepted "quasi-independence," the federal government transferred several functions to the city without providing sufficient resources. The infamous bloated bureaucracy began under the federal government's rule of the District. The three-member commission often hired onto the city payroll friends and relatives of various congressional representatives.

Barry's decision in the 1980s to use the government as the primary vehicle for African-American wealth-building only exacerbated the problem. And, of course, Sharon Pratt Kelly's subterfuge compounded the crisis. By 1994, the city had far too many people working for it. Many had never received proper training. The city's infrastructure was antiquated, and the city's service delivery system was severely damaged by outdated technology.

Following the series of meetings with Kelly administration officials, Gibson, Rogers, and Donaldson projected a fiscal 1996 deficit of between $700 million and $1 billion. "Marion was completely overwhelmed by the problem," recalled Gibson. Two years later, Barry confessed to a reporter that he was "floored by it."

"It was devastating," he said near the end of the second year of his comeback term. "I didn't run for office to be the budget cutter. For the first year, this financial crisis was overwhelming; it almost made me cry. It sucked the energy out of me." Barry never fully recovered from the disaster.

In February, weeks after formally taking office, he announced the looming, suffocating deficit, while attempting to lay out a series of budget cuts necessary for the city to operate. In what he called his miracle budget— it was a miracle his administration could produce one on time, he quipped— Barry called for federal assumption of certain "state-like functions," such as Medicaid, prisons, and the unfunded pension liability, which experts predicted would reach $10 billion by the year 2004. That course, Barry said, was preferable to massive and immediate cuts in city government personnel. During the campaign, Barry called himself a financial wizard. Now he was being laughed out of the water, ridiculed, and accused of using gimmicks, just like his predecessor Kelly.

But two years later, Barry's analysis—that there were structural flaws in the District's relationship with Congress—became the dominant view, advanced by the presidentially appointed financial control board and an independent study conducted by Carol O'Cleireacain for the Brookings Institution in Washington, D.C. President Clinton, following the advice of Franklin Raines, director of the office of management and budget, introduced in Congress, in 1997, legislation designed to provide the aid Barry had called for in 1995.

While many questioned Barry's approach for resolving the city's budget and cash problems, few doubted his numbers. He had proved himself in the fiscal arena decades earlier. When Barry first took office in 1979, then outgoing mayor Walter Washington reported the city had a cash surplus of $41 million—that's how much was in the bank. But Washington's administration used a cash-based financial system patterned after the federal government's.

The link was natural enough. For nearly a century prior to winning limited self-government in 1974, the District had been under the control of the federal Department of the Interior and thus operated as a federal agency. When Congress awarded the District local self-government, it merely transferred some of its authority to local elected officials, but retained its ultimate, sovereign power as dictated by the Constitution. In 1974, after one hundred years of a commission form of government, the District gained the right to elect a mayor and city council. But it lacked any appropriate model for its governance, and continued to operate as a ward of the federal government, framing many of its systems and laws accordingly.

The feds operated on a cash basis, while most state and local governments operated on an accrual basis. Shifting to an accrual system when he took office in 1979, Barry discovered the city was nearly $284 million in debt. Author Derrick Bell in his *Faces At the Bottom of the Well: The Permanence of Racism*, suggests that predominantly black governments typically must confront such debt-ridden legacies. "African-Americans in public office, including the mayors of several major cities, lack resources to address the problems they inherit, and thus can do little to overcome either unemployment or poverty." In many black urban communities around the country, the standard line was that African-Americans came to inhabit collapsing inner city neighborhoods following the suburban march of the Italians, Polish, and the Jews. Blacks, in effect, sat at the bottom of the hand-me-down totem pole, and the only things left when they arrived were termite-eaten frames.

In 1979, Barry's proposed fiscal shift proved a shrewd political gambit, removing his predecessor's performance, or lack thereof, as the gauge for his administration. He redefined local government standards around his abilities and his philosophy, insuring that any assessment of him would be based on what he perceived to be proper and appropriate. Thus, although Barry was the city's second elected mayor, all historical and bureaucratic roads led to him—not his predecessor Walter Washington nor his successor Sharon Pratt Kelly. Both inflicted damage, but their terms in office were not long enough to effect any change in the government structure or in its priorities.

During his second term, which began in 1983 with the implementation of a "reformation" plan, Barry continued to shape the government in his own political image. The city, the government, and Barry, were thus highly entwined prior to 1995. Any evaluation of one was incomplete without consideration of the other two. "For better or worse, the state of the District government is wrapped up with the career of Marion Barry," says American University law professor Jamin Raskin. "It's very hard to separate an analysis of Home Rule from an analysis of how Marion Barry has performed in office. It's hard to remember the Kelly administration. That appears as a brief hiccup in the long reign of Marion Barry."

In finances, Barry was far superior than either of his predecessors— before becoming mayor, he had served as the chairman of the Council's Finance and Revenue Committee. Even *The Washington Post*, Barry's nemesis, acknowledged his budgetary acumen during the 1994 campaign: "As mayor, Barry was at times a brilliant fiscal manager, particularly in his first term, and even in flashes toward the end...Throughout his twelve years as mayor, Barry was tugged between his commitments to responsible financial management and progressive social programs. He wanted to prove that the District's home rule government could manage its money, and he brought the city into the big leagues of municipal finance," a *Post* 1994 editorial noted. "Even Barry's opponents concede he is good with numbers. In recent interviews and council hearings, he has displayed a mastery of the city's figures.

"Former aides remember that Barry introduced the concept of linking the District's spending to its revenue, [thus] balancing its budget. That was a breakthrough for a government that previously had operated as the fiscal equivalent of a federal agency, spending up to a congressionally authorized level, regardless of its revenue," the editorial continued. "Barry's improvements enabled the District for the first time to borrow money on the Wall Street bond market, which offered lower interest rates than the city had paid when it borrowed from the U.S. Treasury. Barry also automated the District's financial management."

But Barry's inattention during the three years of his drug use—1987 through 1990—ratcheted the District's annual deficit upward to more than $300 million. When Kelly took over in 1991, it was $331 million. Still, even during his drug-crazed days, his fiscal management far exceeded hers. In 1990, prior to his arrest, he asked then Brookings Institution fellow Alice Rivlin to head a study on the city's future fiscal health. The Rivlin commission demonstrated Barry's forward thinking and his willingness to tap outside experts to improve his government—even if he didn't always follow their advice.* Rivlin's report remained for six years the blueprint for a District government reform movement.

In 1995, when Barry said the red-ink sea was swallowing the District, no one disbelieved him, save the D.C. Council, whose chairman, David Clarke, accused Barry of manipulating the data. There wasn't any question he had massaged the numbers. As in 1979, Barry reframed the discussion, suiting his needs, securing the advantage. As an executive on the road to redemption, Barry could have sought to camouflage the financial situation, employing contrivances, just as Kelly had for two years. Instead, he presented the worst case scenario and chose the path of least resistance. The resurrected mayor presented the ballooning deficit purposely to flaunt his expertise, hoping to demonstrate his readiness to perform the job much more proficiently than he had in past administrations. Not unlike Anansi, who occasionally fell into traps he set for others, Barry's announcement activated an avalanche from which he never fully escaped.

Initial reaction to the city's dire straits came from Wall Street, which accused the government of lying. That kicked off an investigation by the U.S. Securities and Exchange Commission—the second faced by the District in two years. The first query involved the handling of a bond deal by Lazard Freres, Merrill Lynch, and the city. Wall Street also dropped the city's credit rating to that of "junk status," making it next to impossible to borrow money. Restricted borrowing impeded the District's ability to survive, jeopardizing its payroll and other expenses. Gibson and the other advisers saw their campaign prediction unfolding slowly and painfully before their eyes.

◆ ◆ ◆ ◆ ◆ ◆ ◆ ◆ ◆ ◆ ◆ ◆ ◆ ◆ ◆ ◆ ◆

During the primary campaign in 1994, Barry's "inner-circle" advisers came directly to his aid. They met privately—for the first time—at the swank downtown law office of Beveridge and Diamond. Thornell Page, David Abramson, Gladys Mack, Carolyn Smith, Carroll Harvey, Elijah Rogers and James Gibson—all former Barry stalwarts—attended. All were key members of Barry's Kitchen Cabinet.

A white Jewish businessman who owned a public relations firm, David Abramson had supported Barry from the time the former civil rights activist traded in his dashiki to assume the mantle of traditional black politician. He created the "Taking a Stand" slogan for Barry's first mayoral race. And while other whites, including Jeffrey Gildenhorn, Max Berry, and Robert Linowes, abandoned him, Abramson had not yet left his side.*

Two of his other Kitchen Cabinet members had fiscal expertise—Gladys Mack, a former budget director for the District, and Carolyn Smith, a former finance and revenue director. Carroll Harvey had been with Barry since their days at Pride, Inc.

Surveying the political landscape, the group concluded that Barry could win both the primary and the general election. They wanted to help him prepare for governing, but weren't sure he'd welcome their assistance.

"These were people he's always respected, people he knows and he's comfortable with. They have his interest at heart. They're also independent enough to speak their minds about Marion Barry's strengths and weaknesses," explains Rogers. "You don't work for someone for four years and not get to know them, appreciate them, and what it's like to govern."

Rogers was asked to call Barry to see if he would be interested in attending the group's next meeting. Barry accepted the invitation. "One thing about the mayor: He's always inquisitive," says Rogers.

When they met with Barry, Gibson was to be the group's spokesperson. It seemed strange that such a responsibility fell to the man most strident about Barry, one who had refused to meet with him in a one-on-one setting, fearing he might explode. But Gibson and the others reasoned that, as a group, they could ask and answer the tough questions without anyone claiming personal ownership.

When Barry arrived at the meeting, the others were already seated. He entered and hugged everyone. "He was very emotional when he came into the room," recalled Gibson. Those close to Barry say he has always been quick to cry or show his emotions with his friends, though in public, he kept them under heavy wraps.

Gibson, Rogers, and the others queried Barry about his position on various issues. They asked him if he felt he could adapt to the changing climate, whether the pressure from such an environment might send him back to drugs. Hearing his responses, some were satisfied enough to say that they would publicly support him and readily aid him. Others took a little more convincing. Finally, the group as a whole told Barry they knew he could be elected, but they weren't sure he would be able to govern.

◆ ◆ ◆ ◆ ◆ ◆ ◆ ◆ ◆ ◆ ◆ ◆ ◆ ◆ ◆ ◆

While Barry basked in the glow of his re-election, an ornery bunch of

Republicans grabbed the reins of Congress, brutally kicking out Democrats who had dominated the House for nearly forty years. They eliminated entire committees, sent staffers looking for jobs without severance pay, and stripped D.C. Delegate Eleanor Holmes Norton of her vote.

The Democrats had coddled the District government for twenty years, refusing to intrude in its affairs, failing to scrutinize the activities of elected officials. Barry had enjoyed a smooth relationship with Congress, even as his government became riddled by scandal.

One scandal involved Jeffrey Cohen, a long time Barry friend and wannabe real estate mogul. Cohen purchased property in the predominantly black neighborhood of Shaw in northwest D.C. for eight million dollars, and when he ran into trouble, sold the property back to the city for eleven million dollars. Retained to help develop the project, Cohen earned hundreds of thousands of dollars in fees for himself before finally filing bankruptcy. His father bailed him out of trouble, but the District government ate the loss and completed only one of the projects Cohen had proposed. In the interim, Cohen became godfather to Barry's son, and Barry became a partner with him in a real estate deal in Massachusetts (it failed to make money).

Meanwhile, the city's infant mortality rate skyrocketed, as did teen pregnancy and unemployment. The District's public housing agency remained on the federal "troubled agency" list for more than a decade before being taken over by the courts. By the time of Barry's drug arrest, the District's prison system was under six court orders for overcrowding and for failing to provide various services. Still, Democrats in Congress made no effort to snatch power from Barry, and District residents elected him three times. Had it not been for his arrest in 1990, he would have been the odds-on favorite in that year's mayoral contest. Congress and the majority of District residents, though especially the black poor and disenfranchised, became enablers in Barry's various schemes to manipulate and deceive.

The Republicans leading Congress in 1995 signaled an end to the cushy life of District leaders—leaders who were overpaid but routinely under-performed. The GOP vowed that things had to be different, and to ensure there was bite to its bark, House Speaker Newt Gingrich appointed Rep. James Walsh, a New York Republican, to head the House subcommittee on District appropriations. In previous congressional sessions, Walsh unsuccessfully submitted a dozen motions designed to impose budgetary discipline on the city, and to force massive personnel and program reductions. But emboldened by his new position, Walsh pledged to bring fiscal austerity and accountability to the District—even if it killed the city. Over the next year, he lost several fights, but he kept his promise.

◆ ◆ ◆ ◆ ◆ ◆ ◆ ◆ ◆ ◆ ◆ ◆ ◆ ◆ ◆ ◆ ◆ ◆

When Barry announced the District's dire financial straits, congressional representatives began to talk of placing the city in receivership. There was nothing new about the concept. The state of New Jersey had taken over control of several school systems, including the one in Newark, and Massachusetts had appointed a receiver for Chelsea (a Boston suburb) when it ran into major financial difficulties. The Chelsea receiver helped turned around the city and its school system by imposing strict spending and management reforms.

For Republicans, receivership talk was to be expected. They clearly didn't embrace the notion of a redeemed Marion Barry. And Barry made his own claim of redemption impossible to believe when, during the first few months after his inauguration, another scandal splashed across the front page of *The Washington Post*. Housekeeper Barbara Mouring accused Barry's wife, Cora, of laundering campaign funds for an independent business political action committee.

Here's how the process was said to have worked: The Washington Business PAC sent a check to the Barrys' home in the name of the housekeeper's son who, according to Mouring, never worked for the campaign. Cora Barry nonetheless instructed the housekeeper to have her son cash the check and then pass the money to Cora's brother, Walter Masters.

Mouring relayed this story to a *Washington Post* reporter. Mouring and the *Post* reporter later confirmed that two men in their presence—one a security guard for the mayor, Ulysses Walltower, the other a Korean business supporter—threatened Mouring if she did not recant her story.

The Korean businessman, Yong Yun, had his own problems. He had leased a building of his to the District government for twenty million dollars. During the same period, when negotiations on his lease were reaching a final stage, he helped oversee renovations at the Barrys' new home on Raleigh Street, Southeast, raising questions about whether the city decided to do business with Yun in exchange for his service to the mayor.

The *Post*'s report launched an investigation by the U.S. Attorney's office. Meanwhile, Barbara Mouring's own checkered history came to light. A former drug addict, she had once been arrested for shoplifting. Several weeks after the *Post*'s report, Mouring's son was found dead, shot execution style, in southeast D.C. Nearly a year after it launched its investigation, the U.S. Attorney decided not to file charges against Detective Ulysses Walltower, the mayor's security guard accused of intimidating Mouring into recanting the story she told the newspaper.

But Walltower later ran into trouble when the media revealed he had not been showing up for work and was still getting paid by the city. Others, it seemed, were signing his time sheet. By all accounts, this arrangement had been approved privately by the city's police chief, who owed his job to the mayor. Nevertheless, the department used the time sheet scam as yet another mark on Walltower's record. Consequently, when the District's police department concluded its own investigation of Walltower and the Mouring incident, it recommended his firing. Walltower resigned before the department could take action.

Yun, one of several Korean and Chinese businessmen funneling cash to Barry's 1992 and and 1994 campaigns, according to campaign workers, was indicted on twenty-eight felony counts of making false statements to obtain loans, money-laundering, and conspiracy. In a plea agreement, Yun admitted to receiving the loans in question to purchase and renovate the building, which he leased to the government. He also admitted to taking kickbacks from the loan to help pay personal debts. He was given a sentence of community service and required to repay the money received in kickbacks from the loan.

But while congressional representatives and some District residents may have cringed at the scandal tainting Barry's new mayoral term, and the scandal that had colored his Ward 8 council tenure, Yvonne Scruggs, head of the Black Leadership Forum, said, "A lot of people who vote for Marion don't pay attention to what he does from one day to the next. They don't read the newspaper and they are not voting any ideological position. They are saying, 'Here's somebody who is like me, and if it weren't for the quirk of fate, he'd be just like me.' They vote their own identity. They vote against the whites who run the District. They vote against the Congress that treats us like a colonial preserve. They vote against the separation of white wards. Washington is unlike any other city. It's almost like [formerly apartheid] South Africa."

The Yun scandal, along with Congress' visceral reaction to Barry and the history of his past administrations, convinced Capitol Hill to impose tight reins on the new mayor. To do otherwise, they believed, would be to conspire in the city's eventual ruin.

D.C. Delegate Eleanor Holmes Norton, hoping to derail the "receivership" train, proposed a financial authority or control board for the District, similar to ones established in New York and Philadelphia when those cities faced fiscal collapse. In each case, the control board successfully restored solvency while improving the city's overall credit ratings. With those control boards still in operation, their expertise could be used in setting up one for the District. Tom Davis, a Virginia Republican and chairman of the D.C. Subcommittee, agreed with the control board notion bought the idea and began negotiations with fellow Republicans who insisted on receivership for the District.

Within weeks, it was clear a control board would be created. Norton took the lead, attempting to quiet possible accusations that the white dominated Congress was taking control of a predominantly black government. She formally broke the news to a group of civic activists known as the Committee of One Hundred of the Federal City Council. Even before Norton's announcement, the media and others touted the benefits of a control board. Colbert I. King, editorial writer for *The Washington Post*, cautioned that social ills drove the city's fiscal woes. The control board in Philadelphia had been successful in turning around the city's fiscal ailments, but a Temple University study showed the lives of Philadelphians living in poverty remained unchanged. That control board, King said, "didn't prevent a rise in welfare rolls, slow the exodus of well-paid jobs and middle class residents"—all problems, along with mismanagement and an obstinate recession, that triggered the District's own financial decline.

"Control boards have a critical and limited purpose," King wrote. "They help, if not force, politically paralyzed leaders to face up to the fiscal disasters they've had a big hand in creating."

The control board legislation, Public Law 108-4, was the most significant change in the city's operation since winning limited home rule in 1973. No one could dispute the need for a control board or some financial overlord. Although it maintained a federal staff of more than twenty-five professionals, presumably to review and comment on the affairs of the nation's capital, Congress had done a lousy job of monitoring city finances. Congressman Tom Davis once said the city was "coming apart at the seams" and that the control board legislation was the "cornerstone" of Congress' response. He refuted claims that the District had insufficient revenue and blasted elected officials' propensity for funding everything they wanted and nothing they needed. He said the District's generosity had become overindulgent, and had brought the nation's capital to its knees.

Public hearings were held for Public Law 108-4. The day the Congressional committee stood poised to pass it, Norton invoked her ancestry: "My great grandfather, Richard Holmes, didn't walk from slavery [into the District] only to have his family surrender a century later to financial insolvency," she said. The majority of District residents, especially whites who had grown weary of the government's decline, and who feared Barry would return to his old spending habits, welcomed the move, echoing Norton's sentiments. But others, particularly African-American activists in the civil rights and Black Power movements of the 1960s and 1970s, anguished over the board's creation.

One District government administrator lamented the impression now conveyed around the world— that "those stupid niggers can't run a [local] government. They can't run anything." That assessment was unduly harsh, because the District's fiscal circumstance wasn't unprecedented. Other predominantly white governments fell under the weight of a recession that hit in the late 1980s and stayed around well after.

Always the situationist, Barry wore a smiling face about the imposition of a control board, arguing that without it, the District could not borrow on Wall Street. Interestingly, when Barry's own reconnaissance team had discovered the massive cumulative debt just months earlier, Gibson had suggested that Barry call for a control board. Barry rejected the idea. To ask other professionals into his domain, said Barry, suggested that he wasn't up for the task, and stripped him of the prestige and authority he sought. One month before passage of the control board law, in his "State of the District" address at the D.C. Convention Center, Barry, following Norton's lead, took some credit for recent Congressional developments. Telling the truth about the city's finances, he said, set the District on the road to recovery. "Most of the storm is over," Barry puffed.

But before year's end, it became apparent that Barry misjudged the potential trouble such an independent body could cause, the level of Congressional disdain for him, the District's shifting political landscape, the full meaning of his mayoral victory, and his ability, using his considerable powers of persuasion, to control dissimilar variables and forces. Moreover, he learned that unlike his previous administrations, his political machinery had grown too weak to deal with a frontal attack.

The greatest destruction to Barry's machinery had come with his betrayal of Sandra Allen. Just weeks after Barry had returned to the office of mayor, there was heavy speculation about whom he would endorse to succeed him as Ward 8 Council person. Everyone expected it to be Allen. After all, she'd made incredible sacrifices to remain unflinchingly loyal to him. But when she went to see him at his office in One Judiciary Square, he refused her the endorsement, and said he was throwing his support behind Eydie Whittington, a political novice.

Both Allen and Berea were hurt. Allen's mother and family were devastated. The battle for the seat became fierce. Barry and wife Cora raised money for Whittington, and Cora herself served as Whittington's campaign manager.

Allen lost the race by one vote. Ward 8 residents, including Sandra

Seegars, charged campaign fraud and corruption. She accused several people, including Barry's brother-in-law, of voting, though they weren't Ward 8 residents. The D.C. Board of Elections and Ethics, investigating the charges, determined that at least one non-resident had voted, but it refused to invalidate the election. Whittington went on to serve out Barry's two-year Council term. But Allen and her team didn't stop campaigning. By the next election, they were ready for Whittington, and so were Ward 8 residents. As a statement of their dissatisfaction with Barry and his machine's efforts to steal the previous election, they overwhelmingly supported Allen, and easily pushed Whittington out. Barry's treasonous act had cost him the affection of his base of supporters.

Though still enamored of his Anansi-like skills and rhetorical showmanship, African-Americans elsewhere in the District were generally ready to enter the new epoch of pragmatic politics. Barry's ascent would be short lived, his redemption questioned, and his future cloudy.

◆ CHAPTER TWELVE ◆

ON JULY 13, 1995, DISTRICT RESIDENTS nearly filled the cavernous Department of Agriculture Auditorium at 14th Street and Independence Avenue. They came to meet the new set of overseers installed weeks earlier when President Clinton signed Public Law 108-4, establishing the D.C. Financial Responsibility and Management Assistance Authority. The authority, which months later came to be known, more simply, as the "control board," called the public meeting as a sort of coming-out party, to introduce its five members (and two top staffers) to the public and to hear residents' concerns.

Flanked at each end by the board's executive director and general counsel, three men and two women sat elevated on a long stage, creating the mood of an inquisition, or casting the entire affair as if it were a scene from a slave drama where the servants implore the master to grant their wishes.

Andrew Brimmer, the board's chairman, sat at the table's center. A native of Newellton, Louisiana, the son of cotton farmers, Brimmer received a doctorate in economics from Harvard University in 1957 and served for fourteen years as a member of the Federal Reserve Board. He pushed his way to the top of his profession during an era when hostile treatment of blacks was the rule. He was a director of several major corporations—Bank of America and United Airlines among them— and served as chairman of the trustees at Tuskegee University in Alabama. In 1976, he opened his own economic and financial consulting firm. During her term as mayor, Sharon Pratt Kelly tapped him to lead the mayor's advisory group of finance experts. During that stint, he advocated the imposition of a commuter tax on District workers who lived elsewhere, and urged Kelly to seek from nonprofit organizations and universities a Payment In Lieu of Taxes, or PILOT. Neither proposal passed the council.

On the surface, Brimmer seemed the epitome of an "Uncle Tom"—the figure despised in black communities for his excessive concern about whites and their impression of him. But Brimmer's behavior was deceptive. In his official biography, published by the control board, Brimmer listed the research for which he was proudest—the "testimony he prepared when he was in the U.S. Department of Commerce, which demonstrated the burden of racial segregation on interstate commerce. The U.S. Supreme Court cited it extensively in its unanimous opinion upholding the constitutionality of the Public Accommodations Section of the Civil Rights Act of 1964."

The Rev. Jesse L. Jackson praised Brimmer's appointment to the control board, noting that he was impressed with the economist's role as a "guiding force" in the African-American community on legislative and other matters. While the appointment came without compensation, Brimmer relished the assignment, and told the *Washington Post* that, "Given what I have been able to achieve, and the kinds of other commitments and activities I have, I have no concerns about income."

It would have been hard to find someone more philosophically different than Barry—more at odds with the mayor—than Brimmer. Like Tuskegee's founder, Booker T. Washington, Brimmer advocated hard work and discipline, and had advanced in mainstream society through accommodation and negotiation. A clipped, military style of communicating gave him the aura of an autocrat or dictator, and he preferred working outside of public view. "I see no advantage in trying to do this in public," he once said, citing the Federal Reserve as the model he intended to use in leading the control board. At his consulting firm, Brimmer maintained a schedule that bordered on boring, rising every morning at about seven, and taking vacations each year in the same states and countries: Hawaii, Florida, and Vancouver (the latter for deep sea fishing). He exuded the predictability and dependability that marked most black leaders prior to the 1960s, and draped black America with indubitable confidence during some of its harshest days. He was from the old school, where one's word was his bond, and where an honorable, respectable image was coveted more than gold.

While Brimmer sought to work with and through the system, Barry committed mutiny in every way possible—from his days at Booker T. Washington High School, to his civil rights organizing in McComb, to his Free D.C. Movement in the nation's capital. He could be capricious and recalcitrant, and even his most enthusiastic supporters complained that he often was undisciplined. Although Barry at sixty years old and Brimmer at sixty-seven were products of the same generation, they reflected the opposing views and attitudes present in black America since slavery—differences that were exacerbated by the civil rights and black power movements. The divergent cords of their development promised to cause continuous philosophical and political clashes.

"I knew when Andrew Brimmer was appointed chair that [it] wasn't going to work with Marion," says Cropp. "That was oil and water."

Despite their differences, both men were avid practitioners of the cool pose—Brimmer slightly stiffer than Barry, the elder control board member more emotionless than his younger counterpart. Both were aloof, tough men. Both wore the cool mask, which, according to Majors and Billson, "belies the rage held in check beneath the surface." By wearing it, the black male appears unfazed by anything said or done to him. "Being cool shows both the dominant culture and the black male that he is strong and proud. He is somebody. He is a survivor, in spite of systematic harm done by the legacy of slavery and the realities of racial oppression, in spite of the centuries of hardship and mistrust."

While Brimmer had comfortably arrived at a place in mainstream society where he no longer needed the mask, wearing it had become habit, an integral part of his personality. But he could remove it at any time and not jeopardize his standing in society. Barry was denied such a luxury.

The control board selected Stephen Harlan, owner of H. G. Smithy Real Estate Company—the only white member—as its vice chairman. Later, Harlan, a registered Republican, became one of the board's more outspoken members, at one time calling Barry irrelevant and insisting on increased financing for police and public works. Unofficially, he became the assuager of white and black middle class fears, reiterating the board's intention to change the political and management culture of the city. Harlan's outspokenness caused some blacks to consider the control board part of the infamous "plan". Whites, it was said, wanted to regain political power over the city and would use whatever means necessary to do so.*

Other panel members included Joyce Ladner, a former civil rights veteran with a doctorate in sociology, who served as Howard University's interim president from 1994 through 1995. Highly respected in her field, Ladner became the board's social service and education maven.

Constance Berry Newman, undersecretary of the Smithsonian Institution, and Edward Singletary, former vice president and secretary of Bell Atlantic Corporation, were the board's two other members. By law, each member served a three-year term. They could, however, be reappointed.

Brimmer selected John Hill, a 41-year-old District native, as the board's executive director. While with the General Accounting Office, Hill had led the congressionally-ordered study of the District's finances in 1994. A veteran numbers cruncher, he was considered skillful by his colleagues. A soft voice and self-effacing style camouflaged his fierce, cut-to-the-chase approach. His demeanor matched Brimmer's, except that the young director laughed more freely. Hill hired thirty others to serve as his staff. Most were former GAO personnel. The GAO, like much of the government, had gone through a personnel reduction known as "downsizing." Hill took in many of its refugees.

At first, power seemed to rest with the five member control board, but shortly after his selection, it became apparent that Hill would chart the treacherous course between the city and the control board. "It's clear to me the primary power will be John Hill," Lawrence Guyot said. And while Hill made statements like "Board members are ready to do whatever it takes to get the situation resolved," his even tone suggested that he didn't offer threats, only bankable promises. As the board's clout grew, the respected Hill became the central hope of District residents.

◆ ◆ ◆ ◆ ◆ ◆ ◆ ◆ ◆ ◆ ◆ ◆ ◆ ◆ ◆ ◆ ◆

District activists, many of whom had lobbied aggressively for the creation of the control board, came to the Department of Agriculture Auditorium to ensure that the new body met their needs. Allotted three-minute time slots, they poured out their concerns and challenged the panel. Steve Michael, a spokesperson for ACT UP, an organization of AIDS activists in the District, asked for increased funding. Civic activist Marilyn Groves from Dupont Circle pleaded for better trash collection. Manny Pastreich, a representative of the janitors union, demanded that Brimmer resign from Carr Realty's board (as a director, he was paid twelve thousand dollars a year, plus expenses for attending meetings) and that Harlan step down from H.G. Smithy. The Rev. Graylan Ellis-Hagler, pastor of Plymouth Congregational United Church of Christ, said that Brimmer's and Harlan's conflict might surface in the area of property tax rollbacks and potentially preferential treatment. Both Brimmer and Harlan refused to resign but promised to recuse themselves on matters affecting the firms with which they were affiliated.

Other residents, like Samuel Jordan, representative of the Statehood Party, Kathryn Pearson-West, and Guyot, admonished board members for becoming conspirators in the "nullification" of the vote in the District. "I see no way for this board and local self-government to exist simultaneously," said Guyot. After two hours of being abused—twice as long as the board originally intended to permit for public comments—the panel recessed for lunch.

The morning session proved that District residents, who for years operated under the control of a fickle Congress, had become quite malleable, able to shift allegiances and attention at a moment's notice—and without shame. "There is a plantation mentality," explains Cropp. "A lot of people don't like me to say it like that. But we have accommodated ourselves. We Washingtonians, native or long time Washingtonians, have become pragmatic in dealing with power.

"We understand that the true power in the District emanates from Capitol Hill and therefore your role is to go to Congress as supplicant," adds Cropp. In effect, the control board was Congress's proxy.

When the control board first convened on July 13, 1995, few Barryites —those for whom there wasn't any appropriate substitute for Barry— attended. Most meeting participants turned out to be NIMBYs—the Not-In-My-Backyard types whose myopia could boggle any mind. Few saw the city as a large tapestry. Few regarded their issue as a piece of a larger jigsaw puzzle. Most pursued their interests more or less separately.

Despite his flaws and frailties, one thing could be said about Barry: He was the only leader with the clout to unify the District. Groups coalesced either out of hate, or support, for him. Occasionally, when Barry forgot his personal interests, he galvanized the city around common issues—the boycott of Roy Chalk's bus company, home rule, economic development.

Returning from lunch and determined to complete its agenda, the control board adopted its bylaws, provided clarification about board members' potential conflicts of interest, and plowed into the District's fiscal 1996 budget. Unanimously approved were eleven recommendations that required Barry to make deep cuts in city spending, including the elimination of 5,600 positions. If the mayor went along, said the board, two thousand District employees would find themselves out of work.

The meeting suggested an openness that was short-lived. Within months, the control board retreated to upscale offices at One Thomas Circle in northwest D.C., installing a tight security system that included a locked front door and a surveillance camera. That, along with a public meeting format that restricted public input, severely hampered residents' ability to influence any control board decisions.

◆ ◆ ◆ ◆ ◆ ◆ ◆ ◆ ◆ ◆ ◆ ◆ ◆ ◆ ◆ ◆ ◆

Weeks before the board's July meeting, control board member Joyce Ladner called Marion Barry at his office. An attractive black woman of medium height, stocky build, and fair complexion, she, like Barry, had belonged to the Student Nonviolent Coordinating Council and she had grown up in Barry's native state—Mississippi. After attending historic Tougaloo College, she completed a brilliant, seminal study of young, inner city black girls, published in 1971 and titled *Tomorrow's Tomorrow*. During the waning years of Barry's third administration, she wrote several provocative opinion pieces for *The Washington Post*, blasting the city's leadership for the state of the District, especially in the areas of education, crime, and youth development. Although not a member of Barry's inner circle, she shared civil rights war stories with Barry, and thus had access to him often denied to others.

Ladner urged Barry to cooperate with the board. She intimated that if he were astute, he would take credit for any advancements the board achieved. Similar advice came from D.C. Delegate Eleanor Holmes Norton, who said that Barry could be like Nixon going to China—an analogy that would be repeated ad nauseam throughout his term. Barry listened. Both women were politically sagacious, although they never played the game with his tenacity and verve. Barry's cunning propelled him to advance into enemy camp, under conciliatory flags, feigning a desire to cooperate. When he had gathered enough data, he retreated to devise his own attack.

The story of Anansi the spider riding the tiger proves illustrative of Barry's modus operandi. According to one version of the tale, Anansi bragged to the King that he had once ridden the powerful Tiger. Upon hearing of this, the Tiger took umbrage, tracked Anansi down, and tried to force him to go before the King to recant the bogus claim. But Anansi professed to be too busy. The Tiger demanded that Anansi tell the King the truth, even if the Tiger had to take him. Anansi the trickster loved this suggestion. So he told the Tiger that, if he were to ride on his back, he would need a saddle to brace his feet, a bridle to hold on, and a whip to swish away the flies. The Tiger said he didn't care so long as Anansi came along quickly. So the two arrived at the King's house. The Tiger was galloping, and Anansi was on his back, yelling for the King to see.

Like the Anansi from that story, Barry loved tricking all enemies. He took personal pride in his ability to twist them to his point of view, to outsmart them. In the 1994 election, he attempted to mollify John Ray's campaign when it courted his support. But, even as Joseph Johnson sat before him touting the benefits of his candidate, Barry knew that he intended to jump into the race himself within a few weeks. It was "political jujitsu," the kind for which James Michael Curley was also well known. Curley once faced an election opponent who repeatedly ended his speeches with the question, "Where is this coward Curley?" According to Curley biographer Jack Beatty, Curley attended one of his opponent's events in a disguise. When the man asked the predictable question, Curley stood up boldly and shouted, "Here I am Tom! Right here." Curley's startling appearance stole the thunder from his opponent. Instead of receiving boos as his enemy had hoped, Curley received all the laughs and attention.

In 1995, despite Norton's and Ladner's advice, Barry hoped to use the same tactic with the control board and the Republican Congress. Hoping to seduce Speaker Newt Gingrich, he sashayed onto Capitol Hill. There he held forth with the quick-witted Georgia Republican widely credited with pulling off a revolution that dumped an unprecedented number of conservatives onto Capitol Hill. For a time, it seemed the two had become fast friends, soulmates of sorts. Forging a friendship with Gingrich, Barry hoped, would increase District support on Capitol Hill, or at least send the message that he was "the Speaker's boy and not to be messed with." Gingrich initially saw Barry as providing his party the entree it needed to advance in urban issues and to attract African-American supporters.

Gingrich came to a town hall meeting at Eastern High School in southeast D.C., where he received effusive praise from Barry. Later, Gingrich ran around to various District schools in poor communities waving money and promoting a reading for dollars program. The new speaker won so many accolades that he forced the Clinton White House, particularly Hillary Clinton, to begin its own blitz into neighborhoods beyond the federal enclave. But the honeymoon between the ultra conservative and the ultra liberal faded like a firefly in daylight. Each returned to his respective rhetoric, unable to continue the masquerade. As was his wont, Barry vastly overestimated his persuasive skills and underestimated Congress's contempt for him.

Responding more viscerally than strategically, Congress refused to appoint Barry to the new control board. The mayors of Philadelphia and New York had been placed on financial oversight commissions. In Washington's case, Congress refused to appoint to the board any of the District's elected officials.

D.C. Council Chairman David Clarke posed as great an obstacle as Barry. Rooted in the same civil rights, wealth redistribution philosophy, Clarke was obstinate and emotional, bursting into tirades when events travelled outside the scope of his desires or intellectual capabilities. More than Barry, Clarke believed in using the government as the primary engine for social change.

To wiggle his way inside the tent and to sit at the table, Barry had to play his hand deftly. After his first private meeting with Brimmer, it appeared he had done so. Brimmer emerged saying, "I do not anticipate, do not expect, and have no intention of engaging in any day-to-day decision-making in this city, to either hire or fire or cancel or make contracts, or anything of that sort. The mayor is responsible for the administration of this city, and the mayor with the council is responsible for fiscal affairs." Two years later, Brimmer ate those words.

◆ ◆ ◆ ◆ ◆ ◆ ◆ ◆ ◆ ◆ ◆ ◆ ◆ ◆ ◆

Weeks before the control board's July public hearing, Barry submitted to the Council changes to the fiscal 1995 budget and a projected budget for fiscal 1996. The final budget retained many of the features of his preliminary proposal. It didn't reflect, however, an earlier report that found the city stumbling in its effort to significantly reduce its deficit and rein in spending. Payments for invoices totalling millions of dollars had been delayed—the result of incompetent managers and an antiquated automated financial management system. Some contractors halted delivery of services to the government. Others saw their credit rating jeopardized when the District stalled on its payments, making it impossible for them to pay their creditors. The report predicted a severe cash-shortage for the District by June. The sole hope was passage of the control board's proposed legislation permitting the District government to borrow from the federal treasury. The ability to secure the loan was the major incentive for Barry's support of the law.

By the time the control board met in July, a tidal wave of support emerged for massive personnel and spending cuts. The five-member panel directed the government to cut five thousand positions—3,600 of which were vacant already. "We are prepared to use our authority, and not to let it just rust on the shelf...I am not prepared to wait forever for the results," Brimmer said during a July congressional hearing where he and other board members testified.

In Barry's view, job cuts meant the upheaval of entire families. For every employee laid off, Barry saw three or four other people adversely affected, and the quality of life for each diminished. This left-leaning perspective couldn't obscure the obvious, however. Each job Barry couldn't protect meant the loss of several potential voters. If he wanted to win in 1998, he had to stem the loss of public jobs in the preceding years. Additionally, concerns about the rapid labor reductions pushed by Congressional reformers, especially Rep. James T. Walsh, a New York Republican—and their potential impact on the delivery of services—prompted Barry to hesitate.

During fiscal 1995, Walsh pushed for a total reduction of $140 million in proposed District spending. To achieve those numbers, the city drastically cut its work force, offering lucrative retirement packages. The most skilled and most senior employees took advantage of the offers, leaving behind a government work force that was largely inexperienced. The result was a decline in both quantity and quality of city services. Under Mayor Sharon Pratt Kelly, the District lost hard-to-replace talent because personnel laws mandated low salary ceilings. Only Barry and his city administrator Michael Rogers seemed worried about the impact rapid reductions might have on the city's overall health.

Meantime, the mantra of "bloated bureaucracy" played in the press and in congressional hearings. Barry had built this bureaucracy and his unwillingness to slenderize it was characterized as a staple of the politician's survival kit, rather than distress over the city's future. In truth, it was both.

Barry operated in gray areas, where the lines seem perpetually blurred. He managed a complex world, sometimes complicated by his own fuzzy thinking and inconsistent actions. In one instance, he might call for federal intervention to save the city from red ink. In the next instance, he might admonish Congress for intruding into District affairs. He wanted to have his cake and eat it, too. Political scientist Samuel Huntington, in describing the gap between what Americans believe and the actual practices of their institutions, discusses the notion of "cognitive dissonance," whereby a person simultaneously accepts conflicting beliefs, attitudes, or conditions. A person can respond any of four ways: Try to eliminate the gap (moralism), tolerate the gap (cynicism), ignore the gap (complacency), or deny the existence of the gap (hypocrisy). More often than not, Barry ignored or denied the gap between what he claimed and how his government actually performed.

Responding to the control board's mandate, Barry submitted a revised fiscal 1996 budget that removed from the city's personnel inventory seven hundred jobs held by workers at the Department of Public Housing. He reasoned that since the courts had taken over the agency and appointed a receiver, and the city provided the agency no funding, those workers were no longer District employees. It was a stroke of genius, the kind of edge dancing for which Barry had grown famous throughout his political career—the kind that made other politicians marvel at his intelligence. "Distress creates charismatic leaders," said Beatty. It also allows for greater creativity. To that end, Barry didn't ignore the rules, so much as he reshaped them—a sculptor melting the metal from a flawed model, recasting it for a new molding.

But while politicians and operatives sat in awe of Barry's chutzpah, Home Rule fanatics and other critics called it capitulation. Carroll Swanson, a Shepherd Park retiree, told the *Post*: "If he had been more responsible, he would have developed a different budget and tried to show he was cutting expenses. Instead, he rubbed their noses in it. He is leaving the hard choices to the control board."

But the business community embraced the plan. Black Entertainment Television president Robert Johnson captured the reality of the situation, asserting that the issue wasn't so much the budget Barry proposed as whether the mayor could be trusted to implement it faithfully.

Barry hated to have his veracity questioned, but question it people did. Whenever the media challenged his honesty and integrity during his years on drugs, he dumbfounded them with a display of righteous indignation. True, Barry was never convicted of fraud, graft, and corruption. But his trial did confirm the unreliability of his word.

◆ ◆ ◆ ◆ ◆ ◆ ◆ ◆ ◆ ◆ ◆ ◆ ◆ ◆ ◆ ◆

Everyone initially imagined that Barry himself might slice the District's bloated bureaucracy, making the reduction more palatable to residents, particularly the poor and working classes. But he wasn't imitating "Nixon going to China." Like all politicians, he suffered divided sentiments: His constituency had returned him to office, he thought, to create jobs. He had shaped the District's black middle class. Viewing him as a friend, labor unions had dumped thousands of dollars into his campaign. Business leaders expected a repeat performance of the early 1980s, when Barry turned a deaf ear to competing interests in neighborhoods and invested millions in downtown development.

Now, by demanding that he cut the city payroll, the control board was essentially trying to effect his political disintegration. And business people were warning him that, if he didn't reduce the city payroll, there wouldn't be any money for economic development or for public safety improvements—nothing with which to stimulate the local economy. Torn between his own political legacy and the interests of his constituency, Barry followed the tradition of black politics.

"This is a mayor who, in his entire political career, always maintained contact with, and had been absorbed in, the black community. He never crossed over," notes Ivanhoe Donaldson.

Just as integral to African-American culture is the notion that a leader should never acquiesce without a "principled fight." In order for residents to perceive his battle with the control board as one of ethics and values—not simply a power struggle between rival egos—Barry couched his fight as a question of priorities, drawing a distinction between his goals and those of the control board. He dramatized the control board's value system, as evidenced by its financing agenda. He spoke of its "insensitivity" to the plight of District workers, and its disregard of elected officials. From the beginning, Barry clothed himself as the people's champion, or as the *Washington Times*' Adrienne Washington called him, the "People's Prodigal Prince."

African-American cultural custom required Barry to fight. If he acquiesced immediately to the control board's dictates without at least feigning disgust, without pretending to be prepared to duel, many in the black community would have written him off as a chump. What's more, he had to "kick ass without breaking a sweat." The cool pose was entrenched in the black community, especially the place Barry called home, the place where his political base resided. In the world of Barry constituents, cunning, manipulation and outright dishonesty are part of the theater of playing cool. The individual performs to an adverse audience with panache, telegraphing that his spirit can never be broken.

The achievements of Adam Clayton Powell or Coleman Young weren't the only things that won them respect in their hometown communities. Even those who claimed to dislike the two flamboyant politicians gave them respect because they never gave up. They fought—sometimes foolishly —for what they believed in. And that alone, the willingness to do battle with the establishment, continuously won them accolades. Powell went into Congress "shouting and protesting," says his biographer Charles V. Hamilton. "His adversaries hated him for it; his admirers loved him precisely because of it. Given such inclinations, he could hardly be anything but extremely controversial. The combination of his fiery persona and the touchy racial problem were ingredients of an inevitably stormy political career."

Failing to execute a boxer's pose would have made Barry a laughing-stock not only in various District black communities where his strongest supporters lived, but in the eyes of his numerous fans overseas as well.

"If you have a conquered people, what is your psychology about assimilation, about joining the enemy? There is a deep maintenance of boundaries," explained James Gibson. "To fully collaborate or assimilate to some extent has connotations of capitulation to the conqueror. In a sense, because race is such a factor, as are issues of equity and concepts of fairness, you see Marion trying to find a stance that retains integrity for him and the people he represents."

"All cultures define their own sins," adds political analyst Paul Ruffin. For African-Americans, more egregious than fighting is not fighting for the right reason. So Barry feigned disagreement with the board, landing a couple of rhetorical blows. He accused it and its backers of wanting to decimate the city government by imposing cuts without forethought. He said the reductions had to be more precise, more surgical, with a scalpel and not a butcher's knife. But neither the council nor the control board bought Barry's spin. The council revised his budget, but it wasn't a major improvement over the mayor's. The Council members proposed to reach the required reduction in force by privatizing government services, but failed to fully identify those services.

In August 1995, buoyed by its earlier meeting with residents, the control board held another public hearing, this time at Howard University's Cramton Auditorium. The change of venue came in response to public criticism about the location, time and setting of its previous meeting. Cramton was larger, and a Saturday event more convenient than a weekday for working class people. The board also lowered itself, moving from the stage to the main floor, and putting it on a level equal with the audience. Residents treated the board like a spurned lover. Fewer than one hundred persons—mostly government workers or union representatives who believed their jobs in jeopardy—actually attended the all-day meeting. The morning, as before, was dedicated to citizen testimony, the afternoon to control board business. By the close of the meeting, the board finalized its order to cut the payroll by the end of fiscal 1996, although it did buy into Barry's proposal not to count public housing workers. It voted to include only some of those positions within the fifty-six hundred to be cut.

Barry had achieved a partial victory. Using Muhammad Ali's rope-a-dope technique, he decided to accept the short-term pounding, abuse, and ridicule of not being a responsible leader, convinced that in the final analysis he would win the fight. If he could sculpt the board's cold and swift action into an indictment against it and the Congress that created it, residents, reeling from the pain of austerity, would realize his plan was the more humane. Despite the illusion he created of not cooperating, Barry's administration, by the end of fiscal 1996, had reduced the city payroll nearly one thousand positions more than mandated. But few residents knew this, because the media failed to report it, and Barry's critics coveted the numbers like a secret CIA document.

◆ ◆ ◆ ◆ ◆ ◆ ◆ ◆ ◆ ◆ ◆ ◆ ◆ ◆ ◆ ◆ ◆

The "downsizing" triumph wasn't attributable to Barry's alacrity but to the Herculean endeavors of City Administrator Michael Rogers. Rogers had previously been director of the Minority Business Development Agency of the U.S. Department of Commerce when Ron Brown was the department secretary. He came to the District with a solid reputation in both the private and public sectors for management acumen and political sophistication. He had been the director of the Mayor's Office of Contracts and the Chief Procurement Officer for the City of New York in David Dinkins' administration, where he handled a total budget of seven billion dollars—almost twice the District's. He also had served as vice president for municipal services and executive director of the Jacob Javits Convention Center for Ogden Services Corporation.

And, before all that, Rogers had served as Deputy General Manager of the Washington Convention Center, during its construction through the first five years of operation. He was widely credited with building a first class operation that became the national leader in the convention industry. During Barry's first administration, Rogers served, too, on the staff of the Temporary Commission on Financial Oversight of the District of Columbia, a congressional commission created to develop and install a financial management system for the city. Because of this experience, Rogers knew a thing or two about finances and the District's fiscal woes.

Barry courted Rogers for the City Administrator job for weeks. His distant cousin Elijah Rogers played a role in convincing him to join the administration. Elijah and Michael Rogers had been professional colleagues for a number of years and Barry knew if anyone could convince the reluctant prospect to say yes, it would be Elijah. Barry also turned to commerce secretary Ron Brown as an emissary in his mission.

Since winning the November 1994 election, Barry had hunted for an African-American professional with proven experience, willing to enter a rancorous environment. The city was Congress's fiefdom, local officials were subjected to the whims of a veritable monarchy, barbed remarks were traded frequently, and a history of mutual apprehension challenged every proposal to improve the future.

Initially, Barry sought Bryon Marshall, who held a similar post in Atlanta. During an earlier Barry administration, Marshall had directed the city's mammoth and troublesome Department of Human Services. Stepping back into the District was tantamount to Pandora repeating her first critical performance—this time with gusto. Marshall opted out of a D.C. deal when his discussions with Barry became public—he hadn't yet talked with his boss, Atlanta Mayor Bill Campbell.

After weeks of arm-twisting, including three meetings with Barry, Rogers held firm in emphatically refusing the post. He told his boss Ron Brown that he had declined Barry's offer. Following a Commerce Department trip to Chicago, however, he found his picture on the front page of the *Washington Post* as Barry's nominee for city administrator. Rogers believed Barry leaked the story to exert the ultimate pressure on him to say yes. A new round of calls from his friends encouraged Rogers to accept the challenge. Rogers now had to recant. He surrendered, but demanded more money. If he took the job at the offered figure of $90,000, he told Barry, it meant a substantial cut from his Commerce Department pay, and it would entail higher living expenses. Always wanting to be king, Barry preferred that the new administrator's salary be below his own of $90,000. Barry reluctantly offered $115,000, the largest salary ever paid to a District government employee, the highest allowable under the city's Home Rule Charter, and the first time Barry had exceeded his own salary to bring in an administrator. The quiet squabble over money should have been the first indication to the mayor that Rogers would not be easy to deal with.

When Rogers was appointed on February 3, 1995, Barry and his transition team exhaled. The mayor had proudly announced staffing appointments prior to taking office, but there were major positions still vacant after his inaugural. Barry himself could read and understand a spreadsheet better than his predecessor or any of the current parcel of politicians, but he lacked the discipline and the interest to make the major shift awaiting the District. His terrain involved big-picture stuff, charting the overall course for the government. The details and implementation were the province of others. The Rev. Jesse Jackson once described himself as "a tree shaker, not a jelly maker." The same could be said of Barry. He desperately needed a city administrator who loved diving into details, following the flow of events from start to finish. Barry often became distracted or simply bored with the mundane aspects of managing a government.

Soon after entering the fray, Rogers discovered that crucial spending cuts ordered months earlier by Congress and Barry hadn't yet been effected. Forecasting a flood of annual deficits, Rogers took the bow, overseeing a ten percent slash in employee wages, a mandatory, government-wide, ten day furlough for every worker, and massive layoffs involving more than two thousand persons. By the end of fiscal year 1995, the Barry administration reduced the city's deficit by $150 million—ten million more than originally ordered.

Rogers struck fear into most District bureaucrats. After only a few days on the job, he upbraided a manager during a Capitol Hill hearing for failing to follow instructions about a payment to the region's Mass Transit Authority. Barry, for all his tough talk, couldn't fire anyone. He agonized over possible firings and usually remembered something the person had done for him. Sympathy, instead of sound management, ruled. Barry's inability to give the boot to the deserving resulted in years of mismanaged programs, corruption, and unadulterated waste. Dwight Cropp heard Coleman Young once call Barry a "pussy" because the mayor "whined about everything." Two years into his tenure, Rogers had fired, on Barry's behalf, several members of the mayor's cabinet. He had also shielded his boss and the government from the control board, assuaging fears and reducing confrontation between Andrew Brimmer and Barry. He had become the mayor's protector, and his willing executioner.

Experience with New York's control board vested Rogers with direct knowledge few others in the administration possessed. He understood that without complete cooperation of all parties, the reform agenda was destined for failure. Shortly after the appointment of the D.C. Financial Responsibility and Management Assistance Authority, Rogers broached with executive director Hill and chairman Brimmer, the idea that they develop, jointly, the agenda for right-sizing the government, improving management, and restoring fiscal solvency. Brimmer and Hill bucked, choosing instead to chart the board's own course. The following year, they released their own strategic plan. Before the end of Barry's term, the city was drowning in plans, none of which were extensive enough to successfully resuscitate the District.

The control board's rebuff of Barry's overture demonstrated an arrogance no less nauseating than the mayor's and fed the adversarial relationship that characterized much of the interaction between it and the Barry administration. Brimmer called his relationship with Barry "episodic," but it wasn't all the mayor's fault that board and bureaucracy never worked as smoothly as they had in Philadelphia. The District control board "summoned" Barry—for the first time— to a public meeting, providing the mayor with overnight notice. Members wanted to chastise him before an audience about failing to provide contracting information. Initially, Barry planned to attend the hearing, but he thought better of it. He couldn't acquiesce, although the board clearly held the hammer. After all, in African-American communities, image is extremely important—that's why Cadillacs are sometimes parked outside public housing apartments, and gold chains found around the necks of persons who can't remember the last time they went to a physician.

At the meeting, Rogers substituted for Barry, challenging, with two boxes of documents that had been forwarded as requested, the board's assertion that the administration had been uncooperative. Rogers' body language communicated his readiness to do battle with board members and their staff. The board backed down. In street vernacular, Rogers had posted "no chump" signs, indicating that neither he nor the mayor could be disrespected.

Earlier, during the summer, when Barry and Brimmer were at odds over the budget, Rogers suggested a three-day summit to bring everyone together. The meeting came off, and though it didn't produce the unity he had sought, Rogers received credit for setting the tone for the next year when the mayor, D.C. Council, and the control board produced a consensus budget.

Ten months after starting his tenure, Rogers was winning praise throughout the city. "A lot of people attack the leadership of this city. But Michael Rogers makes it harder and harder for them to do that successfully," said civic activist Lawrence Guyot. *Washington Times* columnist Adrienne Washington tapped Rogers as her 1995 Man of the Year, describing him as the "consummate professional" with a "temper that borders on legend.

"It's ironic that the District finally has found the right person to be its city administrator only to have him hamstrung by a micro-managing control board, a wimpy chief financial officer, an inexperienced inspector general, and a mellowing mayor," continued Washington. "Even so, he's made a difference in the way government works." Business and civic leaders privately wished that Rogers would run for mayor. In 1997, the talk intensified. At least one person suggested directly to Barry that he consider backing Rogers for mayor. The District's beleaguered populace seemed eager to embrace the pragmatic leadership Rogers displayed. Furthermore, his political instincts proved he was more than a corporate-style executive concerned only with the bottom line. Despite his conflicts with the control board, executive director John Hill quietly attempted in late 1996 to persuade Rogers to consider an offer to become an "independent" city administrator.

In a short time, Rogers had amassed an impressive list of accomplishments, including privatizing two major sections of the Department of Corrections, and creating the Water and Sewer Authority, whose board members included representatives from Maryland and Virginia. These maneuvers helped protect the District from a regional insurrection that threatened a major real estate asset and the city's pride. Rogers also pushed through the organization of a separate Department of Health—a proposal former Mayor Sharon Pratt Kelly bandied about for four years but never implemented. He developed the plans for reforming the city's personnel and procurement systems, and with George Washington University, created the Center for Excellence in Municipal Management, which became the primary vehicle for training District managers.

But Rogers was constrained, and everyone knew it. Government insiders reported as much to the control board, and civic leaders like Dwight Cropp and Jim Gibson often spoke of it. The realization that Barry, his chief of staff, Barry Campbell, and his wife encumbered Rogers' management decisions prompted Cropp and Julius Hobson, Jr., to write an op-ed article, which appeared in *The Washington Post*. It called for the appointment of a receiver to take over complete operation of the District's government, extracting all power from Barry. "Michael [Rogers] was the last best hope. If they were going to undercut him, maybe we needed to look at another model and have a city manager come in who was appointed for a four or five year term like the city auditor," says Cropp. "We could have some way of minimizing political influence. We didn't like what we saw. We saw Michael losing influence."

Cropp and Hobson's proposed model was Chelsea, Massachusetts, where in 1991 the state legislature abolished the local government and appointed a receiver. After several belt-tightening years, and the burial of old style politics, Chelsea reinstated its elected government.

The District's control board and others were prepared to lobby Congress for legislative changes that ensured Rogers' independence, making him a de facto receiver. But he declined the offer, citing professional ethics. A city manager, Rogers had been trained to respect and support elected officials. Barry had hired him, and Rogers would support the mayor as long as philosophically and ethically possible. And when that became an impossible task, he said, he would leave the administration. Privately, he expressed concern about being accused of "racial treason." That dreadful moniker, he feared, would leave him without any future employment options—black or white. If he were hired as anyone's second, there would always be the fear he might turn on the person—stab him in the back. Rogers' refusal to accept the offer of independence proved a major tactical error for him personally and for the District.

Rogers rejected the seductive advances of the control board, placing his reputation in greater jeopardy simply by continuing to associate with an executive who couldn't make up his mind whether to play ball with the control board or throw spitballs at it.

But ironically, the mayor, his wife, and his chief of staff plotted the city administrator's demise. For them, Rogers had grown too big. He was constantly and favorably quoted in the media, and few people held a negative view of him. One business leader called him the "one sane individual in the circus passing for a city government." In fact, *Washingtonian* magazine touted Rogers as indicative of the country's "new black leadership," and thereby instigated the sniping and undercutting that marked Rogers' final days with the Barry administration.

The "new black leadership" was not to be confused with the "new black vanguard," say Joseph Conti and Brad Stetson, authors of *The New Black Vanguard*. The vanguard made a break with old-line civil rights tactics. Its members suffered "allegations of racial disloyalty, [but] maintain that the traditional methods of advancing black interest are effete, if not iatrogenic." By contrast, civil rights leaders, like Barry, often wrap themselves comfortably in race-based rhetoric. In the same issue of *Washingtonian* magazine that claimed Rogers exemplified a "new breed" of black leader, Barry was excoriated for his race-based politics.

Shortly after the October 1996 *Washingtonian* magazine issue appeared on the newsstands, Cora Barry pushed to muzzle Rogers. She even suggested to her husband that he look for a new city administrator. Chief of Staff Barry Campbell, who sometimes socialized with the mayor and his wife, fed Cora Barry information about Rogers, stirring the pot of animosity. Things came to a head in March 1997 during a meeting with staff from the Mayor's Office of Communications. The mayor, his wife, and Rogers were all in attendance. Cora Barry criticized the handling of a media story about a District employee who took a government vehicle out of town—where the car was later stolen. Rogers had kept the issue from sticking to Barry, ordering an investigation and appropriate disciplinary action against the employee. Cora Barry said the mayor himself should have responded to press inquiries about the incident.

Tired of being harangued, Rogers, looking directly at Barry, snapped, "Is there something wrong here?" The room cleared, leaving only a few choice ears. "I do not work for your wife," Rogers continued stridently. "If there is a problem with the way I handle things, I expect to hear it from you and no one else." What was wrong, according to Barry, was that his wife believed the city administrator wasn't giving the mayor enough credit for the good things that happened in the administration. Barry said that from his point of view, the mayor should always get the good press and the city administrator should always get the bad press. It was the same policy that Richard Daley had espoused in Chicago.

Rogers took the exchange to mean that the mayor and his wife felt he was too visible. He subsequently took a lower profile, sending all media inquiries to the mayor's press secretary to determine the appropriate person to respond to them. The mayor's strategy backfired. With Rogers restrained from responding, Barry became the District government's primary voice, and critical press reports escalated.

The March 1997 brouhaha wasn't the first time Cora Barry had intruded in her husband's affairs. When Barry served as Ward 8 council member, staff members repeatedly complained about her abrasive, abusive, and masculine style. But the complaints fell on deaf ears. Barry simply told staffers that "Y'all let Cora get to y'all. You should do what I do—ignore her." But he didn't really ignore Cora. He couldn't afford to. She knew his secrets and had ushered him back to office. Furthermore, as a political scientist, she could offer insights that occasionally were brilliant. But her directness repelled most potential allies.

Cora Barry wanted only her husband in the limelight, the way Nancy Reagan wanted balloons to descend and trumpets to blow whenever "Ronnie" entered the room. In previous administrations, the unwritten rule was that all accolades accrue to the chief. But in 1995, no one believed Barry. Many had simply grown tired of his 1960s-style leadership. Others reflected on all those years in the 1980s when he would nearly swear on a stack of Bibles that he wasn't using drugs, only to admit in 1990 that he was addicted. No one was prepared to take anything he said to the bank. Rogers was the appropriate proxy.

Yet, true to form, Barry wimped out. He permitted his wife and chief of staff to persist in their bickering. In fact, the mayor, envious of Rogers' popularity and professionalism, joined the gang attack. Rogers spent weeks completing a plan to reform the city's controversial procurement system, which for years had been flawed by favoritism, cronyism, and unbridled incompetence. Believing that, as city administrator, he would oversee its implementation, he presented the report to the mayor. Hoping to score points with the electorate and the press at a time when the control board was thrashing the District government's procurement system, Barry released the report to the media and touted himself as a savior. He boasted that he would preside over changes. "There is a new sense of urgency. I am driving it. You are going to see a big difference," he said. That declaration became the joke of the week. Barry apparently forgot—or simply refused to confront—his own past. It was yet another manifestation of his "accentuate the positive, forget the negative" mantra.

For years, African-Americans had developed leather-thick skin, casually dismissing all complaints about their leadership. They maintained a bunker mentality born during segregation, when their leaders and their communities faced constant attacks and when any error, misstep, or failing was magnified a hundredfold. Accordingly, Barry's supporters often ignored his flaws or sought to downplay them by comparing them to those of white politicians. But there were real problems. Under Barry's previous administrations, the city's multi-million dollar procurement program devolved into a poorly run patronage system where contracts were awarded to friends, or lovers like Rasheeda Moore, and relatives of friends and former lovers. Regulations routinely were violated, resulting in dozens of reports by City Auditor Otis Troupe and his predecessor Russell Smith.

The Washington Post editorial writers hooted derisively at Barry's procurement reform remarks. Calling it "Mr. Barry's Out-of-Body Act," the editorial said the reassurance "comes from the same mayor who allowed an untrained and poorly supervised contracting bureaucracy to waste millions of dollars acquiring goods and services for a city that can't afford to waste one dime." Ironically, Barry's stab at Rogers backfired on the mayor. Before the end of 1997, he and his administration lost complete authority over personnel and procurement.

The mayor's release of the procurement report devastated Rogers. At every possible juncture, he had sought to protect Barry and to provide the best professional advice and service to him and the city, only to have the mayor deny the value of his contribution and sabotage his efforts to reform the bureaucracy. Even before other dramatic events of 1997 overtook the city, Rogers contemplated moving on. Barry had betrayed him more than once. If he hung around for Barry's next mayoral campaign, things could only get worse.

In September 1997, Rogers submitted his resignation. Word didn't leak to the press, however, until October, and then only because Barry's Office of Communications quietly passed the word around. WRC-TV Channel 4's Tom Sherwood was the first to report the story. Barry's people were telling the press insistently that the mayor wanted Rogers out—that he was being pushed out. But actually, changing events in Congress prompted Rogers' decision. The resignation became as messy as the previous six months had been. Barry, hoping to rope the cow after it was out of the barn, downplayed Rogers' departure, telling reporters his city administrator had had "some successes and some non-successes."

The entire affair embittered Rogers, who had deliberately held back on providing the media news of his departure, permitting the mayor the opportunity to make a formal announcement. In the end, Barry had tried to stick it to him. Fortunately for Rogers, he had more friends than enemies in the media, and his achievements were noted by the press, causing Barry to seem foolish in trying to scapegoat his chief administrator for his own failures.

◆ ◆ ◆ ◆ ◆ ◆ ◆ ◆ ◆ ◆ ◆ ◆ ◆ ◆ ◆ ◆

While Barry dogged his city administrator, he sang the praises of the District's new chief financial officer (CFO). The law that created the control board also established an independent CFO with authority over the government's entire financial operations. The CFO had to certify any budget figures distributed by the mayor. Initially, Barry interviewed Carol O'Cleireacain, a former New York tax commissioner, for the post. Smart and perceptive, O'Cleireacain was also the control board's choice. But Barry refused to hire her after she pushed for a larger salary and increased powers. When he interviewed Anthony Williams, rail thin and balding, he liked what he heard. Williams, a forty-four-year-old numbers cruncher, had served as the first chief financial officer for the U.S. Department of Agriculture.

But the law made Williams' employment difficult. While Barry could hire the CFO, only the control board could fire him. Thus, the five member panel had to be satisfied with him as well. At his confirmation hearing, Williams sweet talked both the D.C. council and the control board, telling elected officials he was the Indian to their chiefs. And, he told the appointed panel, he would pull the city out of fiscal insolvency. On the surface, he appeared a stereotypical accountant—with a bow tie and self-effacing demeanor.

Barry hypothesized that he could ride the tidal wave to success on

Williams' boat. If he aligned himself with the District's finance chief, he could lay equal claim to any improvements in the municipality's condition. This theory echoed advice he'd originally received from Joyce Ladner and Eleanor Holmes Norton. During the campaign, he'd proclaimed himself a financial wizard. The fiscal improvements ushered in by this chief financial officer offered an opportunity for him to be re-crowned—this time with greater and more authentic fanfare.

But Williams, more than Michael Rogers, became the media's darling. And he wore more hats and contradictory masks than Barry, thus complicating his potential use as another scapegoat for the mayor. A former college dropout turned conscientious objector, turned air force pilot, turned deputy comptroller for the state of Connecticut, he had been city alderman in New Haven, Connecticut, and a White House appointee. In short, Williams couldn't be pegged.

He had a wonderfully dry wit, and rarely spoke without making an obscure analogy. Analogies were his life-preserver. He reached for them when pressed into a corner, when confronting a group of strangers, when wanting to scream at the absurdity of affairs in the District, or when his anger with his boss reached a rolling boil. Like Barry, he preferred coded language, making it difficult to track his intended meanings. While Barry's use of language simplified everything for the common man and encouraged racial divisions, Williams' diction swelled, creating a verbal labyrinth accessible only to those with the proper, class-conferred navigational tools. What's more, he often used his analogies to attack with the swiftness of a striking rattlesnake.

Like Lightning in "Amos n' Andy," Barry was slow to catch the true meaning of Williams' words and the substance of his character. It wasn't until the fall of 1996 that Barry realized he had met his intellectual match. He was unsure of a response. Meeting a virtual clone of oneself, up close and personal, can be highly disconcerting.

Even before Williams arrived, however, he proved troublesome for Barry. The mayor had one perception of the role of his number three man, whom he planned to co-opt the way he had most people throughout his political career. Barry's theory was, in essence, "If you can't beat them, buy them." He bought his friends and enemies alike.

Once, during a community meeting in Ward 6, Barry, arriving late, was heckled by several residents. But one young woman was the loudest, calling the mayor rude and obnoxious. When the meeting adjourned, with reporters in earshot, Barry asked the woman if she had a job. Growing quiet, she replied "no." He asked her if she were looking for one. "Yes," she said. "Call me at my office tomorrow," he told her. The woman smiled, thanked him, and exited the building. There weren't any jobs—Barry knew that. But for the media's benefit, he had shown the woman to be a fraud. Never mind that because he offered her something he didn't have, he was scarcely more genuine. But he considered himself the victor in the brief battle, and winning carried a perverse premium in his world.

The control board thought that the District's CFO should be independent of the mayor, and that he should control his own fiefdom. That view didn't jibe with Barry's. Behind closed doors, the two rivals fought. During a public hearing, Brimmer said that the CFO would neither be controlled by, nor take instructions from, the mayor. Brimmer announced that the CFO would have hiring and firing power over all finance personnel. Even Rogers differed with Brimmer's view. The CFO should report to the city administrator, and nothing in federal law suggested otherwise, he contended. Still, the control board chairman believed that, with his pronouncement, he had resolved the dispute.

Within the first six months came indications that Barry had pledged allegiance to the wrong aide. He and Williams fought over almost everything. And unlike Rogers, whose professional ethics constrained his behavior, Williams was so independent that he considered his only allegiance to himself and the job he believed he was hired to do. "The worst mistake Marion ever made was when he got drawn into battle with Anthony Williams…[They butted heads] in five instances, and in all five instances Marion lost," says Guyot.

Barry and his CFO tussled, for example, over payment priority for bills. Roy Littlejohn, a Barry ally, had performed poorly as the operator of J.B. Johnson Nursing Home—patients received far from the best service—yet the District government paid his company according to contract. The city administrator canceled the contract with Littlejohn and Associates after finding out that J. B. Johnson employees had not been paid their wages on time, and that their health insurance premiums also hadn't been paid, although such deductions had been made from employees' checks. Rogers attempted to arrange some payment to Littlejohn. CFO Williams blocked those efforts. Barry seethed over Williams' handling of the affair. But Congress and anti-Barry forces in the city loved it. Finally, they had someone daring enough to say no to the District's political king. Physically smaller than Barry, and initially conveying the image of a pipsqueak, Williams knew how to dig in his heels, call in the troops, manipulate the media, and play to the Barry bashers.

The mayor and his CFO also scrapped over where Williams should locate his office, who to name as outside financial adviser, and who had control over the District's cluster of more than one thousand financial workers—the same issue raised earlier by Brimmer. Once, CFO Williams attempted to steal an employee, Harry Black, from city administrator Rogers. The battle between the two—city administrator and CFO—made the newspapers. Harry Black was Rogers' financial adviser. Williams wanted him transferred to his staff. But before the transfer could be effected, Rogers fired Black. Although he declined to comment publicly, administration insiders said Black, in preparation for his move to the CFO, had begun thrashing the mayor and Rogers. After receiving reports that Black had made disparaging remarks in an elevator, Rogers decided his former protegé could not work anywhere in the administration. He warned Williams that any attempts to hire Black would make relations between the city administrator and the CFO chilly and awkward. The small dispute escalated into a major battle over whom the CFO could hire.

Williams also sought to replace Rodney Palmer, the city's budget director and a Barry appointee. In a private meeting with Barry, Williams raised concerns about Palmer. After the meeting, Barry thought the matter resolved, although he had not fully consented to removing Palmer. But three days later, Barry learned his CFO had gone to the control board, soliciting its help in replacing Palmer. Barry dashed off a letter, chastising Williams about his precipitous action and accusing him of "unprofessional conduct."

Although he initially refused to remove Palmer, Barry held a press conference notifying the public that his budget director was being moved to the Office of Policy and Analysis. He crafted the entire scenario as if he had initiated the action to maintain an air of cooperation. But in fact, there were efforts in Congress to amend the original control board legislation, clarifying the authority Williams held over finance personnel throughout the government. Barry's move softened the blow of the loss but it didn't eliminate it.

Williams, an impish man who once called himself a geek, had won. His willingness to skirmish with Barry won him praise comparable to Rogers' and the control board's John Hill. Indeed, the triumvirate became the city's leadership team. They shared similar styles and offered a window into the District's future of pragmatic leadership, absent race politics. Like Rogers, Williams had the air and talent of the new black leadership. The difference was, he seemed on a mission to disabuse the city of Barry's political style. And Williams escalated his attacks on Barry. During a congressional hearing, he accused the mayor and his managers of believing they had a "right" to overspend. Williams painted a picture of an executive unwilling to make difficult spending decisions, setting a precedent for the entire bureaucracy to ignore the approved budget.

Williams used his assault to deflect attention from his own missteps and failings. He didn't meet the deadline for setting up the computerized financial management system. The District was unable to receive a clean audit for fiscal year 1996 because Williams had not completed certain tasks in time. At the start of fiscal 1997, he claimed that Barry's inattention to management reforms meant the city faced an eighty-five million dollar deficit, and that the mayor's cost-cutting plan was insufficient to rein in the overspending. Williams made the statement to the press, although he sat through rounds of meetings where plans to reduce the size of the deficit were discussed. Once again he proved to be the more agile and effective Anansi. "Some of his own medicine was being used on him," says Cropp, explaining Barry's relationship with Williams. But Barry still didn't understand Williams' plot. In fact, he couldn't fathom that there was one. Each time the CFO was caught with his hand in the jar, he said the press misquoted him. Barry believed it, the way the Tiger, galloping into town, believed Anansi wasn't riding him. A trickster rarely will admit he has been outwitted.

During one budget fight, Barry bragged that CFO Williams was in his corner, calling their alliance brand new. "The point I'm trying to make is that Tony and I had our little rough spots when we first got started—jockeying around and trying to see who was here, who was not here, and the control board wasn't helping," Barry explained. "[But] now we're comfortable because he knows his role." Three weeks later, Williams sucker-punched Barry, sending a letter to Brimmer blasting Barry yet again for not acting decisively. Williams urged the control board to make budget cuts based on Williams' plan—not the mayor's. Getting rid of Williams was next to impossible for the mayor. In addition to being the favored son of Congress, Williams, by organizing and attending community meetings, had built his own local constituency. Barry had to live with him.

From the very beginning, Williams had his eye on the District's assets, particularly its real estate portfolio. The CFO once told a reporter that, after his stint with the District, he might like to get into the development business. Having control over asset management offered a nice vantage of potential economic development opportunities and potential partners. Barry attempted to diminish the importance of the portfolio, telling the press it didn't come under Williams' office. Then he contrived a counter-move, hiring his own real estate manager. At one juncture, the District had two such managers.

But Williams' ace was Congress. There, he was God. When things became too heated, he sought congressional assistance, colluding with Rep. Charles Taylor, a North Carolina Republican and head of the House subcommittee on District appropriations. At one point, Taylor intended to tack thirty-one amendments to the city's fiscal 1998 appropriations bill, and he needed the CFO's aid. In exchange, Taylor proposed placing the real estate portfolio with the CFO. The maneuver, however, drastically affected a control board plan to secure Congressional funds for police raises and school repairs. Williams was publicly rebuked by D.C. Delegate Eleanor Holmes Norton, who accused him of "empire building." Control board chairman Andrew Brimmer said he couldn't trust the CFO's numbers.

Sixteen months after he hired Williams, Barry finally understood he'd been duped from the start by the slick-talking, bow-tie-wearing chief financial officer, who from all evidence never intended to be anyone's Indian. In his "State of the District" speech in 1997, Barry accused Williams of making "key policy decisions."

Williams counter-attacked. "We're not here to get along," he said. "We're here to ensure results. I have respect for the mayor personally and for his office. But if the ship is approaching the reef, I'm going down to tell Captain Hazlewood," Williams explained, using a reference to the Exxon Valdez.*

After the Congressional fiasco with Taylor, Williams, in true Barry tradition, kept a low profile. But when the smoke cleared two months later, Williams had control of asset management, including the city's real estate portfolio. By the fall of 1997, he had received a national award from *Governing* magazine for the fiscal changes he implemented in the District. And, like Rogers, some business leaders quietly talked of him as a possible mayoral candidate. One thing was apparent: Williams had positioned himself quite nicely in his battles with the mayor. Barry was left to figure out which of his tricks had failed.

CHAPTER THIRTEEN

SHE WORE DARK GLASSES, shorts, and tennis shoes. He wore a jogging suit, his right hand clutching her shoulder the way a blind person holds the leash of a seeing-eye dog. An ill-timed smirk cradled his mouth. His eyes stared into the glare of television cameras. Surrounded by the media, the couple made their way through the airport concourse. People shouted questions, but neither bothered to answer. She simply tunneled through the throngs. He slid through the opening she created—a running back following his offensive lineman. He had fumbled, which was the reason they were boarding the plane to St. Louis. The previous week, Barry and his wife Cora had hastily left the District, going into semi-hiding the way Salman Rushdie had after Ayatollah Khomeini issued a *fatwa* against him.*

Barry's plight, like Rushdie's, grew more dramatic each day. The airport scene came one week after the journey began: On April 27, 1996, Barry's press secretary released a statement announcing the mayor's intention to depart immediately for Skinner Farm near Annapolis, Maryland. Barry had spent his first few days after prison at the same facility. His April 1996 trip would not have been any more significant, except that Barry laced his announcement of the Skinner Farm trip with the lexicon of addiction recovery, sending the media and everyone else into frenzied rounds of speculation.

"Step Four of the Twelve Step Program states that every person should take 'fearless personal moral inventory' of oneself. This inventory, one of the cardinal principles of Narcotics Anonymous and Alcoholics Anonymous, should involve a level of 'rigorous honesty,'" Barry said. "I have recently taken such a personal inventory. And being absolutely honest with myself, I have to admit that I have not given proper priority to my health and continued recovery. In my inventory, I see telltale signs of spiritual relapse and physical exhaustion. The Bible says, 'To thine own self be true.' I know myself and realize that recovery is a lifelong process. And I must take responsibility for what steps must now be taken to assure my health and continued recovery." He called the "rejuvenation" trip necessary for a "proper balance in my personal life for continued and successful recovery."

The night before he released this statement, Barry summoned his top aides to his southeast D.C. home. Among those present were his chief of staff, Barry Campbell; his press secretary, Raymone Bain; and the city administrator, Michael Rogers. He passed around a draft of the release he and his wife had written. For hours, the group discussed the wisdom of issuing it. Barry's aides feared that reference to recovery and the Twelve Step program might cause the media to infer that the mayor had relapsed into drug abuse. They argued that he should simply leave and let Bain answer any questions about his whereabouts.

But the mayor insisted on an announcement. Initially, he wanted to release it on Friday, which would have given the media twenty-four hours to play the story repeatedly, the way they had the Vista Hotel sting video tape. He also wanted to hold a press conference—either at Union Temple Baptist Church or his office. Union Temple would have been an eerie replay of those days following the Vista Hotel arrest, when Barry, then married to Effi, stood at the podium confessing his sins: He wasn't addicted to cocaine, but to alcohol, prescription drugs, and sex—not necessarily in that order. But if the media saw him, Barry now thought, that would reduce the speculation. Deferring to the counsel of his aides, he decided not to stage the press conference and waited until Saturday afternoon to release the statement, leaving the media with their vivid imaginations and prodigious curiosity to seek the truth—or at least the facts.

◆ ◆ ◆ ◆ ◆ ◆ ◆ ◆ ◆ ◆ ◆ ◆ ◆ ◆ ◆ ◆

As in 1990, when he conceded drug use but denied the full extent of his problem, Barry's press release failed to disclose fully the events leading to his abrupt "rejuvenation" departure. He didn't even tell everyone gathered at his home that Friday night all of the facts: On April 26, an employee in the Office of Communications, which is located inside the suite of offices that constitute the Mayor's Office on the 11th Floor of One Judiciary Square, returned from a meeting to find Barry in the middle of buying crack cocaine, according to a top-level city government employee. Witnessing his long-time friend exchanging cash for a package, the employee knew the mayor had hit a rough patch in his recovery. Cora Barry and only a few others received a report of the aborted buy, but they went into a panic. How many other times had Barry purchased drugs as mayor? Where had he purchased them? Had anyone seen him?

Actually, the signs of relapse had been present for months, but everyone had conveniently ignored them. Barry had returned to smoking cigarettes, hiding out in his office to puff away. He began frequenting after-hours clubs, where liquor and drugs were freely exchanged. His late-night carousing resumed, prompting a talk from his friend Ivanhoe Donaldson. "I had heard that he was out there, and I know Marion: When he starts doing that, that means there's something wrong going on at home. So I went and talked to him and jacked him up a little," said Donaldson, who denied that there had been any drug buy on the mayor's part.

Another confidante—one of several to confirm the crack purchase reported by government employees—blamed Cora, saying, "She was pressuring him into drinking again, telling him it's okay if he takes a drink. That woman is just plain evil." Barry also resumed his infamous womanizing: *Washingtonian* magazine ran a story in its "Capital Comment" column reporting that radio personality Marty Davis received phone calls from the carousing mayor. Government employees told more than one reporter about the mayor regularly visiting a female bartender at The Coach and Four Restaurant and Lounge on 14th Street NW, inside the Frank Reeves Municipal Center.

After Barry's departure for Skinner Farm, *The Washington Post*, believing the mayor had indeed returned to drugs but lacking the data to substantiate it, assigned a fleet of reporters to track down any leads. Metro reporter Hamil Harris searched 18th Street looking for anyone who had seen Barry making a buy in front of Tom Tom restaurant—the *Post* had received a tip that the mayor's car had been seen in the area.

At Skinner Farm, a few television stations sent helicopters to spy on Barry's activities, taking photographs of him walking the grounds, with aides and security in tow. Meanwhile, a reporter at the *Washington City Paper* received a call about the in-house buy and also was told that the mayor had been visiting a place at 12th and O Street. His latest associate, the reporter was told, was someone called "the Rev." Months later, a full name and face were given to this individual. It was clear that the personal redemption and resurrection of Marion Barry had begun to unravel.

◆ ◆ ◆ ◆ ◆ ◆ ◆ ◆ ◆ ◆ ◆ ◆ ◆ ◆ ◆ ◆

Barry went to Skinner Farm to contemplate his future. Even he was frightened by the downward slide his personal life had begun to take. The Vista Hotel sting had saved him from near-certain death caused by escalating drug use. Being snagged this time by a faithful employee was a godsend, halting him before he completely relapsed. As most recovering addicts know, relapse begins in the mind long before it occurs in the body. Sometimes, intense cravings can be created by the sight of drug paraphernalia, or visits to old hunting grounds where the addict has used drugs. Barry and Cora briefly forgot the need for him to be vigilant.

Many of the mayor's friends doubted he could serve two masters: his recovery and District residents. The issue of dual allegiance had surfaced during the campaign, when even his former associates pondered whether he was returning to public life too soon. Union Temple's Willie Wilson knew Barry needed something to keep him occupied, to make him feel useful, but he had sought to keep Barry out of politics. Gibson and other Kitchen Cabinet advisers wondered whether Barry would resort to drugs to anesthetize the pain and pressure that often accompany a life of politics—a life where every foible is magnified a hundredfold and privacy is practically nil. Barry couldn't afford another public disgrace. Although no one knew it, the first one sent him into a deep depression, soothed only by the presence of Tom and Barbara Skinner, his wife Cora, boxing promoter Rock Newman, the Rev. Willie Wilson, Sandra Allen, Bob Bethea, his mother Mattie Cummings, and his son Christopher.

In April 1996, some people counseled him to get out of the business, to resign immediately, or at least not to seek reelection. Cora argued against resigning, believing it would signal defeat. Barry, she thought, had fought too hard to drop out before the completion of his term. Besides, though she stayed out of the limelight, she relished being the District's first lady. Others were neutral, urging Barry to follow his own heart. For most of his life, Barry's ego had been captain, steering him into treacherous waters even when common sense militated against it.

But while politicians can be notoriously lacking in self-awareness, a huge ego seems to be an essential element of most politicians' character. How else to explain the self-vision that drove Napoleon, that convinced Richard Nixon of his righteousness until the very end, that pushed Bill Clinton to keep going even when national opinion polls suggested he should pursue another line of work, and that soothed House Speaker Newt Gingrich when young upstarts in his own party threatened mutiny?

By week's end, Barry, accusing the media of hounding him, put his rejuvenation show on the road, flying to the Thompson Retreat Center in St. Louis. And just to prove his ego and his need for the spotlight had not been diminished, he advised his press secretary to announce his decision to leave Skinner Farm. She also told the media the time of his arrival and departure from Washington National airport, although she withheld specifics about his St. Louis destination. The media pandemonium at St. Louis and National airports paralleled that of the courthouse in 1990. Who would ask for a repeat performance other than someone desperate for attention—even the wrong kind? Consciously or subconsciously, Barry, for a moment, diverted everyone from the failings, fights, and near disasters of his young government.

◆ ◆ ◆ ◆ ◆ ◆ ◆ ◆ ◆ ◆ ◆ ◆ ◆ ◆ ◆ ◆

Fifteen months into his fourth term, Barry's age and battle scars were visible. He wasn't the young maverick he had been during his first term, reining in a runaway deficit, smiling as he worked fifteen or eighteen hour days. Since taking office, the fights over money, the efforts to maneuver through the control board's supervision, the determination to hold on to his political territory, and the attempts to defend himself against internal and external attacks—all had taken their toll.

Then, in December 1995, he stood before a bank of microphones, accompanied by his wife and two men. He had called a press conference because word had reached him that one of D.C.'s television stations was about to break the story: The mayor had developed cancer. Barry acted much as Arthur Ashe did when he received a telephone call from *USA Today* informing him they intended to run a story telling the world that the great tennis champion had full-blown AIDS. Disclosing matters of such consequence was not just the media's job. For the affected individual to maintain control over his personal life, he had to tell the story himself, and a thorough-going control freak like Barry needed to keep his fingers on all levers, at all times.

Therefore, the sixty-year-old Barry offered details as to how his prostate cancer had been discovered and what course of action he intended to pursue. Two doctors—Alfred Goldson from Howard University's Cancer Center and Michael Manyak of George Washington University—explained the mayor's options. A full biopsy still had to be performed to determine whether the cancer had spread to other parts of Barry's body. The media was stunned. Barry and his wife had decided well in advance just what spin the press would put on a this dismal story: they would praise the mayor for coming forward.

Nearly forty thousand American men each year suffer from prostate cancer; a disproportionate number of them are African-Americans. Former Senate Majority leader Robert Dole had been treated for the disease. Stokely Carmichael, a.k.a. Kwame Ture, also had been diagnosed with the disease, but his prognosis was not good. Everyone expected him to die within a few years.

Three weeks after he told the country he had prostate cancer, Barry entered John Hopkins University Hospital in Baltimore, renowned for its treatment facilities and medical personnel. He decided to have his prostrate removed by noted urologist Patrick C. Walsh, who had pioneered a surgical procedure that bypassed the nerve ending and reduced side effects such as impotence.

Four days later, on December 13, 1995, Barry left the hospital. Doctors predicted a full recovery. But while Walsh and his colleagues successfully removed the prostate, and Barry's cancer went into remission, the mayor suffered incontinence and bouts of impotence for months after the surgery. For a man who had often measured his self-worth by his ability to seduce women, the sexual side effects of prostate removal caused great consternation, and became only one of several factors that guided him to the slippery slope of addiction relapse.

◆ ◆ ◆ ◆ ◆ ◆ ◆ ◆ ◆ ◆ ◆ ◆ ◆ ◆ ◆ ◆

Within days of returning from his cancer operation, the District was hit with three successive winter storms, blanketing the city with mounds of snow. Despite annual visits of the white stuff, the District's municipal services repeatedly displayed total ineptness at handling it. One of the hallmarks of Sharon Pratt Kelly's administration had been its successful snow removal. But few people knew that Betty Hager Francis, then director of D.C. Department of Public Works, often overspent the agency's budget to achieve those results.

Who really cared about such a frivolous issue? The city's murder rate stood comparable to the casualties in a small war. Children were being poorly educated. Unemployment remained higher than the national average. And there were more sick people, per capita, than in any other American city. (The District had astronomical incidences of cancer, hypertension, and rates of HIV infection.)

Yet, residents and elected officials—especially those on Capitol Hill— became obsessed with snow every year. Those from the South simply hated it. Those from states where more snow falls in one winter than the District receives in a decade couldn't understand why the city was unable to remove it quickly and efficiently. Snow removal, a never-ending issue for Barry, arose in 1987 at the start of his third term. While he was in Los Angeles drinking and womanizing, his city struggled with more than twenty inches of snow. Residents read news reports of their mayor sitting curbside in Los Angeles waiting for an ambulance. Initial stories said he experienced symptoms similar to those associated with a drug overdose. While Barry partied in California, D.C. government had bungled the simple task of snow removal. The episode highlighted an administration inefficiency that began to take shape during Barry's second term and continued unfettered during the third. Snow became an indelible black mark in his political history. Each winter, residents braced for the flashback to Los Angeles. The past rode shotgun to the present and the future; Barry couldn't kick it off his train, not even in 1996.

Still out to prove his mettle, Barry paraded about like a peacock when he should have been recuperating. He wanted to project a public image of a dedicated executive. He boarded a helicopter to survey storm damage. Then he staged a press conference, proclaiming snow removal was going well and that major arteries were being plowed as he spoke. It was always difficult for him to restrain his ego, to resist an opportunity to play the District's messiah.

But as he boasted, television stations flashed pictures of residents with cars stuck in mounds of snow at street corners. Thoroughfares such as Constitution Avenue NW, just blocks from the mayor's office, looked as if they had never seen a plow. Frustrated by the government's inability to provide such a basic service, residents who could afford it pooled their money and hired private companies or individuals to plow their streets. It took more than a week before the primary arteries of the nation's capital finally were cleared, and it happened only with help from the federal government.

Wholesale anarchy began. Barry said the city's fiscal crisis bore the blame for the promises he was now unable to fulfill. Private contractors had not been paid for their previous work, and refused to put their trucks and themselves at the District's disposal after the snow storm. Barry named a committee comprised of the city administrator, the comptroller, and others to develop a snow plan, insuring there would be enough trucks, salt, and other resources for next year. He also warned that in the event another storm occurred, neighborhood streets would receive the government's attention first. But Barry made Rogers his point person on the revised snow removal plan; if the effort failed in 1997, the mayor couldn't be blamed. If it succeeded, he could accept the laurels for having the foresight to construct a committee. While the muscle flexing won some praise in local quarters, Barry's pronouncement riled congressional representatives, and they translated it as yet another example of irresponsible leadership.

◆ ◆ ◆ ◆ ◆ ◆ ◆ ◆ ◆ ◆ ◆ ◆ ◆ ◆ ◆ ◆

The release on Valentine's Day, 1996, of his Transformation Plan pulled Barry's mayoralty from the freezer. Dressed in business attire, he held forth for the media in the conference room of Group Decision Support Systems, Inc. Barry declared himself architect of the plan entitled "A Vision for America's First City." The document, which accompanied his fiscal 1997 budget proposal, called for extensive changes to the District government structure, plus the reduction of ten thousand positions by 1999. Though the mark, he said, could be achieved simply by attrition, the number itself made it appear as if the leopard had changed his spots. Moreover, he proposed collapsing several city agencies into one, and completely eliminating others. Barry, who had seemed down for the count, came flying off the canvas.

A few critics dismissed the plan as half-hearted, but mostly it was praised, from One Thomas Circle—where the control board was headquartered—to Capitol Hill. Was it just talk, or a politician feeling the squeeze of an impatient electorate? Was it Barry attempting to reinvent himself for the times, which called for pragmatic thinking, coalition building, and an end of traditional black politics, including its left-wing, wealth-redistribution approach?

Barry's salvation rested in his ability to reinvent himself, as he did in the 1970s when he travelled the distance from rabble-rouser to school board member. Now nearly sixty-one years-old, such wholesale re-engineering seemed highly improbable. Most of his generation had already walked out the back door of black politics, finding an angry crowd waiting out front, demanding metamorphosis. When looked at from the standpoint of his first term, it was possible to believe that Barry could transform both himself and the city. He had used the tactics and rhetoric of his civil rights past to keep the control board and congressional overseers at bay while he and his staff came up with a cogent response to the District's overall financial crisis.

If implemented, Barry's blueprint promised to return order to the District and move it into the twenty-first century. But carrying out the plan meant he had to destroy the very government to which he had given birth. If this were to happen, it would be like the dramatic scene in Toni Morrison's novel *Sula*, when "Mama" Erta Peace, realizing her son, Plum, is on drugs and growing increasingly dependent on her, sets him on fire, closes the door, and walks away.

Barry's 1996 "Vision for America's First City" echoed the 1982 "reformation" in which Barry consolidated various agencies, created three deputy mayors, and diluted the power and effectiveness of the city administrator who, during his first term, had been considered too powerful. The 1982 plan connected his political machinery with the business community, guaranteeing cash for future elections. In 1996, because Rogers was in charge of implementing the plan, Barry once again had lined up his fall guy. If the proposal fell flat, for whatever reason, the mayor could turn the accusing finger away from himself.

Pulling off this transformation in 1996 would be difficult. Unlike 1982, when the bureaucracy was filled with able managers, Rogers was left with the dregs to turn around a government ten long years in poor condition. And not unlike the cancer that consumed Barry's prostate, whole parts of the District government had to be removed if the city were to survive. In 1982, Barry imprinted his seal on the government, insuring he possessed insider knowledge of every system and every agency. The District and Barry were welded. In 1996, he sought to do the same thing.

"We can no longer look elsewhere for our salvation. We must accept responsibility for acting where and when we can. To radically change our future, we must begin with ourselves," Barry said as he released the plan. A month later, in his "State of the District" address at the Lincoln Theater on 13th Street NW, he repeated the "bootstrap self-sufficiency" theme.

It was a masterful sleight of hand—even acrobatic. Once again, Barry rode two horses at the same time. But in his address, Barry dismissed such critical comments as faulty thinking. "It pleases my critics to believe I have undergone some conversion in values or gained a new attitude about government and people. They think that because I have done something they agree with, I have turned my back on who I am and what I stand for. While it is clear my actions are consistent with the values and service I have represented for thirty years, they choose to call it flip-flopping. I call it having a heart. These are times that require change," Barry said.

"Transformation is about changing what the government does and how it does it," he continued. "Transformation is about accepting a new responsibility for our public business. Transformation is about new ways to create personal opportunities for success…Government cannot sweep every sidewalk, hug every child, hire every worker, make everyone take their medicine, or dry every tear. But each person who became a true member of the community and is willing to carry their load can sweep all the sidewalks around the clock, catch every tear from the person suffering nearby, and love every child."

If Barry hadn't changed his values and principles, he certainly sang a different song, and the refrain sounded very Republican. But talking was never walking for Barry. For him, the axiom has always been, "Watch what I do and not what I say." He used language to test the public, waiting for its response before taking any action. And while Newt Gingrich hired a psychologist to aid him in his "Contract with America" movement, Barry, who understood black people in general better than himself, didn't need any assistance. He sailed without anchors or shipmates. In the District, he was the linguistic contortionist, offering zircon and calling it a diamond. He had so meshed illusion with reality that even he forgot the location of the boundaries. His reach for the transformation plan, his linguistic leaps to sound at one moment like a liberal Democrat, and the next like a conservative, reflected his desperation to right the wrong of his much-publicized arrest, conviction, and imprisonment.

"He does not [simply] want to be vindicated. He wants to get 1990 in another perspective, in his life and in history," James Gibson said. "If he can provide leadership in this circumstance, despite all negative presumptions, the lack of benefit of the doubt, and in the face of reluctant allies, he will have achieved his goal." Reaching for visionary documents was a frequent tactic of politicians in trouble. George Bush had tried in 1992 but was unconvincing. The "vision thing" wasn't easy for George Bush. It was nearly impossible for Marion Barry.

In politics, timing is everything. Like George Bush, Coleman Young, and Adam Clayton Powell, Barry's time had come and gone. Unconsciously, he sped his own demise. He had difficulty eliminating his empathetic ways, overcoming the opposition of a council where four members had designs on his job and others—including the media—conspired to evict him from office. But more than anyone, Barry was his own greatest enemy.

In April 1996, he confronted the same issues he had faced in January 1990, except now there was no FBI to contend with. Barry was again displaying a perverse aptitude for acting against his own best interest. Each time he neared his pinnacle, he stumbled, permitting his personal life to take priority over his professional life, or otherwise being recklessly impolitic. Two months after making a splash with his transformation report and proclaiming himself a fit leader, Barry's shadow self again emerged, and this time the city held its collective breath.

◆ ◆ ◆ ◆ ◆ ◆ ◆ ◆ ◆ ◆ ◆ ◆ ◆ ◆ ◆ ◆

Just days after Barry arrived in St. Louis, boxing promoter Rock Newman called a press conference. A pudgy, light complexioned African-American, Newman sported the Afrocentric clothing of a cultural nationalist. He had invested more than fifty thousand dollars in Barry's 1994 mayoral campaign, and served as chairman of his transition committee. More polished than Don King, Newman sought to bring class to the sport of boxing. But while he appeared less outrageous than King—he wore his hair slicked back against his balding head, not spiked like King—Newman exhibited the same street behavior found in the older fight impresario.

At his press conference, Newman read from a statement filled with as many innuendoes as Barry's had been: "For more than a year, sincere and caring friends have participated in a continuing dialogue, where we have constantly urged and insisted that the mayor maintain greater vigilance and responsibility for his health and recovery. Too often, these urgings have been ignored.

"Now, my brother is caught in the throes of a battle for personal survival. I pray that he is able to call upon a heretofore untapped source of strength to make some decision that will demonstrate leadership, character, humility, and faith in God. For I as his friend can no longer remain silent as I witness the personal unraveling of one of this nation's most committed public servants," Newman continued. "Privately, and now publicly, I appeal to Mayor Barry and our sister the First Lady to stop the maddening process towards relapse and personal destruction. Time has now shown that you cannot get well unless you release yourselves from the pressures that lead to behavior counterproductive to your pressing personal needs. There would be humor and survival to be had in your surrendering to a legitimate process of recovery and relapse prevention. To preserve your lives, you must fearlessly accept the truth of your circumstances and confront the demons that threaten your existence."

Then, responding to media questions, Newman said that, if necessary, the mayor should resign. He knew what others didn't—that on more than one occasion, Barry had actually relapsed—but despite intense media pressure, he did not reveal that information. His actions were a bold departure from the 1980s, when Barry's other friends saw him sinking into oblivion and failed to rescue him. They kept his nasty secrets even when it could cost him his life, to say nothing of his political career.

Newman's pronouncement was risky and shook the entire city. It wound up costing Newman his friendship with the District's first couple.

◆ ◆ ◆ ◆ ◆ ◆ ◆ ◆ ◆ ◆ ◆ ◆ ◆ ◆ ◆ ◆ ◆

When Barry returned to town, looking rested and tanned, he held a press conference in the community room at One Judiciary Square, surrounding himself with more than forty-eight government employees who represented levels 1,2, and 3 of his cabinet. The media, including local and national organizations, were confined to two small sections of the room. Barry Campbell, the mayor's chief of staff, opened the session, which had the air of a pep rally. City Administrator Rogers followed, talking of transformation and leadership. Then he introduced Barry, who strolled into the room with heightened importance as everyone, except the media, gave him a standing ovation.

The scene was reminiscent of Zairean dictator Mobutu Sese Seko, when he returned to Kinshasa after months away at one of his several palatial estates in Europe. A journalist by trade, Mobutu had begun his political career innocently enough, wanting to aid his people's development and rescue them from colonial terror. But suffering the misdirection that power often brings, he became everything he had previously detested. He raped Zaire of its resources, while striking fear into the citizens with his brutal army. In the end, he stashed away a reported six billion dollars in Swiss bank accounts—massive holdings for anyone, much less the leader of an impoverished country.

Like Mobutu, Barry and other African-American political leaders had arrived with good intentions. But they, too, became corrupt. Barry, for instance, continued to lead the District of Columbia, despite indisputable evidence he had ruined it.

In Zaire, during an attempted overthrow of Mobutu, African leaders began negotiating the leader's departure. In the District of Columbia, two groups of wealthy business leaders, fearing Barry might indeed become "mayor for life," as *Washington City Paper*'s Ken Cummings had once dubbed him, began to scout out job prospects for him. Some even approached the White House about a possible ambassadorship to one of the African nations. Like most cultural nationalists, Barry had a fascination with Africa, and during his fourth term as mayor, he made several trips to various nations on the continent, including South Africa and Nigeria. His trip to Nigeria, funded in part by the government of General Sani Abacha, drew fire from human rights advocates and from TransAfrica, which had been seeking stronger sanctions against Nigeria's oppressive military dictator and his government. But President Clinton didn't embrace the idea of an Ambassador Barry. Until 1997, he had refused even to be photographed with the mayor.

Then came proposals for an endowed university chair. Business leaders were willing to raise the money and make the necessary contribution to whatever university Barry chose. But when the effort of a group led by William Fitzgerald leaked to the press, all activity on this front ceased. Barry played insulted. Boasting of his academic credentials and his intellect, he said, "I don't need the help of my friends to find employment."

The night before the press conference, Barry's aides drilled him, posing questions various reporters might ask, including those about women whose apartments he had visited, and about his drug use. Once he was facing reporters, Barry didn't wait for their attack. He assaulted them, chastising them for their relentless pursuit of him as he sought rest, rejuvenation, and time to be with "his God." He accused them of reporting innuendoes that needlessly traumatized the city and for which there was no basis in fact. He denied use of drugs and argued that his only mistake had been assuming the press understood the process required by the Twelve-Step Program. He pledged to pay more attention to his health and spend fewer hours on the job.

And when asked about Newman's statement recommending resignation, he said only that he didn't understand what the boxing promoter was talking about. Barry effectively Mau-Maued the media, the way he had labor secretary Willard Wirtz. He had intimidated his attackers while presenting himself as the innocent. One week after his return, the cacophony surrounding the rejuvenation trip quieted. Still, Barry seemed on a Nixon-like mission to expertly slash his own wrists.

CHAPTER FOURTEEN

WHENEVER THE FIRES IGNITED, searing him and his administration, Barry retreated. Whenever he sought the edge, arriving ahead of his opposition, he advanced. Sometimes he wasn't sure whether to advance or retreat, and simultaneously did both.

In 1988, with the U.S. attorney for the District on his drug-using heels, Barry retreated to a meditation center in Neversink, New York, where he had his colon irrigated. When he returned to Washington, he was drinking corn-silk tea, which according to Global Health Limited's *Vitamin Herb Guide* is good for inflammatory conditions of the bladder, kidney, and urethra. (Cornsilk can also be used for hypertension, edema, stones, bedwetting, and an enlarged prostate.) Barry also conducted yoga exhibitions inside his office, and spouted New Age buzz words straight from an enthusiast's glossary.

But the previous year, in 1987, Barry advanced. Spending nine thousand dollars of city money, he and his cabinet met for two days in West Virginia, at the Coolfont Resort, to chart the course of action for his administration, which had come under fire. Barry also traveled to Miami, the Bahamas, and Chicago. It was hard to characterize these trips as either advances or retreats.

In 1996, Barry retreated, advanced, and explored, indicating a conspicuous state of confusion. Chaos seemed to consume not only Barry's young administration, but also the entire city, as the control board kicked into its first full year of operation, demanding budget cuts while eliminating popular youth and social programs.

A new phrase also became part of the Barry lexicon—"transformation," as in Transformation Plan. While Barry talked of a transformation, in reality his fourth-term administration retraced in practice and philosophy previous mayoral terms and earlier political positions. If lightning doesn't strike twice in the same place, the course of events beginning with Barry's 1995 vault into office produced a collective feeling of deja vu. The years 1996 and 1987 seemed identical, each beginning like the other, with a major snow storm which Barry's administration failed miserably to manage. Each escalated into accusations of drug use, investigations surrounding corruption, charges of mismanagement, and Barry's ever-evasive stance. In both years, Barry denied knowledge of any wrongdoing, while touting the achievements of his government even as it crumbled around him. District residents responded the same way each year. Whites became angry. Most blacks were hopeful but complained about "the establishment."

If Barry and the District repeated their own unhappy history together, Congress didn't do any better. When it created the control board in 1995, it repeated actions taken in 1874. That was the year Congress, spurred by Democrats' complaints, established a "temporary" three-panel commission to monitor the city. Although the entity of the 1990s was increased to five members and called a board, not a commission, it wielded the same powers as the 1874 body.

When Barry returned to Coolfont in the summer of 1996, he could have called the two-day meeting with his top-level managers there a retreat. The cancer surgery had left him "temporarily" impotent and suffering incontinence. He had experienced a "relapse" into drug use, fought a war of words with the control board, and suffered a slew of bad national press, including a series in *The Los Angeles Times* and *The New York Times*. And then, there was revelation of his relationship with "the Rev."

Weeks after his rejuvenation return, "the Rev." hit the front pages of *The Washington Post*. A slight, dark skinned African-American who resembled Charles Lewis, the Virgin Island bureaucrat who exchanged drugs with Barry during the 1980s, Rev. Roweshea Burruss exuded sleaze. In fact, he had been convicted of theft, writing bad checks, carrying a gun without a license, forging court documents, and conducting fake real estate deals. His own mother had filed a lawsuit against him, accusing him of coercing her to take a loan out against her house and the church her late husband founded. The Rev. needed the money to pay a debt and to stay out of jail. Why, given this sordid history, would Barry or any other respectable elected official choose to associate with him?

The thirty-five-year-old Burruss had known Barry since 1994, when he rented office space to the mayor's campaign committee. He and the mayor became chummy. "The mayor gets tired. He says, 'Rev, I'm coming over.' I say, 'Come on over because I'm cooking.' I love to cook. He comes over. We always talk about the youth, the programs…People act like the mayor can't have any friends," Burruss told *The Washington Post.*

The FBI raided Burruss' house on 12th Street NW in the spring of 1996—the second such law enforcement action in a year. In May 1995, answering complaints from neighbors about an after-hours party, District police burst into the Reverend's house. Burruss swore he wasn't operating an illegal nightclub, although people stood in long lines with tickets waiting to enter, a live band slapped out a mean beat, and a fully stocked bar served up shooters of gin and tonic. Exhibiting arrogance matched only by his friend's, Burruss took WRC-TV reporter Tom Sherwood on a tour of the facility. Nightclub-sized tables lined the wall. A drum set and piano huddled in a corner, and two commercial-sized refrigerators were plainly visible. Burruss claimed he conducted church services at the house.

Undoubtedly, police pounced on Burruss when they learned of his friendship with Barry. The FBI, collaborating with the U.S. district attorney, was still investigating charges of fraud and money-laundering emanating from the complaint filed by the Barrys' former housekeeper. The feds had been having a hard time penetrating the chain of secrecy encircling the first family. They had become desperate. If they couldn't break anyone in Barry's circle, they couldn't get to Barry. So they put the squeeze on Burruss, asking him about the mayor's possible drug use.

Barry didn't deny his alliance with Burruss, although he downplayed their involvement. He called Burruss "an associate," but disavowed any knowledge of his activities. Barry admitted stopping by the house to "change clothes" and "eat a sandwich." That comment caused tongues to wag. Why did the mayor of the nation's capital change clothes at another man's house, and have a sandwich, when there was a penthouse apartment just above his office, or he could easily travel the few miles chauffeur-driven to his southeast D.C. home?

Months after the raid and his arrest, Burruss was indicted on federal bank fraud charges. He was accused of masterminding an elaborate check writing scheme involving nearly $300,000. He and his associates deposited a check at one bank, then cashed it against an account at another bank. In total, they swindled three banks—NationsBank, Crestar, and Citizens Bank—out of as much as ninety thousand dollars. They also passed counterfeit checks. By year's end, Burruss was found guilty of these crimes and sent to prison. Barry escaped.

The Roweshea Burruss affair, together with the circumstances necessitating Barry's rejuvenation trip—the need to avoid a possible, 1990-like drug arrest—created a popular sense of impending doom. It also provided unsettling answers to a long-asked question in the District and around the world: Was Mayor Barry personally redeemed?

CHAPTER FIFTEEN

THE EROSION OF BARRY'S POLITICAL IMAGE began in earnest with the battle over Vernon Hawkins. A key organizer of the Loretto, Pennsylvania bus caravan, Hawkins played an active role in Barry's 1992 council race and 1994 mayoral campaign. As a reward, Barry presented Hawkins the directorship of the Department of Human Services, the city's largest agency, spending one-third of the District's $4.2 billion budget.

A monstrosity born during the era of program consolidation, DHS included three commissions—public health, social services, and mental health. Each year, millions of dollars in contracts and grants flowed from the department into the business and nonprofit communities. During the 1980s, DHS became Barry's pipeline to his machinery and to his coterie of friends, like Roy Littlejohn. Tens of millions of dollars went to Cornelius Pitts and other homeless shelter providers. Checks were mailed to nonexistent foster parents. And the creation of a community mental health network witnessed the eruption of questionable businesses, many with direct political links to Barry's administration. In fact, everyone who wanted to advance in the District found the right amount of money to donate to one of Barry's campaigns or one of his pet projects, thereby sending a clear message to the mayor about their ambitions.

During his earlier tenure, then-D.C. Auditor Otis Troupe released dozens of reports about contract corruption in DHS. He accused the agency of deliberately circumventing procurement laws by issuing emergency contracts to escape scrutiny. And while dozens of middle class African-Americans benefited from the contracts, the city's poor, also predominantly black, suffered the effects of a malfunctioning service delivery system. Children were hostage to an impaired foster care system, where caseworkers rarely made house calls and adoptions faced multi-year delays. Juveniles held in detention centers suffered rapes, indecent living conditions, and feeble educational instruction. The government was swamped with untrained or poorly trained managers who raised few questions and simply followed orders—no matter how absurd. By the mid 1980s, Barry symbolized the progressive failure of black leadership to improve the destitute circumstances of his constituency. The District became emblematic of urban dysfunction and DHS stood as poster child for management ills that spread like a California brush fire through the city government. By 1994, the agency, which Barry built, operated under several court orders. Later, the District's federal and local judges would seize control of foster care and mental health services.

In 1995, U.S. District Judge Thomas Hogan conducted a hearing about the city's foster care system. Spotting Hawkins seated in his courtroom, the judge couldn't help but comment that he had seen the tall, husky government bureaucrat before: "Now I have people back in place running the agency who were here when the agency collapsed several years ago…I don't know what people are thinking of," Judge Hogan said.

Hawkins joined the District government in 1965 straight from West Virginia State College. Initially, he worked for the Department of Corrections and then advanced to acting social service commissioner within the DHS. When Sharon Pratt Kelly came into office in 1991, Hawkins received a one-way ticket back to the corrections department. Until 1994, when Barry rescued his sagging career, a prestigious position had eluded the fifty-seven-year-old bureaucrat.

A personable guy, Hawkins proved a spectacular failure, although he surely believed otherwise. Still, the broad brush of blame couldn't bypass him. During his first year in office, his agency overspent its Medicaid budget, and ran the Receiving Home for Children in a manner that made it "unfit to house animals." According to a local judge, it had failed to provide heat for St. Elizabeth's Hospital, forcing the mentally ill patients there to sleep in their coats. And it had permitted decomposing bodies and roaches to take up permanent residence in the city morgue. Hawkins' DHS was stripped of its Medicaid funding for elderly patients at the D.C. Village Nursing Home, and the court appointed a special master to aid clients at Forest Haven. Ironically, the hammer slammed down on Hawkins not because of this litany of ills, but because he mishandled contracts!

Soon after CFO Anthony Williams joined the Barry administration, complaints were voiced that Hawkins' staff concealed the agency's overspending by postponing the entry of millions of dollars of bills into the city's computerized financial management system. Hawkins denied the allegation. Then Williams discovered that several hundred contracts had not been formally renewed, and that, consequently, the District was paying businesses and nonprofit organizations even though it lacked any legal arrangement with them. At the request of Williams and City Administrator Michael Rogers, the control board provided automatic extensions to select contractors, but instructed DHS to immediately negotiate new agreements by a specified deadline. Hawkins missed the deadline twice. Control board Chairman Andrew Brimmer and his staff considered Hawkins grossly incompetent, and asked that he be fired. Quietly, the board sought the mayor's concurrence, but Barry failed to act. The struggle escalated, gaining public attention. Rogers stepped in, urging the mayor not to delay. It was eminently clear to him that Brimmer would not abandon his position.

To keep the board from stripping the mayor of power, Rogers requested that Barry assign DHS's contracting responsibilities to his office. The mayor initially resisted. Finally, while on his rejuvenation trip, he acquiesced. But Rogers didn't pull the entire operation from DHS. Instead, he placed several of his own workers at the agency. They were forced to work with the same system that had yielded few significant results under Hawkins. Rogers' rescue mission didn't save Hawkins, but did authenticate the scope of the contracting problems at the massive agency.

Meanwhile, internal and external forces aligned themselves behind the "Dump Hawkins" movement. Williams told *The Washington Post*, "When you accept the mantle of authority in the District government, you accept a certain level of accountability. Vernon's got a lot of priorities. He's got to manage them. It's part of the job. If he's not managing them, you've got to find somebody else who can do the job."

Barry continued to stall, attempting to plot a surrender that retained his and Hawkins' dignity. But any control board watcher knew that Brimmer never stepped out in public unless he had the support of his members and had clearly made up his mind about his course of action. Unlike Barry, he didn't fire blanks. If he made a threat, he followed through with it. He told

Barry to get rid of Hawkins, or the board would exercise its own authority to fire him.

The standoff was reminiscent of a schoolyard scene where one kid dares the other to knock a wood chip off his shoulder. Barry couldn't resist. He ginned up his demagoguery engine, comparing the control board to the Nazi dictatorship—a comment roundly criticized by Jews, who perceived the mayor as making light of the Holocaust experience. Although he lacked the power to go against the control board, Barry couldn't simply abandon Hawkins without a fight. Hawkins had been his boy when everyone else had abandoned him. He was loyal, and nothing, absolutely nothing, mattered more to Barry than loyalty. Indeed, though it was hard to recognize, Barry's code of conduct was not too far removed from that of Mafia bosses, for whom one gesture of disloyalty was the kiss of death. With Barry, the code extended one way: He demanded everyone's loyalty, but he accepted no responsibility for returning it. He could shaft whomever he pleased, whenever he pleased, and not construe his actions as disloyal.

Although Barry denounced Sandra Allen when she decided to run for the seat he had left vacant on the council, he didn't consider *his* behavior traitorous. But, in his view, Allen had disrespected the hierarchical nature of the machinery. She had forgotten who was boss, and that all political decisions required the mayor's approval. Her superior qualifications were inconsequential to Barry. Nor did Allen secure any special treatment because she racked up highway miles travelling to visit him while he sat in a prison cell, pondering his self-destructive streak. Barry had even stiffed the Student Nonviolent Coordinating Committee, which sent him to Washington in the mid 1960s, essentially telling the leadership to kiss his derriere once his own political ambitions became his top priority. In the nation's capital, he tossed aside his allegiance to the group. He never confused his work for the people with his work for Marion Barry. When forced to choose, Barry always won the toss.

The battle over Hawkins became a public soap opera. Barry pleaded with the control board to keep Hawkins on the payroll. He wanted to assign him to another agency. Empathy clouded his vision, impairing his ability to understand that a major public loss would solidify the growing perception that he no longer ran the city he built. He had fought for months to protect the facade and, with Hawkins, he seemed willing to throw it all away.

Brimmer agreed to let Barry move Hawkins out of DHS and to another post, but for only ninety days, at which time the D.C. government veteran would have to resign or risk being fired. Hawkins took up residence at the Office of the Corporation Council, lingering longer than the requisite three months. Brimmer warned Barry that Hawkins' time was up. The aging bureaucrat finally said good-bye. Barry had suffered an indisputable defeat. It was the third one since the control board came into existence. He had been forced to move his budget director. He withdrew his initial selection for the city's official advocate of the handicapped—a position funded by federal dollars—after the control board intervened, urging HHS Secretary Donna Shalala, by letter, not to confirm the appointment. And now he had lost in the fight to hold onto Vernon Hawkins, his loyal DHS head.

The outline for his declining influence began to be filled in. Brimmer, always the autocrat, proved the control board would flex its muscles and not be bullied by Barry. Allies and members of Barry's cabinet, as if in a choreographed dance, stepped away from the executive almost in unison, psychologically shifting alliances that in future months served to undermine the mayor's potential effectiveness and diminish his stature.

◆ ◆ ◆ ◆ ◆ ◆ ◆ ◆ ◆ ◆ ◆ ◆ ◆ ◆ ◆

Undoubtedly his administration had to regroup, assess the damage to its flank, and design an assault strategy for the next phase of the war. Barry advanced by retreating to Coolfont. He brought in his friend Barbara Skinner to generate a sense of bonding among his cabinet members. He wanted them rededicated to his transformation plan, and without fully exposing his political intentions, Barry wanted to position himself to exercise an option on a fifth mayoral term. He signaled a change in the rules of engagement and a stepped-up pace for his reform agenda. Barry played defense for most of the year, a position at which he wasn't expert. But cabinet members also knew that he wanted to choose whether to run for re-election, and this meant two things: that there were no sacred cows, and that anyone could be sacrificed at the campaign altar.

Returning to the District, Barry launched his re-election program, visiting all the city's major print media organizations, including the alternative *City Paper*, explaining his budget and program plans for fiscal year 1997. Intent on distancing himself from himself, Barry shifted gears, seemingly affecting a major constituent base of District government workers. The union leadership saw the change coming. They anticipated a fight over worker benefits from the control board, but thought they could safely rely on the mayor's advocacy. True to form, however, Barry proved that his loyalty was ephemeral.

◆ ◆ ◆ ◆ ◆ ◆ ◆ ◆ ◆ ◆ ◆ ◆ ◆ ◆ ◆ ◆

The bank of elevators in the North wing was locked. Reporters and District government workers traversed the tenth floor labyrinth, hoping to reach Mayor Marion Barry's office on the eleventh floor of One Judiciary Square, where he had called a press conference. The lockdown was odd but deliberate. The aim was to prevent union leaders from intruding. They and the Barry administration were engaged in a low-pitched battle over the terms of new contracts.

Outside, in the bright autumnal sun, union representatives pranced around protesting what they called the mayor's unwillingness to negotiate. The mousy disturbance didn't affect Barry. He strolled into his office and sauntered to the microphone, accompanied by his spokesperson Raymone Bain, and by labor relations specialists Margaret Cox and Fran Thomas. Bain, dubbed the "Ed McMahon of the District" by WAMU-FM political analyst Mark Plotkin, performed her warm-up number, exclaiming, "Here's the mayor!" Dressed in a crisp, cream colored suit, flashing freshly manicured nails and tinted hair, Barry stood before a body of microphones, television cameras, and scribbling print reporters. The sheen of his skin projected the image of a man recently back from vacation, or unusually relaxed in his own body, but more vintage Barry than anything.

"There's been a lot of discussion about labor contracts," he said. "Everyone knows I have been a strong supporter of D.C. government employees and of workers' right to collectively bargain. So I am not a Johnny-come-lately to this situation. But my political support of unions notwithstanding, I have a legal responsibility to ensure [follow] the law." Preempting any charge that he was engaged in union busting, Barry offered an historical recitation of his latest tiff with union leaders. His fiscal 1997 budget called for canceling the optical and dental benefits for fourteen thousand unionized workers. Non-union workers had had those benefits snatched a long time before. As much as twenty-five million dollars of projected savings in the fiscal 1997 budget were at stake. Failure to achieve that goal severely injured the city's effort to balance its budget. Barry and his aides had hoped to get union leaders to the table to agree to the cancellation. But three days after the contracts expired, the unions and the administration didn't have an agreement. Consequently, Barry delivered on his threat: He pulled the benefits.

"Every day they don't come to the table is every day they don't get the benefits," Barry said confidently, unaffected by the flock of questions from reporters challenging his pro-union claim. "No amount of picketing, no amount of anything else, will get any benefits. I am dumbfounded by their strategy. The optical and dental benefits have been canceled, all because of the recalcitrance of labor leaders," he added. The word "recalcitrance" stuck on the roof of his southern mouth. And although his pronunciation was awkward, he repeated the word, over and over again, making a theme of it—the sound bite he wanted the media to grab for the six o'clock news, and to print in the morning papers. And the press would not disappoint. Unconsciously, they were accustomed to "Barryspeak" and connected with his jargon, almost as fellow propagandists, fellow linguists, fellow villagers who speak the same language.

"[This] is a moral position. It's a legal position." And to prove that once again he was ready to kick ass and take names, he told Michael Rogers to check and to make sure that picketing employees had been authorized to take leave. At the start of 1996, department of public works employees, protesting proposed budget cuts, picketed the control board's offices. That act forced the newly appointed "independent" inspector general to conduct an investigation of the rule breakers. She recommended that more than twenty persons be fired. But the mayor refused to fire anyone. Picketing the control board, he thought, is a whole lot different than picketing him, and union leaders had better make the distinction.

"If they take off [time from their jobs], they are not going to be paid. It's not personal. As mayor of this city, I have a responsibility to protect the financial plan and budget," Barry said. The press conference had nothing to do with employees' medical benefits. It was political theater at its finest. Despite the licking he had received weeks earlier at the hands of the control board, Barry was signaling that he was still in command. It was time to forget the cancer surgery, the relapse prevention junket, Roweshea Burruss, and Vernon Hawkins. Barry was back.

"It doesn't take the control board or Congress to tell me what to do. I know what we need and I'm going to be in front of it. I'm going to be leading the charge to change fundamentally how D.C. government operates," he insisted.

But Barry had a knack for stepping on his own toes, permitting some uncomfortable past episode to reappear, tripping him up, and endangering his future.

◆ ◆ ◆ ◆ ◆ ◆ ◆ ◆ ◆ ◆ ◆ ◆ ◆ ◆ ◆ ◆

Political observers, recognizing the preliminary campaign orchestration, knew Barry was testing his prospects for a fifth term. Fear struck the city's elite. They knew they couldn't beat him at the polls. If an election had been held at that moment in 1996, Barry, casting himself as a liberator, would have beat all comers. It was the same message that had always gotten him elected. Them versus Us: the poor versus the wealthy; black versus white; the establishment versus the outsiders; the District versus Congress; the control board versus the people. Barry had an organizer's skill at identifying and crystallizing the enemy in any scenario, even when it was pure fabrication.

The control board and Congress played into his hands. In November 1996, the five-member control panel demoted the elected school board, making its first major assault on Home Rule. While the move riled some residents, most welcomed the deliverance. The city's public schools were abysmal: Buildings were crumbling from want of an aggressive maintenance and replacement program. Students scored well below the national average on standardized tests. There were too many administrators and not enough teachers—all these problems existed while the city spent nearly nine thousand dollars per pupil, per year—almost two thousand more than that of surrounding jurisdictions. Emergency trustees were installed to substitute for the elected school board. The superintendent was fired and a retired army general named chief executive officer.*

In the middle of the school crisis, Barry departed for Seoul to promote business between South Korea and the District. Critics argued that Barry had become irrelevant. On his return, he shot back, enumerating areas where his imprimatur still mattered. "I am the only entity in Washington that can formulate the District's budget as an initiative, put forth programs and priorities," he boasted. But less than a year later, Barry's brag would seem like so much hot air.

To continue drawing boundary lines, Barry pointed to the control board's decision to cut spending at the city's only publicly subsidized college—the University of the District of Columbia. He cast the fight over UDC as one between the rich and poor, between blacks and whites.

The board also sought to eliminate funding for Barry's pet project, the Summer Youth Employment Program, while it increased funding for police and prisons. Singing the classic black politician's song, Barry accused the control board of emphasizing incarceration over education.

The electorate was all but silent, and everyone believed Barry's appeal had fallen on deaf ears. But the mayor knew people were listening and watching. He knew the control board had not made any tangible difference and that residents were growing disenchanted. While three council members had unofficially thrown their hats into the 1998 mayoral race, they weren't considered serious opposition for Barry, who could claim a solid third of the vote. Moreover, drastic measures had to be taken to dilute the Barry magnetism. To beat him once and for all, his critics had to completely erase him from the equation.

◆ ◆ ◆ ◆ ◆ ◆ ◆ ◆ ◆ ◆ ◆ ◆ ◆ ◆ ◆ ◆

In December 1996, the control board, which had refused to collaborate with the mayor on a plan of action, released its own "strategic plan," a weak document that was nothing more than an amalgam of dates —a fancy "to do" list. Realizing the fundamental banality of its plan, the board began its press conference by urging the federal government to assume various state-like functions performed by the District government. Barry had made the same request eighteen months earlier, concluding that the District lacked sufficient revenues to support itself. But he had been ridiculed. Now a presidentially-appointed panel issued the same statement. Using a Barry ploy, the board co-opted the mayor's position. Suddenly, Congress, the White House, and residents embraced the board's position. Barry attempted to lay claim to the headline: "I was the lonely voice in the wilderness," he said. But, in what might have been a shining moment for the mayor, the media and others denied him a reward for his early advocacy of the idea.

The Washington Times, for example, chronicled his call for a federal rescue plan. But, on the same front page, it ran another story. This one was on a U.S. Supreme Court test case over the constitutionality of requiring drug tests for candidates to higher office. The law was passed, Georgia officials said, because they did not want to "face the shame and enormous anguish that Barry's arrest produced in the District."

Months earlier, D.C. Delegate Eleanor Holmes Norton had proposed a fifteen percent federal flat tax for District residents and businesses. And the Brookings Institution stood poised to release an extensive study of the District's revenue structure conducted by Carol O'Cleireacain—the same woman Barry had turned down to be his CFO. The O'Cleireacain study also recommended that the feds assume state functions, to continue their annual payment to the District, calling it a "Payment in Lieu of Taxes," and to reduce the bevy of local taxes and fees imposed on residents and businesses.

Within weeks of the control board's announcement, the O'Cleireacain report was released. The Clinton White House, led by Office of Management and Budget director Franklin Raines, released a plan that embraced the essential features of the control board's proposal. Meanwhile, a group of civic, political, and business leaders calling itself the D.C. Agenda began an extensive review of the District government and its Home Rule Charter. The Federal City Council toyed with the notion of a city manager form of government, a move that would have neutered mayoral powers. The District's power center was shifting from Barry to another group of individuals. Not even the mayor's force of personality seemed sufficient to arrest the course of events.

CHAPTER SIXTEEN

Marion BARRY TOWERED OVER THE PANOPLY of microphones. Behind him, venetian blinds drawn on a bank of windows
obstructed his panoramic, eleventh floor view of downtown Washington. A
standard, cherry-finished desk that once sat in the far-right corner of his
office had been removed. Barry had rarely used it, conveying a discomfort
with at least this one trapping of power. Instead, he appointed his long conference table its substitute. A credenza anchored one end of that table, while
a television and VCR stood at the opposite end, allowing him to monitor
televised city council proceedings. Occasionally, during council debates,
Barry telephoned a member on the dais, instigating action or explaining
some obscure aspect of a bill that may have been puzzling lawmakers.

Unlike his predecessor Sharon Pratt Kelly, who maintained a stormy
relationship with the Council and couldn't find an ally among its thirteen
members, Barry understood the negotiating and massaging critical for securing legislative victories. In his previous administrations, his success rate
prompted some residents to dub the council a "rubber stamp." Undoubtedly,
the characters and climate at the council had changed since those early days,
but Barry still claimed the advantage. During the spring and summer of
1997, however, he experienced major losses. Collaborating with at-large
Republican council member Carol Schwartz, who opposed him in the 1994
General Election, Barry introduced a bill to restore capital punishment for
persons convicted of killing police and public safety officials in the city. The
measure never made it out of committee, although a *Washington Post* poll
found most of the District's African-American residents favored the death
penalty. The proposal demonstrated once again that Barry had his pulse on
the black community.

His version of personnel and procurement reform also took a hit. Its
passage by the city council came with significant compromise. And with the
advent of the control board, Barry's budget documents received greater
scrutiny.

More than a dozen red-cushioned, chrome-rimmed chairs in neat rows claimed the center of Barry's spacious office. African and African-American art, along with black and white photographs, graced the wall. Top-level personnel from the fire department and other cabinet members, including Barry Campbell, Bernard Demczuk, and Michael Rogers, huddled quietly. As chief of staff, Campbell technically served as Barry's in-house political operative. He was familiar enough with the District's political terrain, but he failed miserably at his job, often leaving his boss exposed on a series of volatile issues.

Demczuk, a former staffer with the Rev. Jesse Jackson's Rainbow Coalition and a former union organizer, unofficially retained his link with labor but officially honchoed the mayor's team of lobbyists who walked the halls both at the John Wilson Building, home to the local Council, and on Capitol Hill. While personable, sincere, and comfortable with common, ordinary people, Demczuk wasn't a savvy, sophisticated Washington lobbyist. Handicapped by the product he had to sell, he won few Capitol Hill allies for the cause.

Behind the scenes, during late spring and early summer of 1997, Rogers stalked professionals inside and outside the District government, hoping to persuade them to join Barry's cabinet. Several positions had gone vacant because local laws prohibited anyone from being paid more than the mayor, making it difficult to recruit the desired caliber of personnel manager. Barry won control board and city council approval to change the law, allowing him to wave higher salaries as bait. Immediately thereafter, Rogers tapped a federal Health and Human Services executive, Dr. Allan Noonan, to head the new health department, and Richard Malchow, an executive in New York State's transportation department, to lead D.C.'s troubled department of public works. (Malchow never began his tenure.)

Other major personnel changes were in the works, clearly telegraphing Barry's pre-campaign packaging. He intended to purge his administration of managers whose poor performance had made news headlines, installing less controversial and more efficient individuals in their places. Rogers, more than Barry, could turn his legendary diplomatic skills into a rhetorical AK-47, firing with precision at those who carelessly crossed his path. His talents were crucial to any re-election bid Barry might launch.*

Barry's press secretary Raymone Bain* stood in her usual position, a few feet away from the mayor, ready to provide a cool glass of water or a handkerchief. The mayor perspired profusely under the television cameras.

Everyone had come for Barry's regular Wednesday afternoon briefing. Although he often talked of his strained relations with the press, especially *The Washington Post,* Barry was usually quite accessible to reporters and editors. He adroitly manipulated some, fumbled with others, and enjoyed sparring with all. At the start of his fourth administration, in the spring of 1995, he launched what he called "Breakfast with the Press." But during the very first session, his wife, Cora, lashed out at *Post* reporter Yolanda Woodlee, who broke the story about the Barrys' housekeeper's charge of campaign money laundering, and implicating Walter Masters—Cora's brother. This brouhaha stopped Barry from scheduling another "breakfast."

Two years later, when he began the afternoon press briefings, everyone speculated that it was an offensive maneuver, that Barry had decided to run for mayor again in 1998. Consistent with the wholesale personnel changes, he had begun a re-imaging program. But he danced around the media inquiries about 1998 the same way he had in 1992, when he stood at the Johnstown Days Inn telling the crowd of elderly black men and women that he hadn't decided whether to run for office again, only to announce three weeks later his candidacy in the Ward 8 council race. Barry carefully stored his political cards in his breast pocket.

Normally, the afternoon briefing sessions were uneventful, consisting mostly of the mayor's response to news reports that may have appeared in local newspapers or broadcast over television and radio. Sometimes he announced new appointments, new programs, or other bureaucratic episodes of his government that proved much too difficult for the District's generally lazy press corps to translate into interesting stories. These mundane briefings offered a glimpse of Barry's lighter, more humorous side—the side that causes people like Elijah Rogers to describe him as a "really nice guy."

"He has a good sense of humor. A lot of people don't know or appreciate that," says Rogers. "In all the eighteen or nineteen years I've known the mayor, I don't ever recall the mayor using profanity." Still, no average guy was Barry. Despite all his charisma and warmth, he rarely let down the drawbridge. He was always "Mr. Mayor"—unless he trusted his interlocutor, and there were few, of course, who met that standard.

On July 30, 1997, when Barry stood before the mixed audience of press and government employees, he was tense and strident, exhibiting all the traits of his days as the street organizer who could send federal bureaucrats scurrying to find the only antidote to Barry's venom—money. He had just returned from a trip to South Africa, and the press had been unrelenting in its attack. There were questions about why he chose to take the trip, which was sponsored by former OIC founder Rev. Leon Sullivan, who had authored the "Sullivan Principle" calling for American corporations in South Africa to integrate their staffs. Barry and his wife flew to Africa at the summit sponsors' expense.

Two other government employees paid their own way. African-American leaders from around the country, including the control board's Chairman Andrew Brimmer, made the trip, hoping to strike cooperative and financially lucrative relations between American blacks and those blacks in the resource-rich countries of Southern Africa. Stories about lost baggage and the hotel in which he stayed appeared in the two dailies. Barry rightly chastised the press for its myopia, failing to report on the groundbreaking nature of the summit.

A two-part series on the mismanagement of the District government, by *Washington Post* metro reporter Michael Powell, also ignited Barry's anger. While Powell's discourse offered a useful comparison, it provided dated information and, said Barry supporters, failed to sufficiently incorporate real, tangible improvements made by the Barry administration. The articles appeared during the weekend preceding a critical congressional hearing. They provided sufficient ammunition for several Republicans then firing at the Barry administration. Early in 1997, President Clinton had introduced legislation to provide much-needed financial and programmatic assistance to the District, stimulating congressional and citywide discussion about the future of the nation's capital. A volatile environment existed, comparable to that which preceded the creation of the financial control board.

Even before the two-day *Post* series ran, however, Sen. Lauch Faircloth, a North Carolina Republican, had called for changing the District government from a "strong mayor" system to one which required the appointment of a city manager. Two dozen angry residents, reading Faircloth's comments in local newspapers, stormed his office demanding an audience. The stand-off humbled Faircloth, but it did not dissuade him. When the *Post* articles appeared, Faircloth, chairman of the subcommittee on District appropria-tions, photocopied and circulated them throughout the Senate, building opposition to legislation designed to provide substantial financial assistance to the District unless management reforms were made a part of the package.

Under a "council-mayor-manager" form of government, all powers would rest in the legislative branch. The mayor would sit as chairman of the Council. The manager, hired by the council, would be responsible for the daily functions of the government. The relationship would be much like that of a chief executive officer and his board of directors. A city manager could be fired at any time by the council. The theory was that a skilled professional manager should operate the government while policy and politics remained the domain of elected officials. The District, many believed, suffered its ignoble fall because it lacked skilled, seasoned managers and because there had been too much political interference from the mayor, city council, and the elected D.C. Board of Education. Once, for example, when the superinten-dent considered closing underutilized District schools, the process devolved into a territorial battle, with school board members fighting one another.

In fact, the District's youthful government had failed to groom a cadre of individuals who could assume the mantle of leadership. Even less avail-able were politically-minded persons who also possessed superb management skills. This alone justified Faircloth's call for a city manager. He unsuccessfully auditioned several methods for establishing the city manager form of government. The manager would be appointed by the president and approved by Congress. Or Congress would appoint and approve the city manager. Or the mayor would appoint the city manager and the local city council would approve him.

Back in 1989, the instigator of a city manager form of government came not from the Senate but from the House. Elijah Rogers, the city admin-istrator from Barry's first term, shot down the idea in an article published in the *Washington Post* 's "Close to Home" section. After listing several reasons for his opposition, Rogers concluded, "A council-manager may not be the appropriate model for the District and may turn out to be a colossal flop if it were tried without full Home Rule. No city manager runs anything as programmatically, environmentally, legally, structurally, and fiscally complex as D.C.

"The government and its programs would become extremely Balkanized," Rogers continued, "and the position of city manager could become a revolving door. Instability, strife, and drift could be the order of the day."

He did not say so, but city managers had been successful in several major cities, including San Antonio and Dallas. Rep. Henry Bonilla, a Texas Republican, ignored Rogers' commentary, and drafted 1994 legislation that would impose a city manager on the District. But he held off introducing it in deference to the control board. The D.C. Agenda, which had conducted its own series of seminars on the city's governance structure, declined to recommend any changes to the Home Rule Charter, although the data clearly indicated the shift would produce far superior results than what the District had seen during the previous decade.*

Eleanor Holmes Norton, following Rogers and, more recently, the D.C. Agenda, overreacted to Faircloth's renewed and unrelenting call for a city manager. She sent out hysterical signals, causing local elected officials and key civic leaders to characterize the proposal as an attack on Home Rule, and vowed to fight it. As a compromise, Norton submitted—in the form of a memorandum to Faircloth—an alternative proposal to create reform committees, comprised of the mayor, a representative from the city council, the control board, the head of each of the District's nine most troubled government agencies, and expert management consultants. Faircloth liked Norton's plan, but in the dead of night, his staff tacked on clauses that gave the control board complete authority over those nine agencies. The amendments also set out nearly impossible deadlines to select directors and consultants, and to produce reports to Congress that outlined reform agendas. Norton allegedly didn't see the language until the next day—after the Senate vote. She had been too worried about the financial portions of the National Capital Revitalization and Self-Government Improvement Act.

Under the measure, passed and signed into law in August 1997, the federal government assumed control of the Lorton prison and the city's court system. The federal Medicaid contribution increased from fifty percent to seventy percent. The federal government also picked up the unfunded pension liability it transferred to the District at the start of Home Rule and proposed providing about $300 million in federal tax reductions and incentives.

But the act robbed the District of an annual federal subsidy of $660 million, paid to the local government in lieu of taxes. More than forty percent of the vacant land in the city was owned by the federal government, and local officials were forced to exempt it from both taxation and any form of development. Moreover, Congress maintained restrictions on the height of buildings in the District, and the city's ability to tax commuters and organizations such as the Federal National Home Mortgage Association (known as Fannie Mae), and the World Bank. The tax restrictions alone denied the District more than half a billion dollars a year in revenue.

The act's fiscal shortcomings didn't stoke Barry's ire. But he was visibly angry on July 30th about the authority that had been stripped from the office of Mayor. The federal legislation enhanced the control board, giving it the power to hire and fire District agency directors, who, according to the Home Rule Charter, were members of the mayor's cabinet. The board's ability to direct the reform agenda meant it now officially and more directly set public policy—a power coveted by any elected official. Barry was unprepared for and shocked by the Congressional savaging.

Norton had convinced him and the council that she had everything under control. She had encouraged Barry to take his trip to Africa, advising him to leave negotiations on the final recovery legislation to her. After all, his presence couldn't add any currency to the city's position. For all intents and purposes, Barry remained a pariah on Capitol Hill, more tolerated than welcomed. His relationship with Gingrich had deteriorated within months after the two started referring to each other as "political soulmates." Jack Kemp, who had offered various proposals for rescuing the District, stepped away, working more closely with Norton. The Congressional Black Caucus, which unanimously supported imposition of the control board, voted for the National Capital Revitalization and Self-Government Improvement Act. The caucus had been urged by Norton to support the legislation, not realizing that the Senate, following Faircloth's lead, would strip Barry of significant power. Because Rep. Julian Dixon, a California Democrat, had effectively turned cool to the District, viewing it—like Republicans—as a city out of control and sorely mismanaged, it was unrealistic to believe that Democrats or the Black Caucus might fight to get the city money and keep Congress out of the local government's daily affairs.

Norton herself continued to maintain good relations with the White House and Speaker Newt Gingrich. But her deftness as an intermediary had been grossly overstated. She sustained a significant loss during negotiations surrounding the creation of the control board when she failed to secure a seat on the panel for Barry or any other elected official. She proved unsuccessful in getting the White House to restore to its legislative proposal the annual $660 million federal payment, desperately needed by the city—at least during the first year of the five-year recovery program.

Norton also lost during budget negotiations in 1996, and was forced to run to Gingrich for relief from Congressman James Walsh, who wanted to append forty-one restrictive amendments to the city's appropriations legislation. Despite these setbacks, she and others somehow were convinced that during the intense and cantankerous talks surrounding hundreds of millions of dollars in federal aid and District assets, she could dramatically influence the turn of events. This was naive, especially for a non-voting member of the House.

But Barry believed it and paid dearly with the loss of basic executive branch powers. He couldn't reshuffle the deck to pretend a Jack was a King. Afterward, he faced a considerable dilemma. If he lashed out at Congress or the control board, he would further tar himself as culprit for the city's abysmal financial and managerial condition. If he allowed events to take their course, he couldn't legitimately claim credit for any improvements, corroding a potential platform for any 1998 mayoral bid. He appeared to be in a lose-lose situation.

Barry's circumstance paralleled that of Jason Warfield, the fictional founder and leader of Quad A. In his book *Faces at the Bottom of the Well: The Permanence of Racism,* author Derrick Bell has Warfield saying in a radio interview: "Militant black leadership is like being on a bomb squad. It requires confidence in your skills and a courage able to survive the continuing awareness that you're messing with dynamite, but that someone has to do it. One mistake, and you're gone! Sometimes you're gone whether or not you make a mistake."

Barry ingeniously played his hand: At the July 30th press conference, he read an incendiary statement, deflecting criticism of his historic mismanagement of the city and his foibles: "The Republican Party's history has not supported full freedom, full democracy, and full self-determination for the residents of the District of Columbia. If you look back to 1973...there were only a handful of Republicans who supported [Home Rule].

"When you look forward at the 1994 District budget, you will find that only thirteen Republicans, including Newt Gingrich, supported the District...The majority of Republicans, at every chance they get, will work to take power from these local officials.

"The people who want to make this a Marion Barry problem need to look at all of this a bit closer. Marion Barry had nothing to do with Eleanor Holmes Norton losing her right to vote. Marion Barry had nothing to do with the elected members of the D.C. Council being stripped of their power.

"Again, all of these actions confirm the majority Republicans' desire to seize control of this city by diminishing full self-government and self-determination...Prior to 1973, this colonial attitude on the part of some members of Congress was at its heyday. We have come full circle...Recolonization is being promoted by several key members of the Republican Party," Barry continued.

"Senator Faircloth, who has led the effort to re-colonize the citizens of the District, has raped Democracy and freedom. Those who would do this will have to at some point pay the political price."

Barry knew his language would agitate long-time statehood advocates and cultural nationalists. He accurately offered a view of continued congressional oppression while titillating racial concerns. Gingerly and subtly, he raised the specter of race, the way he had in 1996 when he accused D.C. Council member Kathy Patterson of wanting to deny poor District residents a right to an education. Patterson, a white representative of affluent Ward 3, had proposed—along with other council members—closing the University of the District of Columbia.

The city could ill afford a state educational institution, they said. Besides, the school did not offer a superior undergraduate education. On this criticism they were a bit unfair, failing to fully appreciate the fact that UDC, as an open-admission school, was obligated to accept all comers. Despite a large remedial program—the deplorable state of District elementary and secondary schools each year destined many high school graduates to remedial English and Mathematics courses—UDC boasted an extremely high graduation rate.

Although Barry refrained from using the words white and rich to make Patterson the object of his criticism, insiders trained in "Barryspeak" knew what he meant. A few months later, Barry held a "Day of Dialogue" aimed at promoting racial and class healing in the city. Patterson was invited, but the damage had already been done.

At the press conference, Barry's veiled threat reminded everyone of 1994, when voters, remembering the 1990 FBI sting and media rejoinders, tossed logic to the wind, returning to office a recovering addict who, during his last term, had mismanaged the city spectacularly.

Barry—the master manipulator, the expert political packager—intended to couch the summer and fall events of 1997 to his benefit. And playing the race card was one of the most effective weapons in his arsenal. The District had engaged in a quiet racial war most of its life. It had been a place where blacks were auctioned as slaves to the highest bidder, or transported to other slave-holding states. When the local government abolished slave trading, many resident blacks and those who were to find their way to the nation's capital still were met with hostility. City blacks received the right to vote in the middle 19th Century. When the government ran into problems between 1868 and 1874, Negro Suffrage was blamed for the District's mismanagement, although Negroes represented less than twenty-five percent of those serving in the city's elected offices. In 1919, the city had race riots. Until 1974, when the District received Home Rule, white congressional representatives, none of whom had been elected by the city's predominantly black population, ran the nation's capital.

History would not deny the District its racial animosity. Barry merely continued a tradition wrought by the city's own past and a brand of racial and ethnic politics eagerly practiced throughout America by people like Chicago's Richard Daley, Boston's James Michael Curley, and New York's Adam Clayton Powell. But while Powell delivered to his constituents throughout much of his career, Barry produced mixed results. Although he had successfully used jobs and contracts to expand the black middle class, he had failed to go beyond that patronage system to sustain economic growth. In fact, much of the District's economic power remained in the hands of whites. This, combined with the decline of his government beginning in 1986, begged the question—at least in the District—of whether blacks were being empowered by the election of other blacks, especially in Marion Barry's case.

By 1987, Barry became the logotype of "failed black leadership." Middle income residents, black and white, fled the city in droves. Some wanted to escape the District's escalating crime, its dirty, pot-hole-riddled streets, and its deplorable public education system. But not all the outward migration could be attributed to Barry and the mismanagement of his government. In all fairness, blacks had finally arrived in the middle class, and like their white counterparts, they wanted big houses, two-car garages, fresh air, and better schools for their kids.

In 1995, Barry genuinely sought to alter his image as a "do-nothing" who had run the city into ruin. But without solid, consistent media reportage, the perception persisted that corruption, waste, fraud, and abuse ran rampant in the District government. The past is an awesome force. It commands recognition, despite attempts to eviscerate it—and a compelling longevity that invites re-interpretation. Thus, many African-Americans— especially the District's poor and disenfranchised—remember Barry's past administrations fondly, perhaps because, in some way, they were empowered by his bravado, even if he failed to provide them adequate municipal services. Whites, by contrast, were imprisoned by the past. With the specificity of Frank Seymour retelling Loretto, Pennsylvania's history, they recounted the inadequacies of Barry's terms in office. They were unable to open the blinds on a new day, forcing the city to become a Barry jail-mate. Consequently, *The Washington Post* could publish the results of a District poll in which black and white views were antithetical: Whites thought the control board was doing a good job, blacks didn't. Whites didn't trust Barry; blacks did.

Without any exertion by the mayor, the media's political coverage of Barry in 1997 was seen the same way as it had been in 1990, 1992, and 1994—as determined by "the white establishment." By passing self-government legislation, Congress unwittingly provided yet another opportunity for Barry to pass under the cloak of "them against us." The issue of democratic rights became inexorably linked with him, obscuring the performance of his past and present administrations. The city's complex situation evolved into a series of overlaid mazes, none ever producing an escape route. A mostly white Congress blamed Barry for the circumstances in which the city found itself. Others accused Congress, which was bewildered by Barry's 1994 election, and intent on exacting revenge. By robbing Barry's office of essential powers, Congress set him up for renewed martyrdom, similar, though less dramatic to the FBI's efforts in 1990. It primed the landscape for a 1998, fifth term victory for Barry, if he chose to run.

Shrewdly, Barry refused to answer any questions at the July 30, 1997 press conference about his political plans, and he deflected opportunities to lambaste Norton for her failure to negotiate acceptable terms with Congress. The following Friday, during WAMU-FM's "Derek McGinty Show," Barry pledged to cooperate with the control board. Although Congress had tried to emasculate him, Barry was publicly playing the role of conciliator, the good civic leader taking responsible action. He told McGinty and WAMU's political analyst Mark Plotkin that he intended to work with the board to insure that management reforms were implemented. His placating tone befuddled reporters, but Barry had to hold out the olive branch, even if he intended to shred it within the next ten minutes. For him, it was another, perverse variation of landing the first blow.

By playing the innocent, he put the control board on the defensive. If it did not respond in kind, Barry could say he had tried to be cooperative and that the control board carried "white folks' water." Privately, Barry egged on his camp of supporters, together with statehood activists enraged by Congressional inaction on their aging proposal. Already they were devising plans to conduct demonstrations and other forms of civil disobedience. Barry claimed not to have participated in the planning. In fact, he did know the blueprint, although he hadn't seen its details.

On August 4, 1997, as Barry met with Control Board Chairman Andrew Brimmer, demonstrators led by Umoja Party Chairman Mark Thompson, and Democracy First Chairman Tim Cooper, staged a demonstration in front of the White House. More than three hundred persons walked the picket line shouting "No Justice, No Peace," and "No Taxation Without Representation." Thirteen demonstrators were later arrested. Before the end of September, numerous other acts of civil disobedience were staged. Buses of more than four hundred District residents departed for North Carolina to join with local citizens in a massive protest outside Sen. Faircloth's home.

Later, on September 3, 1997, with Congress reconvening after its summer recess, more than a thousand residents, including students from Howard University and the University of the District of Columbia, rallied on the steps of the U.S. Capitol. Nationally-known activists, such as Dick Gregory and the Rev. Jesse Jackson, appeared with other civil-rights and elected leaders, including Congressional Black Caucus Chairman Rep. Maxine Waters, a California Democrat. Days later, the Rev. Al Sharpton, former New York mayoral candidate and civil rights activist, picketed the Dirksen Senate Office Building.

Barry left the meeting with Brimmer on August 4 believing two things: that there would be collaboration, and that the control board would refrain from using all its power. But the characters Anansi once fooled had learned a few tricks of their own.

♦ ♦ ♦ ♦ ♦ ♦ ♦ ♦ ♦ ♦ ♦ ♦ ♦ ♦ ♦ ♦

A long folding table, draped with white cloth, replaced the altar customarily used for Sunday services at Luther Place Memorial Church. Located at Vermont Avenue NW near 14th Street, the church had an aggressive ministry of social activism, operating a homeless shelter and building several transitional housing units for women and families. It also served during the early 1990s as the meeting site for more than a dozen ministers who vehemently opposed the death penalty, then being pushed by Sen. Richard Shelby after the murder of one of his aides in downtown Washington, D.C. In 1996, when the five member control board orchestrated a hostile takeover of the District's elected school board, the church opened its doors to the control board for a meeting. Control board members and staff believed holding the meeting in the church would defuse possible violence.

With the public schools, there was a major underlying problem—they were in unfathomable disarray. A study conducted by the control board found that the longer a child stayed in District public schools, the worse the child performed academically. With that kind of record, most citizens welcomed radical action, hoping it would end the District's culture of educational failure. Amidst turmoil over passage of the National Capital Revitalization and Government Self-Improvement Act, the control board returned to Luther Place to hold its public meeting. Its plan was to pass resolutions implementing aspects of the law.

Unclear until the last minute was where the meeting would be held. Initially, the board announced the site as the Martin Luther King Jr. Memorial Library on 9th and G Streets Northwest. The library had become the standard location for the board's meetings. However, on Tuesday August 5, 1997, news articles published in the daily papers indicated the Luther Place Memorial Church as the meeting location. Protest planners were stuck stationing one part of their group at the library and another at the church—just the kind of thing Barry might have done.

But when they knew for sure the church was the place to be, the demonstrators at the library walked the dozen blocks to Luther Place. Brimmer already had begun the meeting when they stormed into the building. When the group reached Brimmer, he stood, pleading with them to be silent. A look of befuddlement crowded his face as he tried to determine what to do. The protesters who had disrupted the meeting were angrily reading a letter demanding that the board adjourn. Finally, Brimmer called in the police. The Special Tactics Unit of the Metropolitan Police Department charged in as if it were breaking up a riot instead of a small demonstration of three dozen residents. The church became a battleground instead of a sanctuary. Officers violently pushed protesters from the risers, pulled a wheelchair-bound citizen onto the main floor, and knocked an elderly man to the ground, tussling with him as they handcuffed him. "Look at that! It looks like old South Africa," cried Clifford Lee, a thirty-year District resident who attended the meeting. The entire melee was captured by television cameras. By the time it was all over, twenty-three persons were arrested. The control board's meeting proceeded as planned.

But Brimmer reneged on his arrangement with Barry. Rather than confine its action to reforms, the board voted unanimously to assume complete and absolute control of the nine troubled District agencies cited in the federal legislation. By the end of the meeting, Barry had lost authority over most of the District government. What the control board didn't take, the courts already had through lawsuits and receiverships. Barry, outsmarted by the autocratic, stuffed-shirt Brimmer, called the board's actions "shameful." Unabashedly proud about outwitting Barry, Brimmer boasted to the press that he had told the mayor who to name as temporary heads of the nine agencies, and not the other way around, as Barry had indicated during a press conference earlier that day.* That prompted a rebuke of Brimmer from *Post* columnist Colbert King, one of Barry's staunchest and most consistent critics. He said it "was no way to treat a mayor, especially one who had already been publicly, unceremoniously, stripped of his epaulets by Congress."

It had been a tumultuous two weeks in the nation's capital. But all of it—the control board's greedy power grab, the police aggressiveness at the board's public meeting, and the *Post*'s admonishment of Brimmer—played right into Barry's game plan.

◆ ◆ ◆ ◆ ◆ ◆ ◆ ◆ ◆ ◆ ◆ ◆ ◆ ◆ ◆

One week after Congress passed the National Capital Revitalization and Self-Government Improvement Act, Barry unofficially launched his 1998 re-election campaign. He conducted an impressive media blitz, appearing on several local television stations and national network programs, including NBC's "Today" and ABC's "Nightline." The local newspapers made much of his "Nightline" appearance, because the show featured a segment in which Barry used his car's emergency siren to speed him through rush-hour traffic to a tennis game. But many African-Americans in the city dismissed the implied critique. They liked the idea of a black man able to move other cars to the side so the mayor could pass. Some remembered living in the deep South, when they or their parents had had to step aside to let a white person pass on the sidewalk or the road. What others might condemn as the mayor's excess, poor African-Americans saw as one of their own finally "arriving" in a country that for years had kept them under its thumb.

Articles about Barry's assault on Congress also appeared in newspapers around the country, including *The Los Angeles Times* and *The Times-Picayune* in New Orleans. The mayor called on the NAACP, the National Urban League, Blacks in Government, and the National Council of Negro Women to join in the fight to return Democracy to the District. And while these prestigious black organizations lent their names to the struggle to return to the mayor's office powers stripped away by Congress, they also added credibility to the resurrected Marion Barry. Not surprisingly, Barry didn't seek support from the American Civil Liberties Union. Nor did he approach any predominantly white organizations. The fight was becoming more definitely one of blacks versus whites. Dwight Cropp once said of Barry that "every time he's besieged, he plays the race card."

By the end of the first week of Barry's media assault, Norton and Rep. Tom Davis, the Virginia Republican whose subcommittee crafted the House version of the legislation, were shuttling between the control board and Barry trying to work out an acceptable arrangement. The White House's point person, OMB Director Franklin Raines, chastised Congress for even including the management reform amendments, and the control board was deciding how to take a more diplomatic approach to dealing with Barry.

Round one belonged to Barry: He offered the control board a glimpse of the trouble he could cause if there was any attempt to completely isolate him. By cloaking the battle in racial terms, he embarrassed President Clinton and his administration, which months earlier had launched a "national dialogue" to promote conversations and healing among the country's various racial groups. Such racial tension right under the president's nose did not augur well for building a legacy around racial harmony.

◆ ◆ ◆ ◆ ◆ ◆ ◆ ◆ ◆ ◆ ◆ ◆ ◆ ◆ ◆ ◆ ◆

The fight between District residents, Barry, the control board, and Congress couldn't have been more propitious for the mayor. The elements fell into place, almost as if Barry had orchestrated the entire play. And perhaps he had. At times, he seemed to be reading from a book only he could translate, puzzling many with his reactions. But he knew Congress would never be satisfied until he had been permanently dethroned. Like a poker player, he watched and waited. He strategically drew and discarded, separating himself from the control board. He would play his hand later, making a chronological defense of his efforts to respond to his constituents and to redeem the District.

Barry could point to his effort to save the University of the District of Columbia, which was forced by the control board to sell its jazz radio station, a city landmark. He could mention the $10 million in economic development funds he sought to add to the 1997 budget for poor communities east of the Anacostia River.

And while the control board cut it out, Congress, in an economic tax incentive program written into the self-government improvement act, cited poor neighborhoods as the beneficiaries of its plan. Barry could say that Congress' action in that regard reaffirmed the wisdom of his budget plan. He could talk about the summer job program, and studies that proved structured activities reduce the incidence of crime.

Barry could also legitimately claim credit for changes in the police department. He had begun the first discussions about "zero tolerance" when he and his police chief Larry D. Soulsby agreed on a model that duplicated—at least in construction—the successful crime-fighting plan implemented in New York City. He did this well before the control board, using its authority, yanked the police department from the mayor's supervision, placing it in the hands of a so-called "memorandum of understanding" partnership. The MOU partnership included representatives from the council, the courts, the U.S. attorney's office, the mayor, and the control board. By the end of 1997, police reform had turned to charges of police corruption and three separate investigations were launched.

The litany of changes Barry had ushered in would be enough to keep his base of disenfranchised and poor voters happy. And even some middle-class residents, the ones who frowned upon congressional intervention, might lend a hand to any banner Barry lifted in 1998. But the election was nearly a year away; he had to continue carving the division he sought.

Three weeks after he was virtually stripped naked of power, everyone thought he might quietly die in his corner. After all, Barry even lacked authority over his own cabinet. He held the reins of a few agencies: the libraries, the office of tourism, and the department of recreation. But a spider can entangle his enemies quicker than they can kill him.

At his regular Wednesday press briefing on August 20, 1997, Barry announced he had authorized an extension of summer hours for all recreation departments. His action followed a decision by D.C. Public Schools Chief Executive Officer Julius Becton to delay by three weeks—until September 22—the fall opening of all public schools. The school administration decided in July to begin roof repairs on forty schools, not anticipating that D.C. Superior Court Judge Kaye Christian would bar anyone from entering the school buildings until the work was completed.

Parents United, a citywide advocacy group, had sued the school system. That lawsuit led to a three year battle, which in 1995 and 1996 caused some schools not to open on time. School CEO Becton decided that, rather than stagger openings, he would keep all school buildings closed. Parents, many without other child-care options, were enraged. They demanded that the school system provide alternatives. And they insisted that Becton had been derelict in his duties. Where parents had initially praised him and the control board, they now were calling for the retired general's resignation and lambasting the control board. Barry's decision to extend recreation department summer programs and hours received widespread support. Even the *Post* lauded his efforts. The potential sticking point in his proposal was this: the control board would have to approve a $400,000 reprogramming of funds.

The control board now faced a major dilemma. If it refused the mayor's request, parents would be further angered by the board's insensitivity. If it approved the proposal, providing even partial funding, Barry could claim victory, and use it in his 1998 campaign literature. His lose-lose predicament had metamorphosed into a win-win opportunity. It was a stroke of genius, and accomplished in just three weeks.*

Barry stood hobbled, stripped of most of his power and authority, but refusing to retreat. The powerful voice of his band of protesters was reduced to a whimper. The press lost interest in Barry, focusing more day-to-day on the control board, where daily operations and municipal power now lay. Barry pranced around, attending ribbon cuttings, giving opening remarks, introducing Etta James at the annual Taste of D.C. Festival, and making other inconsequential, empty gestures and appearances. Though neutered of his fundamental powers as mayor, Barry was posturing as the man in charge. The multitude simply ignored him, and his friends pleaded with him not to run for a fifth term.

BARRY during an emotional moment at his 1995 mayoral inaugural

Barry with fourth (and current) wife CORA MASTERS
BARRY, considered a powerful and strategic force behind
Barry's political comeback in the District

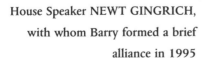

House Speaker NEWT GINGRICH,
with whom Barry formed a brief
alliance in 1995

AND THE EMPEROR HAD NO CLOTHES

· PART FOUR ·

Chapter Seventeen

IN 1994, TWO YEARS AFTER RETURNING from prison, a newly elected Mayor Marion Barry seemed the perfect subject for a tale of redemption—one that cast the former civil rights activist as a victor unfazed by the predominantly white power establishment, and destined to leave a celebratory and remarkable legacy on his adopted home town. By 1998, that story had shifted dramatically. At the end of his fourth term, Barry had reversed his own fortunes. He had become like nearly every other African-American politician from his and the previous generation, including Adam Clayton Powell, Gus Savage, Charles Diggs, Richard Hatcher, and Coleman Young. The man who had arrived in the nation's capital in 1965 to lead a liberation movement had, by 1998, contributed greatly to its recolonization and to the renewed victimhood of its residents.

What's more, Barry, as a peripatetic, ineffective mayor, became emblematic of the crisis in the nation's black leadership, the growing impotence of race-based politics, and the unfortunate decline of the American political system.

How had this happened? The road to ruin, few realize, began long before Barry's 1994 mayoral resurrection. In truth, it was already in progress in 1979, the year Barry became the District of Columbia's second elected mayor. African-Americans of the time may have believed that electoral enfranchisement would lead them to economic parity with whites, but political success nationally already had been thwarted by misdirected intentions, personal greed, and blatant devaluation of the civil rights battle. Many politicians, some with only tangential connections to the civil rights movement, were giving a bad name to a cause that had annihilated Jim Crow laws while permitting African-Americans full participation in the country's democratic system.

"Leadership after passage of the Voting Rights Act became leadership that stopped taking its cues from black people, stopped making decisions based on what black people wanted to do, and instead became leadership on the basis of what could be extracted from white people," says Charles E. Cobb Jr., a former member of the Student Nonviolent Coordinating Committee.

Put in starker terms, Barry had become like his political peers—a chief purveyor of African-American-extortionist politics. By squeezing whites for as much as possible, he helped redefine the civil rights movement. During the 1950s and 1960s, blacks, especially those in the deep South, did not flinch in the face of fire hoses, the Ku Klux Klan, and white citizens councils. They stood their ground as state police officers with attack dogs protected white domain over restaurants, businesses, transportation, schools, and just about every other service.

In those days, the essence of the civil rights movement was "black self-help." African-Americans, refusing to wait for the government to act, took up their own cause. They displayed a fundamental understanding of their own economic power, advocating boycotts against bus companies and against retailers who discriminated against them. Blacks of that era showed a keen appreciation for the strength of united communities, often providing living arrangements for out-of-town activists—sometimes at personal risk and sacrifice. By words and actions, they repeatedly told the world they were prepared to stand up and do for themselves.

But the love-hate relationship with whites, born of extortion and carried on by Barry and other African-American leaders of his generation, created an unprecedented dependency. Blacks came to see their advancement and future almost wholly predicated on what crumbs whites tossed them, rather than on the development of coalitions where each coalition member offered contributions of equal value.

As a one-time key player in the civil rights movement, Barry knew better. Yet he helped perpetuate a model of African-American dependence and powerlessness that shaped the black leadership of the 1970s, 1980s, and 1990s. Any African-American leader deviating from his example was viewed as inauthentic. Thus, for more than 30 years, new generations of African-Americans cultivated a philosophy and political foundation of powerlessness, forgetting about their past of self-sufficiency and self-determination.

In 1994, blacks in the District chose to forget this larger history, not to mention their own dismal past with Barry. They sought a miracle to rescue them from the ineptitude of Mayor Sharon Pratt Kelly. They deeply feared the return of white dominance, and the continued physical and social decay of their city. Feigning amnesia, they reached for a known commodity.

They forgot the thousands of murders that had occurred during Barry's 12-year reign. They forgot the city's record high unemployment, and the 1989 funding cuts to neighborhood health clinics serving the poor. They forgot the erosion of public housing, when more than $40 million of federal money earmarked for repairs at various complexes went unspent from 1983 through 1987. They forgot Karen Johnson, the Barry girlfriend who went to jail for refusing to talk about her relationship with the mayor. They forgot Joan Medina, the city official who died in 1984 of a drug overdose attended by Barry associates. They forgot the dozens of Barry administration officials who pleaded guilty to corruption and fraud. They forgot the millions of dollars in D.C. contracts that went to Barry friends like Jeffrey Cohen and Cornelius Pitts—businessmen whose projects failed to deliver the government services for which they had been paid. The voters forgot how Barry betrayed the city's poor. They forgot Barry's lackluster performance between 1993 and 1994 on the D.C. Council, replete with scandal and lethal doses of demagoguery.

Before that fateful day at the Vista Hotel, the District had become the kind of environment that African-American leaders at the 1972 National Black Political Convention had vowed to obliterate—the kind that caused author Harold Cruse in 1989 to declare that American blacks were leaderless: "The black mayors, congresspersons, cabinet officers and the rest are unable to deliver on promises and programs to ameliorate conditions in their communities, and increasingly even consider themselves leaders of American institutions who happen to be black." Marion Barry was self-consciously black, and yet still couldn't effectively deliver government services.

For more than a decade, the District's elected leaders, Barry chief among them, deflected blame for this. By raising smoke screens of federal negligence, a declining middle-class population, and a hostile region for economic development, they distracted the public from the true reasons for the city's deterioration. Undoubtedly, the District was born facing enormous challenges, but instead of attempting to compensate for disabilities imposed by the federal government, Barry and others permitted the onetime black Mecca to become the poster child of urban dysfunction. And because he and his colleagues were African-Americans, their victims—who were also black—suffered under a self-imposed silence.

"If whites had been in charge of the District of Columbia, and things happened in this city over the 17 years I've been here...citizens would have been up in arms. There is no question about that," said former city council member John Ray.

Like hundreds of other American politicians, indeed, like such black counterparts as Adam Clayton Powell, Coleman Young, and Kenneth Gibson, Barry became addicted to power and its perks. He was Odysseus happily caught on Calypso's island. He found the pleasures of political power seductive. He feasted, without consideration for those waiting in poor neighborhoods for deliverance.

In 1994, District residents may have been profoundly absent-minded, but they were also aided by Barry's artful repackaging of himself. He manipulated his own history, masking the negative and accentuating the positive. He created an image for himself as savior, the man who righted every wrong, the man, who like Mother Teresa, waded into the poor communities where many politicians feared to go. Reminding residents of his Dashiki-wearing days, he told them of how he had helped their bank accounts grow. He bragged that he had fathered a generation of African-American professionals. He told them that he had inspired a previously inactive and hopeless group of people, urging them to assume control of their own lives, teaching them that only through sustained, aggressive action could they gain any sense of independence and self-respect. He told residents that he had discarded the words "retreat" and "surrender" from his vocabulary, and that they had done the same. He replayed the image of Marion Barry as a sweaty, Bible-thumping, country preacher at a tent revival, touching with electric hands the residents of a sleepy, hybrid town—one that wore Northern makeup over its Southern personality.

Barry knew the District the way lovers know each others' bodies. He understood the way the District thinks and the pain it feels. He turned his spotlight on its racial fears, using national events like church burnings, corporate cases of discrimination, and the *Washington Post's* legitimate, though relentless, criticism of his previous terms. These, he boasted, lent credence to his coded claims of untethered white supremacy in the District. He was African-Americans' answer to "the plan," at least for those conspiracy theorists who reasoned that whites planned someday to come looking for *their* nation's capital.

Some blacks still held to that belief. "There has indeed been an ongoing plan by Congress, by a handful of politicians who report to a group of financial supporters, allies and friends who want to be able to cut deals just like they did years ago, when rednecks in Congress ran the city," Rock Newman told the *Washington Post* in 1997, just days after the president signed into law the National Capital Revitalization and Self-Government Improvement Act.

With Barry in charge, most blacks believed whites couldn't force or finesse their way into the upper echelon of District politics. The mayor would protect them from the subjugation of white rule. District residents, in effect, became Anansi's aides-de-camp.

◆ ◆ ◆ ◆ ◆ ◆ ◆ ◆ ◆ ◆ ◆ ◆ ◆ ◆ ◆

The stars were clearly misaligned for Barry to succeed during a fourth term as mayor. National events, an impatient electorate, a paucity of talented professional managers, poor physical health, personal demons, a blurred political philosophy, and a growing public disaffection for race-based politics—all converged on Barry and D.C..

The first significant indication of aborted success came with the election of a Republican-dominated Congress, something few people accurately predicted. Barry hadn't paid much attention to the forces on the right lining up to assault the country and his city. He was, after all, in the throes of his own uncertain political campaign. When he looked up, he saw a bunch of white

Conservative men, like the ones he'd left down South, suddenly in control of both houses of Congress. Twenty years earlier, when pushing for the end of Jim Crow laws and the rise of black political power, Barry had traversed a racist landscape. Many southern whites subsequently ceased wearing their racial and class politics on their sleeves—Barry did not.

While 1979 may have seen a shrewd, confident politician, 1995 found Barry confused and arrogant, without a political compass, and ignoring the reality of the terrain on which he found himself. He faced a city and country imbued with an awesome conservatism and a deadly narcissism. He ignored the prediction and advice of his "Kitchen Cabinet," which warned him he could be elected, but might not be able to govern. And, he dismissed suggestions that he himself call for the creation of a financial control board to rein in the city's mushrooming deficit.

Had he been the aggressor, initiating the request for outside intervention, he might have sculpted the composition of the panel and the extent of its power. Instead, he permitted D.C. Delegate Eleanor Holmes Norton, who had nothing to win or lose politically from the creation of such a body, to lead the charge for fiscal solvency. By taking a passive role, he subjected himself and his future to the whims of Congress. In his fourth mayoral term, as before, he frequently provided his enemies the tools for his own destruction.

With the creation of the control board came a large opportunity for Barry to demonstrate his understanding of the conservative mood sweeping the country—including the District. National sentiments dictated that government step away from its historic omnipotent role. People had to be taught to fish, not be given fish. The moment called for complete reinvention—not a continuation of Anansi's style. But still draped in the jargon and philosophy of the 1970s and 1980s, Barry only half-heartedly divested himself of his wealth-redistribution philosophy, fueling his differences with the presidentially-appointed financial control board.

Adding to his weakness was his administration's dearth of African-American managers, seasoned and capable of carrying out the mayor's much-touted Transformation Plan. With the exception of his city administrator, Barry's cabinet consisted of the inexperienced, the unpolished, the lazy, or the disloyal. It included holdovers from Sharon Pratt Kelly's admin-istration, bureaucrats whose careers had been molded in the District government, which spoke volumes for their talent. It also included political types who went wherever Barry went, like appendages unable to function without him. Barry couldn't even rely on himself. City administrator Michael Rogers and Chief Financial Officer Anthony Williams became the primary advocates of transformation. Barry waffled.

The combination of his own obstinacy, the insubstantial nature of his staff, and repeated confrontations with the control board left Barry politi-cally debilitated at the conclusion of his first year in office.

Hoping to maintain his stature in the public's eye, to demonstrate a moral high ground, he continued—Anansi-style—to play a 1960s radical and socialist. But instead of reading his actions as those of Mother Teresa, District residents saw his protestations as a fixation on personal vindication and redemption—not as a commitment to the District's survival or to improving the plight of the poor.

In fairness, Barry understood that a politician without budgetary control was a politician without influence and power. Lacking complete control of the city's $4 billion purse-strings, he couldn't produce anywhere near the stellar showings of his first mayoral term. But as they watched Barry in action, the public saw personal motivations dominating institutional restraints. Full exoneration from his fall from grace became increasingly unlikely.

A deadly paranoia and myopia set in. Barry's rhetoric became more colored, more racial in connotation and denotation. Instead of taking a "Nixon Going to China" tact, Barry embodied the "Titanic On its Way to Sinking."

A *Washington Post* poll released in 1997 captured residents' disgust with the acrimony between the mayor and the control board. The overwhelming majority believed the five member panel had done little to improve the quality of life in the city. While the majority of African-Americans said they still trusted Barry to "do the right thing," they also did not want him to run for a fifth term in 1998. Barry, in their view, had become the obstacle to progress. To him, he was the reason the control board had not made significant changes. Barry had hoped to crystallize the enemy. Instead, in the public's mind, he had *become* the enemy.

◆ ◆ ◆ ◆ ◆ ◆ ◆ ◆ ◆ ◆ ◆ ◆ ◆ ◆ ◆ ◆ ◆

It wasn't that African-Americans hated Marion Barry. They simply tired of playing his designated dual role of victim and victor. They had fought alongside him for more than 20 years, switching costumes, masks, and lexicon whenever he demanded. By 1998, they, like him, were worn out, even exhausted.

Control board Chairman Andrew Brimmer* described his relationship with Barry as "episodic." The same could be said of Barry's relationship with the city. Unlike his previous administrations where he appeared to know exactly how he wanted to shape his government, a fourth-term Barry failed to chart a clear direction for himself, despite the release of his Transformation Plan. The depth of the fiscal crisis, the election of the Republican Congressional majorities, and the creation of the control board—all caught Barry off guard, unprepared. Though an air of distrust surrounded his return, he ad-libbed his response to the new developments. He projected himself as both insider and outsider. One day he wanted to work with the control board, following its dictates to the letter. The next day, he raised a stink, refusing to acquiesce.

The see-sawing left many blacks uncomfortable and disgruntled. They wanted more than just talk. But it was clear that the man who described himself as a situationist was unable to adapt to the new situation. Residents needed jobs. They wanted an end to the senseless killings in their communities. They wanted improved education for their children. They wanted clean, pothole-free streets. And they wanted their trash collected. Barry had lost his quarry. Residents concluded that if they continued to follow him, they stood a good chance of going hungry.

Barry couldn't measure up, but not because he didn't try. He was lost in a time warp. Even at the start of 1998, he seemed unsure of his next step:

whether to run for re-election, admit defeat, or retire, taking credit for the few improvements that had occurred during his fourth term.*

But, if seeking political office is chiefly about garnering power and influence, then Barry knew that winning at the polls in 1998 did not spell victory afterward. He knew, though he would never admit it in public, that he could never again reposition himself as leader of the nation's capital. The control board, he recognized, probably wouldn't be dissolved until the year 2002.

Marion Barry now lacks authority over major portions of the city government he built. Most cabinet-level directors don't report to him. A Chief Management Officer, appointed by the control board, heads the daily operation of nine major city agencies. The city's budget can be passed without the mayor's approval, and millions of dollars of contracts can be awarded, without his signature, to people who wouldn't dream of voting for him.

Barry's place on the historical charts plummeted in 1990. It rose, expectantly, with his twin-step rise to power, in 1992 and again in 1994. From 1995 through 1998, he hoped for a dramatic upward trajectory. It didn't happen. On the charts after that, he spiraled downward without stopping.

Barry had more than one opportunity to fully exert his authority over the city's revival, but as each opportunity arose, he was distracted, out-of-town, misevaluating events, or using trite tactics. As he moved toward the conclusion of his fourth term, few doubted that Barry had squandered the District's 1994 validation of him. The final chapter of his political career evokes sadness, not because of his personal demise, but because, like most Americans, blacks want to see their governmental heroes, their crusading pioneers, ride off into the sunset, unsullied. Barry had desperately sought to restore his reputation and to leave a more glowing legacy, but in both respects, he had clearly failed.

ANDREW BRIMMER, the control board's first chairman,
and the autocrat the Congress and President brought in to whip Barry
and the District into shape

ANTHONY WILLIAMS, District CFO, who promised to be an Indian and turned out to be a chief. He matched, and even outdid, Barry's Anansi-like maneuverings.

Marion Barry pushed MICHAEL ROGERS out as district administrator. Taken with his new style of black leadership, private-sector executives have urged Rogers to run for mayor.

JOYCE LADNER, one of five original control board members.
A former SNCC member, she urged Barry to cooperate with the board.

JOHN HILL, control board executive director

LAUCH FAIRCLOTH, a Republican senator from North Carolina and former hog-farmer, made slop out of Barry's political comeback as mayor

ELEANOR HOLMES NORTON, D.C.'s non-voting delegate in Congress.
Barry relied on her to negotiate the powers of the mayor—and lost.

Congressman TOM DAVIS, a Virginia Republican who
holds sway over the District's governance

Free At Last

· A CODA ·

OF THE MILLIONS OF AFRICAN-AMERICANS who came of age during the waning years of the southern Civil Rights Movement, most understood that they had somehow become America's conscience, its soul. Despite the degradation of being denied service in restaurants, being admitted only through back doors, being forced to urinate in bathrooms marked "colored only," and being denied water from "white only" fountains, African-American humanity remained intact. "We seemed the sole oasis of simple faith and reverence in a dusty desert of dollars and smartness," W.E.B. DuBois wrote in his seminal work, *The Souls of Black Folk.*

African-Americans held onto their dignity because they believed a better day would arrive. They thought it would come with the election of fellow blacks to major political office. They placed their hopes for advancement in the hands of these political figures, many of them participants in the civil rights movement. They envisioned their leaders to be morally superior.

But even before the public self-destruction of Marion Barry, that dream had been deferred. The sacred heirlooms of black America had been severely tarnished, in some instances completely destroyed. By following their leaders, whole sections of black America became victims, adopting the language of pity and bitterness. The vision of a better tomorrow became one of gray storm clouds. Some black leaders, as racist as the whites they deplored, practiced their own brand of corruption, becoming the black equivalent of the white politicians whose methods they had once decried. To the poor, they denied basic services and resources, discriminating against them solely because of their color and class.

That roster of black leaders is extensive and growing. Too many African-American leaders had become of little value to their communities: Adam Clayton Powell, Gus Savage, Charles Diggs, Mel Reynolds, Coleman Young, Kenneth Gibson, Marion Barry. "Most present day black political leaders appear too hungry for status to be angry, too eager for acceptance to be bold, too self-invested in advancement to be defiant," wrote Cornel West in his book *Race Matters*.

"And where they do drop their masks and try to get mad, their bold rhetoric is more performance than personal, more play-acting than heartfelt," West added.

Barry seemed to prove, as West asserted, that "rigor mortis" has set in on black politicians and intellectuals. Pundits often claimed that Barry's style, his reign, and his subsequent demise were unique. But within the context of both mainstream American politics and its subset of black politics, the man who dominated the political scene of the nation's capital for more than thirty years is actually quite typical. He practiced ethnic and patronage politics with the same bulldog tenacity as Richard Daley and James Michael Curley, albeit with lesser skill. He exhibited the same huge ego, the same propensity to manipulate and charm, in order to advance his career. And like other American politicians, his intent to improve the lot of his people became misdirected by his own greed and quest for power.

Certainly, Barry's career replicates the over-extended political lives of other black politicians. By their communities, these political leaders had once been invested with enormous promise, considered vessels of goodwill and abundant opportunity. Re-routed by the search for influence and personal gain, and held back by their failure to build solid foundations, these leaders left African-American communities with mostly temporary and fleeting improvements—akin to castles in the sand. Some American cities were in worse shape in 1997 than they were in 1967.

Consider the case of Coleman Young. Young adopted Detroit as his home city, cutting his teeth and claiming fame for his work as a labor organizer. In 1973, just as the District of Columbia was close to realizing its dream of independence, Young was elected mayor of Detroit. His city had been dominated by whites, mostly businessmen connected with the auto industry. It was they who had traditionally driven public policy and development. When Young came into office, African-Americans expected things to change for the better.

Young, like Barry, set about removing barriers to black progress. He reduced incidents of police brutality while integrating the police department. When he took office in 1974, Detroit's police department was 18 percent black, with less than 4 percent serving as sergeants and lieutenants. In 1976, Young turned the police chief's office black and kept it that way. He spurred economic development, primarily in downtown Detroit and along the river. He brought in Hollywood films and improved the overall park system. But perhaps Young's greatest contribution was symbolic: his presence increased African-American pride. Like Barry, he instigated greater enfranchisement of blacks—people who once believed their participation in the political or economic system was useless.

But, throughout Young's five terms as mayor, personal and political scandals abounded. There was the case of the young woman who filed a paternity suit against the mayor, claiming that Young fathered her son. Genetic testing confirmed her charges. In 1991, Young's police chief and deputy chief were indicted for embezzling $2.6 million from a fund used to pay informants and to make drug purchases. The next year, Police Chief William Hart was convicted and sent to prison. Detroit's police department problems were eerily similar to the corruption scandals that later erupted in Washington, D.C. In 1997, a top-level lieutenant, Jeffrey Stowe, was arrested and charged with embezzling more than $10,000 from a similar fund. He also was charged with extortion and making false statements to a federal grand jury. Police Chief Larry Soulsby, who was white, was forced to resign following news reports that he and Stowe together rented a posh downtown apartment and received a discount after telling the landlord the apartment would be used for an undercover police operation. Soulsby had been Barry's hand-picked chief of police. By year's end, there were calls for the creation of an independent police commission to ferret out police corruption.

There were other problems shared by the two cities. Under Young, Detroit, like the District, indeed like other black-majority cities, hemorrhaged its middle-class white population. By 1990, it had lost more than 1.1 million people. The city was 76 percent black.

While African-Americans were entertained by Young's urbane, profane communication style, they realized that Detroit was slowly dying under him. A similar style—and the same poor results—were evident in Gary, Indiana, where two different blacks served as mayor before the electorate shifted back to white leadership. Newark, New Jersey experienced similar destruction, as did, to a lesser extent, New Orleans and Los Angeles. Like their white counterparts, African-American mayors were becoming career politicians at their constituents' expense.

But black citizens were growing beyond the leaders they elected. They were beginning to recognize that the dominant theme in the country was shifting (at least slightly) from race to class. As they matured, they began to understand that without becoming business owners and land owners, their economic advancement was only tentative and temporary. For them, it was no longer enough to get government jobs and government contracts.

The changing attitude surfaced in a national survey conducted by the *Detroit News* in 1992. With their answers, most African-Americans seemed to be saying that organizations like the NAACP and the Southern Christian Leadership Conference, and big-city mayors like Coleman Young and Marion Barry, were relatives who had overstayed their welcome. They had feasted at the table, but failed to plant any crops in the field. For a majority of African-Americans, race was no longer the number one concern. In its place, said the survey, was economic development, followed by housing, education, and crime. According to the survey, many African-Americans saw their black leaders as more interested in pursuing their own careers than in resolving their citizens' greatest concerns.

Despite the influx of black elected officials, crime in many black communities, particularly those in urban areas, had increased. Unemployment was on the rise; schools were deteriorating, and economic opportunities were virtually nonexistent.

"Big-city black governments have generally pursued policies and programs of minority appointments and employment, contracts to minority businesses, and efforts to restrain police misconduct in minority communities, but little in the way of policies that might affect the underlying problems of ghetto poverty and dispossession," notes Robert Smith in his book *We Have No Leaders.*

Undoubtedly, some of the problems for urban blacks and their leaders can rightfully be traced back to conservative policies, like those implemented by President Ronald Reagan, and on an overall anti-city climate in the country. But African-American leaders like Young and Barry exacerbated blighted conditions with myopic, misguided public policies and antiquated economic development strategies. And because they were so wedded to race-based politics, they often alienated people and organizations that could provide resources and expertise.

The same year of the *Detroit News* national poll, *The Detroit Free Press* revealed that four out of five Detroiters wanted Coleman Young to retire in 1993 instead of seeking a sixth term. Only two out of five approved of the job he was doing—horrible numbers for a five-term mayor.

"People are tired of a lack of city services, the scandals, the crime, the city's bad image, the whole nine yards," Detroit city councilmember Keith Butler told the *Detroit Free News*. "His [Young's] administration is no longer effective."

Poor health, declining popularity, and a pool of eager political opponents influenced Young's decision to retire as mayor. In 1993, announcing his plans to call it quits, Young said, "I've decided twenty years is enough. I'm tired." The people of Detroit, like those in the District, were tired, too.

"The black community is coming to a point where it is a bit more sophisticated in what it wants in its leadership," explained William Boone, associate provost of Clarke-Atlanta University. "The expectations have moved from symbolism to substance."

◆ ◆ ◆ ◆ ◆ ◆ ◆ ◆ ◆ ◆ ◆ ◆ ◆ ◆ ◆

It was always supposed to be about substance. The Rev. Martin Luther King, Jr. and other civil rights activists weren't merely interested in desegregating schools to create a pleasing appearance. He didn't simply deliver his "I Have a Dream" speech because the words were lyrical. Rather, civil rights stalwarts wanted substantive, long-term change for African-American and poor communities around the country. At first, the best route to a changed life was thought to be through political enfranchisement. Later, around the time of King's death, a gradual, quiet shift toward economic empowerment began.

King's "lieutenants," especially people like Jesse Jackson, did not pick up on the shift. For the past 30 years, Jackson has focused almost exclusively on race. He evidently missed the true import of King's great speech in Washington in 1963. And that 1968 day in Memphis, he also misinterpreted King's support of striking city sanitation workers.

A generation of African-Americans, just on the edge of segregation and integration, was the first to benefit from King's efforts. It would come to understand King's true objective, more succinctly and more innately, than others. Mainstream America characterized this group as "Baby Boomers." In black America, they could be called "transitioners," with one foot set firmly in the past and one firmly in the future, ready to pass the baton, but only after certain conditions were met.

Unfortunately, only since the 1990s has it been possible for this generation to lay claim to leadership roles. Leaders from the generation of Jackson, Young, and Barry, as well as the previous generation, have been disinclined to remove themselves from the political stage. Their failure to take their curtain bow has caused stagnation within African-American communities, and kept them inside a kind of time warp. Consequently, a city like the District of Columbia, which boasts one of the most literate African-American populations in the country, can harbor an astronomical crime and unemployment rate, a failed economic development system, and an atrocious educational system. And it can retain racial divisions comparable to those in existence before 1970.

But two things have occurred within the past decade to produce the inevitable eviction of the "old guard" civil rights leaders—including Marion Barry—and their philosophical approach to solving problems affecting African-American communities. First, a large number of blacks have entered the middle class, adopting traditional values and attitudes. They want to be full, participating members of mainstream America and are, therefore, reluctant to evaluate everything through the prism of race. Prodded by this transitioner generation, a new style of black leader has emerged.

Secondly, even poor blacks have come to appreciate the meaning of the free enterprise system and capitalism, as seen in surveys by both the *Detroit News* and the Joint Center for Political and Economic Studies. Poor and working class African-Americans have come to realize that continued emphasis on race has not appreciatively altered the quality of their lives nor their status in society. Consequently, they, too, have adjusted their lens to focus more on economics, and to look at race alone only when it relates to their ability to achieve economic parity.

In this shift of focus and strategy, blacks have not demanded larger pieces of government contracts, but an influence on economic development and urban planning. They want to build solid business foundations on which their communities can grow. To them, race-identifying leaders like Marion Barry have become irrelevant. "There has been this slow process of transition from the civil rights leaders to these new leaders who are not as ideological," explained Kojo Nnamdi, a political analyst and talk show host in Washington, D.C. "But in some respects, [these new leaders] have their eyes more closely on the prize than the civil rights leaders did. The prize has changed. It's now quality of life and how to take the resources to improve that quality of life."

♦ ♦ ♦ ♦ ♦ ♦ ♦ ♦ ♦ ♦ ♦ ♦ ♦ ♦ ♦ ♦

America's "new black leaders" have moved beyond rallies and protest marches, ushering in an era of competent, professional stewardship of cities long wracked by crime and poverty. They combine corporate savvy and management acumen with street smarts and political sophistication. Unlike Marion Barry, Coleman Young and other "old guard" African-American leaders, they embrace African-American culture but are not imprisoned by it. They understand the nuances of racism, including insidious institutional racism, but do not wear it as their albatross.

They are not simply blacks in fancy suits with Harvard vocabularies. As a group, they walk toward universal humanity, and they fully embrace democratic principles and the existing political and economic systems. They know that if African-Americans are to do justice to their past, the future must be met with excellence and content—not color.

Dennis Archer (Young's successor in Detroit), New Orleans' Marc Morial, Seattle's Norm Rice (who stepped down after very successful two terms), Baltimore's Kurt Schmoke, Prince George's County's Wayne Curry, and Atlanta's Bill Campbell—all members of the new breed of black elected leader in America—understand how to leverage politics into economic advancement. They no longer perceive African-Americans as bit players in the larger game, but as primary participants in the American and world markets, with nearly $500 billion of buying power in 1998.

Take a brief look at Cleveland's mayor, Michael White, who has presided over his city's transformation from bad joke to nation's envy. While White's support of work-based welfare reform and private school choice placed him in direct opposition to old guard black leaders, it mirrored African-Americans' growing acceptance of these proposals as viable solutions to decades-old problems. The Joint Center for Political and Economic Studies found in a national survey conducted in 1996 that 48 percent of African-Americans support a voucher system that would allow parents to receive government subsidies to send their children to public or private schools of their choice.

When Prince George's County Executive Wayne Curry faced Washington Redskins owner Jack Kent Cooke across the negotiating table, few expected him to snare the prize of the Washington metropolitan region—a stadium for the prestigious NFL franchise—without paying a heavy economic price. But Curry, a boardroom-sharp dresser as comfortable in a corporate executive suite as to a political rally, wasn't going to roll over for a billionaire who wanted to build a stadium on prime county land and call it his own. Using hard-nosed negotiating techniques that few African-Americans would have dared use with such a powerful adversary, Curry sealed a deal that brought more than just rhetoric and promises. For the land on which to build his privately-financed stadium, and in exchange for securing state government construction of needed infrastructure, Cooke agreed to provide Curry's county minority participation in stadium construction and concessionaires, season tickets for county residents, $1.5 million in scholarships for county youths, and $3 million toward the construction of a high-tech recreation complex.

Curry's coup compared well to White's. Though he lost Art Modell's Cleveland Browns to Baltimore, Mayor Michael White stood at the exit, extracting an incredible deal for Cleveland, including the retention of the name Cleveland Browns, a multi-million dollar escape payment, the fairly immediate return of NFL football to the city, the NFL's partial funding of a new football-only stadium, and, with a major push from Art Modell himself, a guilt-free expansion club rather than one stolen from another city. White and his brand of economic politics even garnered him a prime-time TV spot during the 1996 National Democratic Convention.

In sharp contrast to both White and Curry was how Barry handled negotiations over a downtown D.C. arena to house an NBA basketball team and an NHL hockey team. By pointing to the District's weak fiscal condition, Barry convinced team owner Abe Pollin to finance his own arena. And Barry's administration also won minority construction and concession agreements. But it nonetheless agreed to $70 million in infrastructure improvements. In the fall of 1997—two months before the MCI Center was scheduled to open—controversy erupted. Having failed to secure the most obvious perk—a no-cost or discounted luxury skybox—city officials decided to spend $675,000 of government money to finance the lease of a skybox. Residents' opposition torpedoed the idea. Barry was left to return to the negotiating table with Pollin, in a position clearly weaker than his pre-construction days. The Arena opened in December 1997.

"We've had mayors in place for 10 or 15 years," noted University of Maryland political scientist Ronald Walters. "Young blacks have acquired certain skills the first generation didn't have. It's very logical. They are the class of people we went into the civil rights movement to produce."

But the chasm between Marion Barry and his younger city administrator and chief financial officer, indicates the old guard's discomfort with what it has produced. So, too, did the 1997 mayoral race in Atlanta, Georgia. Incumbent mayor Bill Campbell was challenged by Marvin Arrington, one of the first blacks elected to the city council and a member of the old guard. Although Campbell made a few mistakes and displayed an abrasive style unfamiliar to most Atlantans, he retained the strong support of many African-Americans and whites. He was the top vote-getter in a crowded field and the clear winner in a run-off election against Arrington.

But by 1997, there was tangible evidence that the new black leaders weren't just talking. They had seen old-style leaders like Young and Barry resort to what Robert Smith called "ritual political posturing as a means to cover up or disguise their inability to lead."

The new leaders had already begun to reap measurable results. Cities like Detroit and Cleveland were showing economic growth or stable populations, while the District of Columbia continued to lose residents to the suburbs and parts beyond. D.C.'s fiscal health was improving, but much of the financial terrain had been given over to a "new, younger black leader" —Anthony Williams.

◆ ◆ ◆ ◆ ◆ ◆ ◆ ◆ ◆ ◆ ◆ ◆ ◆ ◆ ◆ ◆

The rise of the new breed of black leaders does not negate the 30-year contribution made by Barry and that early group of civil rights activists. They were the country's first generation of African-American politicians. Undoubtedly, they were what the country and African-American communities needed during those historic times. But practically everyone becomes outdated.

All of Barry's counterparts have been pushed out, have resigned, or, like Detroit's Coleman Young, Chicago's Harold Washington, and Cleveland's Carl Stokes, have simply died.

"Young, [Harold] Washington, and Stokes—these guys were more than political figures. They were titans," said Democratic pollster Ron Lester after Coleman's death in 1997. "The Archers and the Whites will never get that kind of adoration. It's not that they're not good at what they do, but they came along at a different time, and their names will never be synonymous with black political empowerment.

"They're like the Barry Bonds of politics," continued Lester. "Barry Bonds is a pretty good baseball player, but he's never going to mean to people what Jackie Robinson meant."

Had it not been for the FBI and its Vista Hotel sting, District residents might have sent Barry out to pasture in 1990 or 1994. Instead, the city's African-American majority invited him back in 1994, simply to prove to the federal government and to the white power structure that it would choose its own leaders—flaws and all. Three years later, District blacks loudly signalled their willingness to join the rest of black America, moving to the next stage of political maturation.

A passing generation is never quite comfortable with the next—never quite sure that it has transferred all the essential values, idioms, and motifs, never quite sure that the young upstarts will remember history, remember which paths lead to home. Sometimes, this fear keeps the old generation holding on to power too long, and thereby stunting the growth of the entire community. It was that way for a while in Gary, Indiana, in Newark, New Jersey, and in Detroit, Michigan. Certainly it was the case in Washington, D.C. in 1997 and 1998 as Marion Barry continued to hold together the fraying threads of his political career. He faced a new generation of blacks far more qualified than he to lead the city. But because politics had always been his life, he didn't really know what would become of him without political office. He did not know if history would treat him well.

◆ ◆ ◆ ◆ ◆ ◆ ◆ ◆ ◆ ◆ ◆ ◆ ◆ ◆ ◆ ◆ ◆

Pollster Ron Lester is correct. There will be few Anansis among the new breed of black leaders in America. Few will dazzle with their words and chutzpah, as Barry, Coleman Young, and Adam Clayton Powell once did. This, though, is for the good. Politics and political antics have disrupted America's civic culture, particularly in African-American communities. While national statistics in 1996 showed an increased number of African-Americans registered to vote on election day, turnout has been decreasing. In the District, less than 10 percent of eligible voters came out in 1997 to cast ballots for the chairman of the city council.

Reviving black interest in the political process won't happen with candidates who switch masks and lexicons—actions for which Barry and his generation were notorious. Instead, "a politics of integrity is...needed to draw people back to their faith in our democracy," asserts Stephen Carter in his book *Integrity*.

But the political soil must first be tilled and a new model of authentic black leadership sown. "Quality leadership is neither the product of one individual nor the result of odd historical accidents," writes Cornel West. "Rather, it comes from deeply bred traditions and communities that shape and mold talented and gifted persons."

The Archers, Currys, Williamses, Rogerses, Campbells, and Whites of America are readying the ground for the next generation of black leaders—consciously and unconsciously. By their actions, they will help free our nation from the weight of racism, myopic politics, victimhood philosophies, deficient public policy planning, and misdirected economic development strategies. What's more, in dislodging the Barrys and Youngs from their perches as the era's leaders, they will add an important new chapter to civil rights history.

Twenty years from now, if today's new black leaders provide for their own timely exits from the political stage—something their predecessors failed to do—they will help realize the dream of civil rights era activists. The next generation of leaders, neither race-identifying, as was Barry, nor race-transcending, but "prophetic," will assume their place as stewards of America.

"To be [a]...an elected...prophetic leader requires personal integrity and political savvy, moral vision and prudential judgment, courageous defiance and organizational patience," observes Cornel West.

"Prophetic leaders" will have been nurtured by the history that created Marion Barry, but not embittered by it. Such leaders will have acquired and improved on the political savvy and sophistication of the Dennis Archers, Michael Whites, Marc Morials, and Kurt Schmokes of our cities. But most importantly, they will understand that progress can only be realized when everyone joins hands to build coalitions. By avoiding confrontation, racially divisive rhetoric, empty symbolism, and bravado, and by reaching out to the vast array of potential partners, these 21st Century leaders will reconstruct governments and communities from durable cloth. For many African-Americans, who waited through aborted political promise, prostituted goodwill, and squandered potential, the final change from symbolism to substance will have come none too soon.

ACKNOWLEDGEMENTS

In my junior high school yearbook, a classmate, Marie Slade, wrote that she looked forward to one day seeing my name on the cover of a book. Her words shaped my initial image of myself as a book author. Since then, other people have offered inspiration, opportunities for growth, and a good kick in the rear-end when necessary.

I am eternally grateful to those who have helped guide my career in journalism: O'Field Dukes, Clarence Hunter, Francis Murphy, Kojo Nnamdi, Adrienne Washington, Deborah Simmons, Vincent McCraw, Tyler Tucker, Vanessa Gallman, Harry Jaffe, Jack Limpert, Ed Foster-Simeon, Tod Lindberg, Meg Greenfield, and, most especially, Jack Shaffer, formerly of the *Washington City Paper*.

But special thanks on this project go to: Yolanda Woodlee, my friend at *The Washington Post*, for recommending me to Bancroft Press; James Gibson, who never hesitated to answer my calls, of which there were dozens; to Ivanhoe Donaldson, who I thought would never sit for an interview, but did, and made numerous telephone calls to track my progress and to provide support; to former D.C. City Administrator Michael Rogers, who frequently offered words of encouragement; to Dwight Cropp and Ronald Walters for referring me to other important reading materials; and to the folks at the Washingtoniana Division of the Martin Luther King Jr. Memorial Library in the District of Columbia for providing invaluable research assistance.

My dear friends Misty Brown; David Carr, current editor of the *Washington City Paper*, George Miller; Adrianne Flynn; and Wesley Pruden, editor-in-chief of the *Washington Times*, often rescued me when I was plagued by doubt. And Roy McKay, who patiently read every manuscript and led me to wonderful Barry treasures. Few editors have won my all-around praise, but I have only accolades for Bruce Bortz, my editor on this book and the publisher of Bancroft Press.

Lastly, I'd like to thank Russell for being there.

p. 10 ◆ Census reports indicated a continued decline in living standards. For example, 40.4 percent of black families were headed by women, and the median income for black families was $11,651—only fifty-seven percent of that earned by whites.

p. 11 ◆ Later, she was named in an elaborate kickback scheme involving D.C. city council member H.R. Crawford. The negative publicity had cost her clients and damaged her reputation. Some observers believed Barry had been her downfall, but Clarke maintains to this day a solid relationship with him.

p. 19 ◆ The Freedmen's Bureau was then under the leadership of General Oliver Otis Howard for whom Howard University later would be named.

p. 20 ◆ The cultural nationalist philosophy was anchored in the Black Power movement of the late 1960s and 1970s, and saw blacks clinging to African motifs, asserting the superiority of their race, praising the artistic contributions of blacks to the world, and insisting on African-American political empowerment and economic development undergirded by a "buy-black" philosophy.

p. 36 ◆ Powell's sense of entitlement—akin, as it was, to that flaunted by white men—may have derived from the fact that he had once passed for white. According to biographer Charles Hamilton, Powell "passed" when he was in college at Colgate University. "He pledged a white fraternity. He lived in a white dormitory," Hamilton said on the C-Span program "Booknotes" during an interview in January 1992. "He was found out by the fraternity when they investigated his background." Hamilton added that Powell's sister also "passed" in the 1920s, when she worked "on Wall Street in a secretarial job."

p. 38 ♦ Years later, the head of the city's Office of Campaign Finance also would succumb very publicly to the lure of crack.

p. 53 ♦ The campaign repaid Barry $3,500 of the original loan. As of March 1998, the remaining balance had not been paid. Barry's 1992 campaign ran up a $14,331 debt (as of March 1998).

p. 60 ♦ Tony Cheng's name does not appear in any 1992 reporting statements submitted by Barry's 1992 campaign. Also, finance officials say it would be impossible for them to track cash contributions unless they are reported. It is possible, officials add, for a campaign to not make specific reports of cash because the law allows a campaign to bundle all cash contributions collected at a fundraiser where the fee or donation limit was under $49. There is evidence that, on some occasions, such bundling was reported by the Barry for Council campaign. However, it is impossible to know— other than through campaign sources—if all cash was reported.

p. 73 ♦ Seegars became one of Barry's chief nemeses in the city. She embarrassed him at town hall meetings, accusing him of lying to residents. With taxi cab drivers, she helped mount a recall campaign that failed.

p. 76 ♦ Independent expenditures and the activities of PACs would haunt the Barry campaign, leaving unresolved fiscal issues well after the election.

p. 77 ♦ Years later, however, Barry would be unable to sustain and mobilize this new group of voters, confirming his critics' perception that he continually used, then neglected, poor and disenfranchised citizens who came to his aid.

p. 79 ♦ In a small unsuccessful effort to relieve the situation legally, D.C. council member William Lightfoot had sought to shift the city's drug laws, providing for more leniency in those cases where violent crimes had not occurred. Five years later, the number increased to fifty percent of black males in contact with the criminal justice system.

p. 87 • The city's Office of Campaign Finance failed to thoroughly investigate charges of campaign finance violations.

p. 87 • He had captured seventy percent of the black vote and five percent of the white; eighty-seven of the city's eighty-eight precincts; nine of the twenty-three racially mixed precincts; and none of the twenty-nine that were predominantly white.

p. 92 • Turnout for the Democratic primary was the highest the city had seen in years; 49.1 percent of the District's 304,387 voters came to the polls. Democrats saw 52.1 percent—or 143,082 of their 274,533 registrants—participate in the election. Barry won 66,777 votes as compared to John Ray, who raked in 52,088, and the incumbent Sharon Pratt Kelly, who garnered a mere 18,717. In Wards 7 and 8—Barry strongholds and predominantly black—Barry received 51.6 percent and 45.9 percent of the vote, respectively.

Barry won fifty-six percent—or 102,884—of the 186,316 votes cast on November 8, 1994. Schwartz pulled in 76,902—forty-two percent. Her strongest support came from the predominantly white Ward 3, which provided 25,671 votes. In Ward 2, also predominantly white, she attracted 13,552 votes, and in Ward 1, a mixed area, she won 9,308. But in the predominantly black, middle class communities of Wards 4 and 5, Schwartz did miserably. In Dwight Cropp's' Ward 4, where black residents had shown their anger with the white power establishment by voting for Barry, Schwartz received a mere 7,069 votes. In Ward 5, she won only 4,929 votes. It was clear that even with his flaws and his past public disgrace, the black community supported Marion Barry in 1994.

p. 100 • Isaiah Montgomery, founder of the all-black town Mound Bayou, Mississippi, and the lone African-American member of the Mississippi Constitutional Convention of 1890, supported the conditions placed on voting rights. For doing so, other blacks labeled him "traitor" and called him "Judas."

p. 103 • There are conflicting reports about Marion Barry's early years. For example, he once told a reporter that he was still a toddler when his father died. This is indeed what his mother once told him—to answer young Marion's concerns about his father's absence. Later, Marion Barry, Jr. learned the truth about his father.

Likewise, there is at least one contradictory story about the Barrys' life after leaving Itta Bena, Mississippi. In his book *The Children,* David Halberstam reports that Mattie and Marion Sr. moved for a time to West Helena, Arkansas, where Marion Sr. worked in an oil refinery. Dissatisfied with the job and with life in Arkansas, he decided to move back to Mississippi, whereupon the family split, according to Halberstam. One daughter went with the father, another was already in Chicago living with her maternal grandmother, and Marion moved with his mother to Memphis. For a time, she worked in a cattle and hog slaughter house there. Halberstam reports that this is where Mattie met and married Prince Jones, "a top butcher" then working at the packing house, who had three daughters from a previous marriage. Mattie and Prince had two daughters together, bringing their brood to eight, although only five actually lived with them. It is unclear whether Prince Jones and David Cummings are one and the same person. But all the basic facts surrounding their lives—jobs, number of children, etc. —seem to be the same.

p. 106 • Other versions of the same story suggest that Till precipitated his demise by merely whistling at a white woman.

p. 109 • The group of Fisk civil rights organizers also learned a trick or two from Myles Horton. According to Juan Williams, Horton, in 1932, founded the Highlander Folk School in Monteagle, Tennessee. Initially, the school focused on labor unions, workers' rights, and race relations. It gradually became a training center for civil rights activists. Rosa Parks attended a Highlander training session the summer before she helped launch the Montgomery bus boycott.

p. 125 • A decade later, Treadwell was indicted on federal charges related to the operation of Clifton Terrace Apartments, and ended up serving fifteen months of a three-year prison sentence. By 1997, Treadwell was back in trouble, though Barry had given her a sixty-thousand-dollar job in his office of policy and planning. Several years earlier, Treadwell was elected to an advisory neighborhood commission, a network of community representatives who served as a sort of sub-chamber to the city council. As chairman of her ANC area, Treadwell had access to the group's budget. She admits to having stolen as much as ten thousand dollars. This could have earned her five years in prison. Many District residents believed Treadwell should have been placed in jail and the key to her cell thrown away. She pled guilty to defrauding residents of the same neighborhood she had defrauded in the 1980s, raising as many questions about Barry as it did about his second wife.

In 1971, Barry permitted himself to be persuaded to run for an at-large position on the D.C. Board of Education. He beat his opponent Anita Allen, winning fifty-eight percent of the vote. "When he was president of the board, his interest was not education. His interest was political growth and expansion," Dwight Cropp told Harry Jaffe and Tom Sherwood for their book.

p. 128 • Moving through the ranks of seniority, Dellums later became a member of the House Armed Services Committee.

p. 141 • The tension and stress associated with such a unique position may have been the culprits, and expectations certainly ran high, but the poem "On The Pulse of the Morning" fell flat. Privately, many literary artists rejected it, characterizing it as a jumble of metaphors that took the reader for a chaotic, disjointed voyage.

p. 143 • But unlike Langston Hughes, Brown's work could be remote and overly intellectual at times. It probably didn't help that he created his work from within the halls of academe, serving before his death as a professor at Howard University.

p. 144 • Skinner died before Barry could return to his former office. However, Barry selected Skinner's Bible for taking the oath of office as a silent tribute to his mentor and counselor.

p. 145 • "He [is] a guy [who] says, 'Accept me on my own terms. I'm no saint—I'm born again, I'm resurrected.' There is too much of Marion Barry in too many of us for him to be made the demon," says Lawrence Guyot.

p. 164 • The story in the District was that nothing of consequence happened in the city unless the Federal City Council gave it its seal of approval. But when Gibson offered his services to Barry, he was a consultant to the Federal City Council.

p. 167 • During Bill Clinton's first term, Rivlin went on to become the director of the U.S. Office of Management and Budget.

p. 170 • By the end of Barry's fourth term, however, Abramson would jump ship, lending his support to D.C. Council member Jack Evans in his bid for mayor.

p. 181 • Near the end of his term, Harlan would be mired in controversy of his own, and his credibility would be severely marred.

p. 208 • From his interview with Rob Gurwitt, which appeared in the June 1997 issue of *Governing* magazine.

p. 209 • The author allegedly had blasphemed Islam in his novel *The Satanic Verses*.

p. 242 • He would leave just after the start of the new fiscal year.

p. 243 • Bain holds a law degree, and has moonlighted as a representative for several entertainment and sports figures, including singer/songwriter Baby Face.

p. 246 ♦ By 1998, the control board had hired Camille Cates Barnett as chief management officer. She became the de facto city manager.

p. 255 ♦ Months later, at the start of 1998, the D.C. Court of Appeals would rule against the control board in a lawsuit brought by the D.C. Board of Education. The ruling would substantially weaken the board and add fodder for a Barry attack.

p. 259 ♦ The model used by the control board duplicated in many respects that used by Chicago.

p. 272 ♦ Interestingly, by the spring of 1998, Brimmer himself became the target of a mutinous bunch of control board members, who leaked to *The Washington Post* their refusal to serve a second term with the imperious chairman. Their actions prompted Brimmer to hold a hastily called press conference to publicly announce his resignation effective the end of his term in June 1998. Initially, Brimmer had wanted to resign effective the day of the *Post* article, but Franklin Raines, Director of the Office of Management and Budget—President Clinton's point person on the District—prevailed on him to hold off. Brimmer was effectively outdone by the same tactics he had used on Barry, who privately gloated about the elder economist's ultimate come-uppance.

p. 273 ♦ In April 1998, it was still unclear what Marion Barry might do, though business leaders and his supporters were working overtime to secure him a soft landing. They had raised enough money to establish an endowed chair with the Consortium of Universities. To be housed in a District office on Connecticut Avenue, and to be given his own staff, "Professor" Barry would offer lectures and seminars in urban politics at all or some of the city's 12 universities. When university presidents gave the plan mixed reviews, Barry waffled as to whether he would run again or not for mayor.

SOURCE NOTES

Material for this book was drawn from a variety of sources, including my own direct reporting of District government affairs since 1984. I also conducted interviews with dozens of individuals, including Ivanhoe Donaldson, Elijah Rogers, Michael Rogers, Dwight Cropp, Lawrence Guyot, James Gibson, Ronald Walters, Yvonne Scruggs, Sandra Allen, Bob Bethea, Edyie Whittington, Jamin Raskin, Sam Smith, Sandra Seegars, and Willie Wilson. Some Barry confidantes, District government workers and members of the control board were interviewed, but requested anonymity.

Marion Barry refused to participate in the research for this book. Initially he agreed to sit for a short interview, but then declined. Wherever there is a direct quotation from Barry, it came from previous interviews conducted by me, or press conferences, community meetings, hearings, and other events I attended at which the mayor was present—unless otherwise noted.

The archives of *The Washington Times*, *The Washington Post*, and the *Washington City Paper* also were used.

SELECTED BIBLIOGRAPHY

Agronsky, Jonathan I.Z.—*Marion Barry: The Politics of Race,* British American Publishing, 1991.

Anderson, Alan B. and Pickering, George W.—*Confronting the Color Line: The Broken Promise of the Civil Rights Movement in Chicago,* University of Georgia Press, 1986.

Beatty, Jack—*The Rascal King: The Life and Times of James Michael Curley,* Addison-Wesley, 1992.

Bell, Derrick—*Faces at the Bottom of the Well: The Permanence of Racism,* Basic Books, 1992.

Carson, Clayborne—*In the Struggle: SNCC and the Black Awakening of the 1960s,* Harvard University Press, 1981.

Christian, Charles—*Black Saga: The African-American Experience (A Chronology),* Houghton Mifflin, 1995.

Conti, Joseph G. and Stetson, Brad—*Challenging the Civil Rights Establishment: Profiles of a New Black Vanguard,* Praeger, 1993.

Cousins, Norman—*The Pathology of Power,* W.W. Norton Company, 1987.

Edwards, Audrey and Polite, Craig—*Children of the Dream: The Psychology of Black Success.* Doubleday, 1992.

Hamilton, Charles V.—*Adam Clayton Powell: The Political Biography of an American Dilemma,* Atheneum, 1991.

Hamilton, Charles V. and Carmichael, Stokely—*Black Power: The Politics of Liberation in America,* Vintage Books, 1967.

Jaffe, Harry and Sherwood, Tom—*Dream City: Race, Power and the Decline of Washington, D.C.,* Simon and Schuster, 1994.

Keane, John—*The Power of the Powerless,* Palach Press, 1985.

Majors, Richard and Billson, Janet Mancini—*Cool Pose: The Dilemmas of Black Manhood in America,* Simon and Schuster/Touchstone Books, 1993.

Marable, Manning—*Beyond Black and White: Transforming African-American Politics,* Verso, 1995.

Marable, Manning—*Black American Politics: From The Washington Marches to Jesse Jackson,* Verso, 1985.

Melder, Keith edit.—*The City of Magnificent Intentions: History of the District of Columbia,* Intac., Inc., 1983.

Meyers, Edward—*Public Opinion and the Political Future of the Nation's Capital,* Georgetown University Press, 1996.

O'Cleireacain, Carol—*Orphaned Capital: Adopting the Right Revenues for the District of Columbia,* Brookings Institution, 1997.

Royko, Mike—*Boss: Richard J. Daley of Chicago,* E.P. Dutton & Co., 1971.

Smith, Robert—*We Have No Leaders: African-Americans in the Post-Civil Rights Era,* State University of New York Press, 1996.

Smith, Sam—*Captive Capital: Colonial Life in Modern Washington,* Indiana University Press, 1974.

Wiley, Ralph—*What Black People Should Do Now: Dispatches from Near the Vanguard,* Ballantine Books, 1993.

Williams, Juan—*Eyes on the Prize: America's Civil Rights Movement 1954-1965,* Viking, 1987.

INDEX

FURTHER PRAISE FOR
THE LAST OF THE BLACK EMPERORS

I wasn't that interested in the subject of Marion Barry when I was given this book, but once I started it, I couldn't put it down. *The Last of the Black Emperors* is a terrific piece of writing and an exciting read. Barras' metaphor of the folkloric spider is very appropriate for Marion Barry. Especially impressive is her ability to place Barry's leadership style not only in a political and historical landscape, but also in the emotional landscape of American racism. Barras teaches us a great deal about the development of black leaders over the last four decades, and delivers a compelling story of Marion Barry, the person, and Marion Barry, the emblem.

— **LORI SHPUNT**, Professor of English,
Trinity College, Washington, D.C.

The most comprehensive and descriptive study to date of the elusive Marion Barry. Because of her thorough background and research, Barras has managed not only to capture the essence of one of America's most complex political personalities, but also to help us understand the sinister dynamics fueling Barry's political juggernaut.

— **DWIGHT S. CROPP**, Associate Professor of Public Administration,
George Washington University

The Last of the Black Emperors is invaluable for all those who've never been able to figure out the enduring love affair between Marion Barry and Washington D.C. Barras uses the prism of African-American folklore to crack the code of Barry's appeal and fatal flaws. The nation's capital is on the cusp of ending its affair with Barry. Barras offers the kind of ferocious insight and outstanding historical reporting that make *The Last of the Black Emperors* a huge step in understanding one of the most controversial leaders in contemporary American politics. — **DAVID CARR**, Editor, *Washington City Paper*

Information is power and, in this book, Barras serves up a heaping helping. With compelling anecdotes, brilliant insights, and real data, she takes you inside Washington politics and into the psyche of African-American voters across the country. With unwavering conviction, she explores myths and master plans by examining Barry the man, and Barry the legacy. For the casual political observer, *The Last of the Black Emperors* is a magnificent treat. For pollsters, pundits, and campaign operatives, it's a must read.

—**SONSRYREA TATE**, author, *Little X: Growing Up in the Nation of Islam*
(and third generation Washingtonian)